THE IDEA OF GOD

HISTORICAL, CRITICAL CONSTRUCTIVE

BY

CLARENCE AUGUSTINE BECKWITH

ILLINOIS PROFESSOR OF CHRISTIAN THEOLOGY, CHICAGO
THEOLOGICAL SEMINARY

New York
THE MACMILLAN COMPANY
1922

BROWN BROTHERS, LINOTYPERS
NEW YORK

PREFACE

"If you do not ask me, I know." Of no question of intimate human concern is this more true than of the idea of God. Since our earliest childhood we have been familiar with the word "God": we were taught it at our mother's knee; we have uttered it in the Lord's prayer; it is the background of all we learned in the Sunday-school; it is the atmosphere of our religious reading and our church life; it is the inspiration and support of our Christian experience. We have never stopped to define what the idea means to us, but have taken it for granted as we take the air, friendship, education, and democracy. We have shrunk from exact definition, since we preferred to leave it in the region of feeling; in its very vagueness lies much of its power to quicken reverence and awe and to appeal to simple trust; even if in this way God is removed far from us, he is yet brought near. In avoiding definition we have hoped to escape the aridness of an abstract notion of God and the bitterness of controversy over a logical concept which has only a remote and equivocal bearing on religious experience. Moreover, there is the feeling that to drag this sentiment out from its reticent retreat and turn on it the cold light of reason, force it to give an account of itself and to justify its existence on pain of rejecting it, is nothing less than the unpardonable sin.

On the other hand, in response to a legitimate demand of the human mind, the idea of God has been made a subject of thought and treated with profound reverence and with all the resources available to rational inquiry. Experience, reason, tradition, psychology, metaphysics, the Scriptures and the mind of Jesus, the scientific world-view, history,—indeed, every avenue of approach, every principle of interpretation has been laid under contribution, and each has brought its gift to the enrichment of this, the greatest of all ideas. In this procedure, then, we are not only following a natural impulse, but also acting under the sanction and encouragement of other "seekers after God."

We do not arbitrarily go in search of our theme as if it were a matter of caprice to select this instead of some other equally indifferent subject. Vast fundamental changes in every branch of science—in physics, biology, history and psychology, the powerful impact of present-day systems of thought, as Radical Empiricism and the New Realism, and not least the clothing of this idea in appealing literary form, free from every dogmatic fetter, —all of these present fresh problems and make imperative a re-interpretation of "the meaning of God in human experience."

This work aims at such a presentation of the idea of God as will enable it to function anew in the life of to-day. In the attempt three leading interests are combined—historical, critical, and constructive. Wherever a historical survey would elucidate our problem, this has been undertaken. Because both past and present conceptions of God contain many unequal and discordant elements, these have been subjected to critical inquiry with the view of sifting out such as are of permanent validity. And in order that the results thus reached may not be left floating around as *disjecta membra* on a sea of thought, they have been helped to form themselves according to their natural affinities into the authentic features of the Living God.

The reader who notes the absence of an explicit metaphysics may console himself with the reflection, first, that the material required to make good such a deficiency would necessitate the writing of another volume, and secondly, that the positions of the present work are such as may be trusted to verify themselves in his religious experience and to harmonize with the spiritual element of the Scriptures and the scientific view of the world.

Finally, the author would not extinguish the torch by which his path has been lighted, but would hand it on to others that they, guided by its flame, may discover further and more precious meanings in him who is for us the Living God.

This foreword must not close without an expression of unmeasured indebtedness to President Ozora Stearns Davis for his generous encouragement in the carrying out of this task, and then for the fact that he, together with Mrs. Grace Tinker Davis, in their cottage at Sunapee Lake and afterward read the manuscript of this book and offered suggestions which led to the simplifying of some obscure and many difficult paragraphs. The author is, however, solely responsible for the judgments herein expressed.

CLARENCE AUGUSTINE BECKWITH.

Chicago Theological Seminary,
   5757 University Avenue, Chicago.

CONTENTS

I.

CAUSES NECESSITATING CHANGE IN THE IDEA OF GOD

II.

HISTORICAL SKETCH OF THE IDEA OF GOD

CONTENTS

CONTENTS

CONTENTS

XIII.

THE LIVING GOD

THE IDEA OF GOD

I. CAUSES NECESSITATING CHANGE IN THE IDEA OF GOD

I

UNTIL recently the idea of God has been regarded as among the most permanent and unchanging of all human conceptions. This idea as defined by the Council of Nicaea in 325 A. D., seemed destined to perpetual validity. Later the so-called Athanasian Creed elaborated with infinite refinement the definitions of the Nicaeno-Constitanopolitan Creed and demanded assent to the dogma on pain of eternal damnation. It thus became the corner-stone of the great systems of theology; it provided the keynote of sermons by celebrated divines; it was accepted as final by the vast majority of Christian believers, whether Greek Orthodox, Roman Catholic, or Protestant; and even now Jewish theologians regard this dogma as the authentic and irreformable word of Christian teaching about God. This conception has not maintained itself without challenge from various quarters, especially from metaphysics and ethics. Its metaphysical basis was most seriously called in question by Spinoza, Kant and Hegel. The ethical objection came from the Socinians, and later the Unitarians and Universalists. Yet in spite of these criticisms, any one of which if it had prevailed would have profoundly modified the traditional doctrine of God, the official dogma remained for the most part unaffected by these and other influences. It was felt to be so entrenched in tradition, so fortified by impregnable arguments, so much at home in the sentiments of the common people, so essential to the welfare of the church, that it appeared to be destined to last as long as human life on the globe. It has been assumed that whatever changes took place in any other department of man's life, the form of this dogma would persist inviolate to the latest time.

Two considerations, however, invalidate such an expectancy. The first arises from the fact that the traditional idea of God was the product of conditions of the time in which it appeared. Those who formulated the ancient doctrine did so under the assured conviction that they were putting into authoritative and permanent form only that which had been given by divine revelation; all later additions to the definition, so far as these have been sanctioned by the church, have been supposed to be coined from the same divine deposit of truth. There are, however, constituent elements of this dogma which have no other source than the consciousness of the time. These elements are derived in part from political ideals, in part from ethical beliefs, in part from the prevailing philosophy, and in part from the peculiar religious experience of those who formulated the dogma. Accordingly, the dogma can be dated by an analysis of its contents and comparison of these with the ruling ideas of the time. Historically every doctrine represents two functions: first, to unify and express the social ideals and customs of an age, so far as these bear on the subject at hand,—it becomes thus an incarnation; secondly, in its precision of statement, to condemn and set aside competing tendencies which are struggling for the mastery. This is the more evident according as the idea is greater and the interests involved in it more absorbing and influential. At no moment in the history of the Christian church has a single

idea meant so much or drawn to itself so many elements
of the prevailing thought and life of the time as when
the Nicene doctrine of God was formulated. And if the
historical conditions of which it was the exponent could
have continued unchanged, it would have remained a fixed
and changeless dogma, adapted to the permanent intellectual and religious needs of the church. That the dogma
has persisted for so long a time bears witness to its greatness and to the fact that social and other conditions have
until a comparatively recent period suffered no radical
change.

The second consideration is that since the idea of God
is functional and conditions have arisen far different from
those in the early centuries, we must expect a corresponding change in this idea. In the following paragraphs
some of these changes will be indicated. Meantime we
need to remind ourselves that an attempt so to define the
idea of God as to keep it wholly aloof from the modern
view of the world is to place it in extreme jeopardy. All
the sciences have been born since the fourth century, and
have changed the meaning of the universe for all thoughtful men. The social order has undergone profound modification. The simple fact is that the Nicene idea of God
does not interpret the world to the modern man; between
that idea and the world of to-day is an impassable gulf.
If the alternative is either that idea of God unmodified
or none, then the conclusion must be—no God. Such an
idea cast in irreformable dogma is the greatest possible
encouragement to atheism. For several years now the
difficulties of this position have steadily increased. Men
have been stigmatized as unbelievers, sceptics, or atheists,
not on the ground that they repudiated all reference to a
Power in the universe higher than themselves,—no one
has ever held such a view,—but solely because they could

not reconcile their thought of the universe with the common dogmatic definition of God. Moreover, additions to the idea of God have been made by theologians, so that in successive generations these newer ideas have become an integral part of accredited orthodoxy. It has even happened that although the basic portion of the earlier conception was retained, yet the additions, as in Calvinism, when judged by ethical standards, were even more objectionable than the original elements.

If the idea of God could have received final statement in the fourth century, it is the only idea of the human mind of which this may be said. An idea, no matter in what field, which has ceased to grow is either moribund or dead. Those who betray greater anxiety to preserve the exact form of the ancient definition of God than to find the meaning of it in the changing conditions of each new day, treat it as if it were safe only when mummified, shut away from light and air, bound fast in the grave-clothes of tradition. Whereas this idea is the most vital and energetic, the most changeable and yet the most enduring, the most susceptible to external influence and the most capable of varied statement—always partial but always suggestive—of all the ideas of men. There is no cause for alarm that this idea has been taken down from its pillared security and subjected to the same analytic scrutiny, the same impartial judgment, the same liability to revision which has marked the consideration of economic and other social problems. In these latter fields immeasurable progress has been made; theories having the sanction of immemorial and undivided tradition, shown to be no longer tenable, have given place to others which more fully interpret our modern world. And we have a right to expect a similar result with reference to the idea of God. In any case no change which could come to it would

be as dangerous as keeping it apart from the thought and
experience of the modern spirit.

II

If now we inquire what are the causes which impel to a
restatement of the idea of God, we may discover some of
them in the following conditions, to a consideration of
which the remainder of this section will be devoted.
There is first the impulse from the changed views which
have taken place in all other departments of human interest. There is not a single subject on which the content
of men's thought remains the same as it was no longer
than fifty years ago. To feel the force of this suggestion one would have only to pass in rapid survey a few
of the great outstanding judgments and beliefs of that
time. The point of view, the instruments of investigation, the method of inquiry, the things sought for and
discovered, the particular interests involved, all are different. And when we come to religious questions, the
same is true. Of the historic doctrines of the church,
aside from the idea of God, not one but has undergone
redefinition—inspiration, revelation, the Scriptures, authority, creation, providence, the supernatural, sin, the
person and work of Christ, conversion, prayer, the world
to come. This fact creates a strong presumption and
expectancy that a corresponding change will mark the
present-day idea of God.

III

We have to recognize the dominance of the scientific
spirit as compared with the spirit which prevailed during

the period when the idea of God was formulated. The scientific spirit is marked by certain characteristic tendencies and habits. Its approach to reality is through observation and experiment. It relies upon inductive verification. All questions which involve human beliefs, customs, and ideals are subjected to historical inquiry. In no field of interest is this method more fruitful than in the study of religion and the contents of dogma. These are traced through the various stages of their development to their sources, in order to discover the permanent and unchanging elements in their multiplicity of forms. Here the whole question of authority has to be reviewed and revised. No scientific man thinks of wholly rejecting authority in his search for truth; he simply modifies its meaning. Instead of yielding assent to a position on the ground that this has been demanded by a body of men, he first assures himself that they are reliable witnesses of that to which they testify; and his assent is qualified by the reservation that the conclusions are subject to verification and revision. He is thus committed to the attitude of historical criticism, in the light of which it is seen that no belief retains its validity unchanged through perpetual generations. The presumption is thus created that a doctrine such as the idea of God, which originated in modes of thought alien to the modern scientific spirit and world-view, requires restatement, in order to become acceptable to the scientific temper and intelligence of to-day.

IV

A changed view of the world cannot fail to influence our idea of God. The traditional idea was connected with certain conceptions of the world which are no longer

possible to us. The world, for example, originated in
an absolute creative act, due to an instantaneous divine
fiat. All the various orders of existence, especially living
beings, were created in their present forms, fixed and
incapable of transmutation. The Ptolemaic astronomy
provided the setting for the relation of the earth as central not only to the solar system but to the rest of the
finite universe. As the world had an absolute beginning,
so it was to have an absolute end. God was free to create
or not to create, and free at any moment to withdraw
his sustaining power, in which contingency the world
would sink into nothingness; his power was also unlimited
in respect to every single thing, to allow it to exist as it
is or arbitrarily to change it. While therefore the world
was utterly dependent on God, he was in no sense
dependent on the world. His inner (Trinitarian) life
remained wholly unaffected by the creation.

If anything in the world appeared to oppose God, this
was referred not to a property inherent in it, but solely
to the limitation which God before the origination of it
saw fit to impose upon his own action. In view of the
fact, on the one hand, that in the nature of the world
as we know it, there is not a single thing which argues
for an absolute beginning of its existence,—and "revelation" is silent concerning this,—and, on the other hand,
that there is the same reason for assuming that the ultimate constituents of being are eternal as there is for
holding that anything exists now, the idea of God begins
to take on a very different character. There are also
certain realities which lie wholly beyond the region of
possible creation, which are by their very nature changeless and eternal, as, for example, time and space, number, the principles of logic, and also the principles of
change. Nor must we here overlook the evolutionary

doctrine of the world, which holds that the entire process
of development is to be referred to resident forces, operating according to ascertainable fixed laws, implying, if at
all, a vastly different divine activity from that which tradition alleges.   Moreover, there is evil in the world which
is no less inherent and indestructible in it than is goodness; this which does not originate by divine permission is
not to be overcome by divine power.   Furthermore, when
we consider personality and the social aspect of the world
we become aware of the serious limitations set by these to
the power of God.   The naïve notion of him revealed in
the beautiful story of the Garden of Eden is unworkable
and out of place in relation to conditions of modern civic
and industrial communities.

V

The present-day use of the Scriptures opens a way to
a changed view of God.   The Bible is no longer equivalent
to a treatise on systematic theology from which one may
cull proof-texts to substantiate and expound doctrinal
positions.   Instead of this, the writings which are here
brought together under one cover represent the progressive ideals and achievements of the Hebrew people under
the most varied conditions.   If we confess that it contains
for us the final standard of faith and practice, this must
mean not that it offers a logical and ultimate form of
belief on all matters affecting our life, but rather that
the principles and aims which are fundamental in it are
permanently valid for the highest and farthest reaches of
individual, social, and religious life.   We cannot, however, without further ado find in the Scriptures our final
idea of God.   For we should have first to inquire which

of the many ideas there presented is to be received. It could not be precisely that of Moses or of the Judges, or of David, or the prophets, or of Paul, or even of Jesus, and that too for several reasons. (1) While each of these ideas of God was in turn adequate for the particular period in which it appeared, it became progressively insufficient for later conditions. (2) It is impossible for any generation to push back its thought-forms into the exact molds of any preceding time, and this is especially true of two ages so dissimilar as the first and the twentieth centuries of the Christian era. (3) Since every idea assumes a definite content as it functions for a given condition, under different conditions the idea will necessarily undergo serious modification. No idea of God which arises under historical conditions is permanently valid for the rational and religious consciousness.

Even if we supposed that the idea of God was given by revelation, this would not solve our problem. For on this supposition the different ideas of God in the Scriptures would have to be referred to revelation, and since all of these would have to be ascribed equally to revelation, we would be left without a criterion by which to judge which was binding on us. Again, even assuming revelation as the source, we know of no revelation which is not historically conditioned. We would accordingly be unable to distinguish ideas which owe their origin to revelation and those which emerge in the personal and social development of consciousness. Moreover, the Scriptures themselves make no claim to finality but point beyond themselves to other times, to richer experiences, and to further disclosures of God for the meaning of life. The ideas, instead of being full-grown and rigid—an arrested development—having therefore exhausted their initial impulse, are on the contrary germinant, with all the marks of a living organism; they are continually changing, with exhaustless adaptability to circumstances, capacity of self-renewal, with a certain directive control over the raw material of experience for self-maintenance, and susceptibility to certain varieties of stimulus by which they take on different forms.   The ideals of the Hebrew religion are consciously incomplete, the New Testament looks forward to a further unfolding of the meaning of its faith in which God will appear in yet more glorious revelation of his creative will.   Already to their simple idea of him, derived from the prophets, Jesus, and their own limited experience, the apostles began to add material from Greek and other sources, and so opened the door for still further assimilation and enrichment.   They seem not to have reflected upon what was involved in this process, which was indeed inevitable.   But they were radically right in their central conviction that the deepest and most permanent need of humanity is justice, love, forgiveness, purity of heart, sympathy, peace, loyalty, and that wherever these are, there God is and is essentially defined by them. To these moral qualities, properties of a metaphysical nature were added, and a sanction was therefore provided for further accretions which were certain to follow from contact with other types of rational religious thought.

VI

A transformation of the notion of authority involves a change in the idea of God.   As long as authority was conceived of as external, the only hope for a change in the idea of God lay in the possibility that the leaders of the churches might revise their doctrine and send it forth under the same sanction which attended the earlier dogmas. Such a hope was, however, destined to be unrealized. Now by far the vast majority of Christian believers in the world—the Greek, Roman Catholic, most of the Lutheran, many Episcopalian, and indeed great numbers of other churches—hold a doctrine of God which in its essential features is practically identical with that in existence fifteen hundred years ago. Essential to this position are peculiar conceptions of revelation, reason, faith, and the autocratic right to impose beliefs.   (1) Revelation is regarded as a miraculous communication of truth to which the recipient brings only a passive acquiescence. Since the content of revelation transcends the capacity of the human mind to discover, it comprises mysteries which, if they do not contradict what is held to be true in other regions of thought, and in certain instances even if they do contradict, are to be accepted. While it is conceded that some knowledge of God may be had from the order and ends in nature, from history, and from the moral consciousness, yet the chief, the ultimate reliance is placed on revelation. On the other hand, the official doctrine of God contains elements which can by no possibility be justified by any theory of knowledge, as, for example, the metaphysical affirmations concerning the inner Trinitarian life; these, therefore, if their validity were questioned, would have to be referred to revelation. (2) In harmony with this notion of revelation, the reason is conceived of as an instrument not for arriving at the highest knowledge of God, but for dealing with secondary matters, for judging of the credentials of a supposed revelation, and for arranging in logical order the truths thus communicated. (3) Accordingly, faith is an attitude of mind to which the revelation is addressed—waiting, passive, receptive. Since the revelation is enshrined in dogma, faith becomes assent to propositional notions. **(4) Going**

along with this is the unquestioned trustworthiness which
belongs to the Scriptures, to the decisions of councils, and
to the prestige of great names. This entire point of view
is well summed up as follows: "There must be some central authority whose duty it is to lay down the broad
lines along which and within which those who wish to be
in a state of salvation may travel." [1]

The notion of authority has, however, undergone a
radical change. It has been shifted to an inner court.
It has emancipated the individual conscience from ecclesiastical control. It holds to the self-evidencing power of
truth. It appeals to the subjective as well as to the col-
lective judgment of men. While it adheres to the social
aspect of authority, it finds the meaning of this in the
fact that if truth has been already arrived at by a few,
yet this is equally open to the experience and justification
of all others. It consecrates the findings of scientific men,
providing material for the idea of God which is no less
valid than the decisions of councils solemnly affirmed by
accredited theologians.

According to this view, there are many aspects of
authority: the authority of history, the authority of
experience, the authority of the purposive ideal, the
authority of the rational judgment, the authority of
moral values, and the authority of religious yearnings.
In this light several new meanings become clear. Revelation is a disclosure of the purpose of God through the
interpretation of history and experience and social well-
being. Reason is the power and the only power by which
the meaning of the divine will is ascertained and formulated. Faith is not static, as assent to propositional
statements, but is dynamic and teleological, surrender to

---

[1] F. W. Wormley, *The Theology of the Church of England*, p. 34.

the ideal as this authenticates itself in consciousness. So radical a change in the elements which are involved in authority cannot but impel to a corresponding change in the idea of God,—a change which shall represent the free and boundless movement of the human spirit in its search for the Ultimate Reality.

VII

The idea of God is subject to further change through a redefinition of the supernatural. The conception of the supernatural has a long and significant history. From its earliest appearance in consciousness on into present-day theism it has undergone so many modifications that we can with difficulty detect traces of the earlier in the latest view. Yet with diminishing emphasis the characteristic feature has persisted: the absolute freedom of the divine power and its superiority to the forces of the world in which it operates. In earlier times this divine power was conceived of as acting with pure unhindered arbitrariness,—a point of view which still survives in the doctrine of the absolute sovereignty and predestination of God; yet gradually the scope of its manifestation has been narrowed until now it has nearly reached the vanishing point. Its functioning has been variously defined. It has, for example, been brought into play to account for great moments in the history of our world, as the creation, the beginning of life, the origination of consciousness, and the appearance of the moral consciousness in man. It has also been requisitioned in connection with miracles and answers to prayer. According to some thinkers, miracles have been restricted to Old Testament and apostolic times; accordingly, all so-called ecclesiastical miracles occurring

since the last of the apostles are stigmatized as counter-
feit. Others maintain that, although the supernatural
continues to manifest itself in miracles and answers to
prayer, yet these must be comparatively few, lest their
too great frequency destroy our belief in the order of
nature and the uniformity of the divine action; in any
case, even if God does not interfere, his power to do so is
strenuously upheld. Owing to the pressure of modern
thought, defenders of the supernatural have been divided
into two camps. One, recognizing at length the untenability of its former contention, has reluctantly yielded its
positions one by one and accepted the scientific view of
the world, together with its implications. The other camp,
repudiating modernism and the scientific interpretation of
reality and retreating into positions abandoned by the
advancing intelligence of educated men, is still advocating
antiquated and indefensible theories of creation and miracles. The motive urging to this procedure is indeed com-
mendable, since it springs from the feeling that only in
this way can the idea of God be guarded from mistaken
and destructive interpretations. But the apprehension is
groundless. The reality of the supernatural depends not
on any theory of creation as an absolute origination
of the world, or of miracles as suspensions or violations of
the laws of nature. No such doctrine is found in either
the Old or the New Testament. And now for a long
time, ever since Spinoza and Leibnitz, and especially
Hume, a definition of miracles has been sought which
would be relieved of difficulties originating in metaphysics,
science, and experience. At the present time two suggestions are frequently met with. One is to the effect that
miracles, regarded as phenomena, are unusual or
extraordinary events; the other is that miracles consist
essentially in the coincidence between an event and a

prophet's word,—in which the ghost of Leibnitz is seen to walk once more.

In the interest of a theistic interpretation of the world, the tension between the natural and the supernatural is relieved by regarding these from different angles, as the causal and the teleological. From the point of view of their cause, events are natural, so far as referred to uniform and concomitant variation among phenomena; they are supernatural so far as referred ultimately to the will of God. From the point of view of end, the distinction between the natural and the supernatural is seen not in an essential difference between the events in which these are embodied, but solely in the degree of their value for religious experience. The profound change in the meaning of the supernatural which has been thus described will contribute its part in the reconstruction of the idea of God.

VIII

We now turn to the newer conception of the historical origin of the idea of God. The common theory refers it to two sources, reason and revelation. (1) From the point of view of reason, God is defined as an "infinite and perfect Spirit in whom all things have their source, support, and end." This is claimed to be a rational intuition or a first truth, the marks of which are universality, necessity, and independence and priority in relation to all other truths. Other views concerning the Supreme Being are referred to perversions or misinterpretations of the intuitive conviction. All of our knowledge and mental processes, our certainty that the universe is a unity and has rational ends involves belief in God. This intuition implies that men know what God is as the ultimate reality of the world,—Perfection of Reason, Power, and Personality. The idea of perfection results from three processes: negative, denying to God all limitations of the creature; positive, affirming of God all perfections of the creature; and by way of causality, maintaining that he is the ground of all effects in the world. (2) Revelation does not so much originate the idea of God in the sense of creating its first beginnings, but rather aids in illumining, guiding, correcting, and completing it as it emerges in the rational intuition which it presupposes. This revelation appears in nature, history, the moral consciousness, and the Scriptures. From the Scriptures are derived all those qualities of God which are involved in redemption— the Trinity, the decrees, the divine mercy as subordinate to justice, the will to forgive sinners through an expiatory sacrifice, and the final judgment.

These two explanations of the origin of the idea of God refer it not only to two different sources, but to sources so disparate that the elements thus derived can be harmonized with each other only by a mechanical process. To derive the idea from an intuition of reason and then supplement it by revelation is a purely arbitrary procedure; to hold that supernatural revelation communicates truth which is otherwise inaccessible to the reason is to allege an impossible definition of reason and revelation. In any case, both of these explanations, each for a different reason, is wholly inadequate for its task. The origin, including the development, of the idea of God is to be sought in the historical conditions through which the different races of men have passed. The aim of every religion has been to enable men not only to overcome in the struggle for existence, but even more to attain fullness of life. How to escape sin, suffering, sorrow, and death, how to win compensations for the frustrations of endeavor, how to discover the values which are possible to experience, how to find courage and strength for the common social tasks,—this is the aim of every religion, and these are the conditions which determine the content of the idea of God. Accordingly, different peoples in different ages and countries, and the same people in different times and conditions, develop different ideas of God. In fact, however, people are not the same when conditions change. Two conclusions follow: (1) An idea of God which suffices for one people cannot answer for another people at the same or at another age of the world, nor indeed for the same people at a further stage in its own history. Whatever may be alleged of the finality of the great dogmatic definitions of God, as that of the Council of Nicaea, the fact is that this idea as it appears in Augustine, Thomas Aquinas, and the leaders of religious thought in modern times reveals progressive modifications which reflect the changing conditions of thought and experience. (2) Since all ideas are functional and no idea of God meets all the varied needs of all Christian people at a given time, there must be many variations of it to embody the requirements of different groups. A cross-section of present-day religious thinking discloses a rather bewildering diversity of ideas of God, as these appear in Calvinism, Arminianism, Socinianism, monism, panlogism, voluntarism, vitalism, pluralistic pragmatism, and the New Realism,—each one an attempt to solve the problem of existence from a different point of view and in answer to a particular set of needs. Nor are we at the end of these endeavors, which should be welcomed by all who are in search of truth whose only function is to serve the well-being of men. The gains of the recent past should assure us that the future will open new paths into the meaning of God.

IX

The discovery that the traditional idea of God is a
blending of two types of thought—Semitic and Aryan—
which will later be subjected to more specific exposition,
is significant. The derivation of the entire metaphysical
content of the official doctrine of God from Greek speculative thought, to which attention was called by Hamp-
den,[1] by Ritschl [2] in 1850, by Harnack,[3] and by Hatch,[4]
raises several interesting questions. One is, whether the
Greek elements originating in a different world in answer
to a philosophical rather than an empirical religious need
should not be eliminated from our interpretation of God
from the Christian point of view. If this course should
not recommend itself, on the ground that the Nicene
Creed added to the Semitic conception of God only those
materials from Greek thought without which it could not
function in the religious life of those whose ideals were
determined by the Greek culture, then two further questions arise. (1) Whether the Greek metaphysics, both
in its form and in its content as it appears in this Creed,
is now an indispensable element in our idea of God. (2)
Whatever answer we given to this question, a further
inquiry emerges: if the Hebrew and the earliest Christian
conceptions of God were necessarily transformed by reason of having to function for the Greek consciousness,
does not the same law hold good as this idea makes its
way in the ever changing conditions which confront it as
it passes from one stage of civilization to another, from

---

[1] Bampton Lectures, 1832, on the *Scholastic Philosophy Considered
in Its Relation to Christian Theology.*
[2] *The Origin of the Old Catholic Church.*
[3] *History of Dogma,* 1886-1890.
[4] Hibbert Lectures, 1888, *The Influence of Greek Ideas and Usages
on the Christian Church.*

simpler to ever more complex and exacting moral and spiritual demands? Of two alternatives open to the idea of God, that of remaining on the Nicene foundation or advancing to meet the needs of to-day, the first would be suicidal; in the second alone lies the hope of its continuous ministry to the life of the world.

X

The bearing of the new study of Jesus Christ on the idea of God is profound and far-reaching. In orthodox circles, until less than one hundred years ago the doctrine of God remained wholly unaffected by reference to the historical Jesus. The Socinians had indeed interpreted God in the light of Jesus, but since this interpretation ignored or discredited much of the theology of the schools, it was rejected as dishonoring God. Kant had placed the knowledge of the metaphysical content of the divine nature under grave suspicion. Schleiermacher found in the God-consciousness of Jesus the supreme disclosure of God. Strauss by his negative criticism stimulated the study of the historical Jesus to an astonishing degree. In addition we may be reminded of the more recent attempt to make theology Christocentric. All these movements have contributed to withdraw attention from the purely dogmatic, speculative idea of God to the ethical content of his personality. There are still published elaborate works on theism where the traditional arguments for the being of God are advocated. God as the Absolute is still presented in writings of great cogency; but the attention of Christian thinkers is surely moving to another field of interest. Men are seeking for that idea of God which will make a difference in their lives. This

they find in the conception of Fatherhood, as reflected in
the spirit of Jesus. There are those who say that Jesus
Christ is the only God they know; others maintain that
God must be like Jesus. Such positions greatly restrict
the scope of the activity traditionally attributed to God
and preclude reference to qualities in God which are
proper subjects of inquiry; they ignore many questions
which have only a speculative interest, which is indeed
legitimate enough in its place; and they tend to make that
controlling for thought which is believed to be central in
the life of God and most influential in the life of men.

Nothing more truly defines the bearing of Christian
thought to-day than its reference of all ideals of conduct
to Jesus Christ. The Christian character finds its spirit
and aim embodied in him; and the social welfare is safe
only in adherence to the principles of his teaching and
life. Plain men who have become confused and weary
with the scholastic definitions of God, partly because they
do not understand them, and partly because if they do
understand them they are not able to see what relation
they have to actual human experience, find Jesus intelligible,—not the Jesus of the theologians, with their bewildering doctrine of nature and substance and person, but
the Jesus of the Synoptic gospels. If they look beyond
him for some one who shall mean more to them than he
does, such a one must mean at least as much as he means;
and if such a one perchance means more, the more must
be interpreted in the light of what is most real and precious in Jesus. Thus the new values which have been
discovered in Jesus Christ are carried over and incorporated into the idea of God. Welcome is every fresh exposition of the gospels, every new interpretation of the
secret of his life for the sake of the light thus thrown
upon the highest spiritua lends.

XI

The transition from the philosophy to the psychology of religion is radically significant for the idea of God. The psychology of religion occupies a different point of view and presents other materials than those which have hitherto been available. It is in no way concerned with metaphysics. It deals with reality as dynamic rather than static. It knows and can know nothing of an aspect of reality conceived of as at rest behind the changing forms of phenomena. It is therefore silent on many of the subjects to which systematic theology has devoted prolonged attention in the doctrine of God. The theistic arguments find no place in such a study. Its presentation of the divine attributes is at a far remove from the traditional treatment of them: self-existence, immutability, eternity, immensity, omniscience, omnipotence, omnipresence, the transcendent Trinity, and divine decrees, so far as these are based on metaphysics, are ignored, with the result that to those who are accustomed to the dogmatic method in theology, the contents of the psychological treatment seem meagre and disappointing. This is, however, due to the fact that we have been so long accustomed to seek our material for the idea of God from quarters which sustain no organic relation to experience, which could neither arise nor be verified in the utmost ranges of possible experience. The doctrines in question may correspond with reality, but since their truth can never be established, their bearing is purely speculative and without influence upon practical life.

The psychology of religion shows that religion is only another way of describing an aspect of the highest personal and social interests of men. When these life-interests of a given group are summed up and unified, they

represent an idea of God which, in however fragmentary
form, expresses a true, even if imperfect, notion of the
divine. The characteristic note here is the consciousness
of value. The idea of God thus becomes another name
for the highest ideal values of men. Since these values
are undergoing continual transmutation, at one time ceas-
ing to function, at another passing into higher meanings,
the idea of God changes to correspond. This idea is
further shaped according to the type in which these
values have taken form in the social experience, as in
the nomadic, agricultural, and national, whether autocratic or democratic. The values thus enshrined in the
idea of God have no other basis or guarantee than what
they derive from the consciousness itself. This is indeed
subjective, open to all the dangers of subjectivism, but
with all its liabilities to mistake, it must be accorded its
full worth. There are those who find in the consciousness
of value the essential content and the convincing test of
reality. Yet to any who wish to supplement the idea of
God as it appears in the psychology of religion by reference to other points of view, the way is not closed.

XII

The change from the static to the dynamic conception
of reality is fraught with promise in its influence upon
the idea of God. From the conception of atoms as inert
substances moved by an external force, taking form and
serving ends for which they have no inherent fitness, the
entire universe is resolved into energy which is disclosed
in the equipoise of action and reaction, or in change where
the action for the moment exceeds the reaction; but
always with a tendency to return to dynamic equilibrium.

This does not indeed do away with atoms and electrons, since these are resulting equipoises between uniformly acting dynamic forces. In the psychical region the dynamic view is still more impressive. Here, instead of postulating a mind-substance, one, indivisible, unchangeable, attention is directed to the fact of consciousness where what appears to be static as habit is the equilibrium established between perpetually active dynamic elements. However deep we push our inquiry into the nature of our world, we are never able to pass beyond energy into a substratum of inactive and changeless Being. Everywhere is action, movement, freedom—a dynamic universe. This changed point of view compels momentous changes in the conception of God. It necessitates a different meaning to creation and providence, but also to the very nature of God. If God has anything to do with the creation of the world and with control in it, then he must be the kind of Reality which answers to the world as we know it. And if energy is the characteristic principle of the intelligible universe and there is nowhere revealed a resting substratum which is fixed and changeless while the universe is subject to continual flux, an irresistible presumption is created that the Most Real Being will likewise be energy, activity, and will; accordingly the terms essence, substance, and nature must be interpreted not as a resting basis, but in terms of energy, that is, of will and purposive activity.

XIII

Closely allied with this is the part assigned to experience in determining the idea of God. There are two points of view from which this may be considered. (1) Experience is conceived to be the sole source of the knowledge of God. This theory has never been consistently worked out, but it represents a strong tendency of religious thinking. According to Scheiermacher, the basis for the idea of God lies neither in the *consensus gentium* nor in the fitness of the human soul for religion, but in religious experience, and more particularly in Christian experience. Experience is then resolved into the feeling of absolute dependence. This in turn involves absolute causality as the corresponding fundamental property of God. In the reciprocal relation of dependence and causality as this is focused in the Christian consciousness is revealed the character of the divine attributes. These attributes are, however, not to be affirmed of God as he is in himself, since we have no valid objective knowledge of him; the divine attributes are not separate forms of the essential being of God, but only ways in which we interpret our feeling of dependence. In this feeling of dependence there are given three aspects of our knowledge of God: (1) in relation to the world and strictly limited by the world, God is eternal, active, omnipresent, almighty, all-knowing; also one, unlimited, simple; (2) as disclosed in the contrast of sin and grace, God is holy, since he legislates duty to the conscience, and righteous, since he connects evil with sin; the essence of God is love as revealed in the will to redemption; (3) the idea of God in the Trinity—the union of the divine with the human in the person of Christ, and continued in the common spirit of the Christian community.

(2) The other point of view from which experience is made the determining condition of the idea of God is not so much theoretical as practical. The powerful movement of religious life introduced by Wesley, while it carried along with it the dogmatic definition of God, yet, by its emphasis upon experience, tended to retire into the

background all those ideas of him which did not lend
themselves to the immediate uses of faith and practice.
The preaching necessary for the great revivals of religion
and in general the character of the people to whom for
the most part this kind of preaching has ministered, have
made it imperative that the message of the gospel draw
its power from the moral and redemptive side of God.
So far as those who occupy this point of view have encour-
aged religious revivals, engaged in social reforms, in the
inculcation of civic virtue, in the constant and everywhere
necessary ministry to the sinful, the sick, the suffering,
and the dying, they have drawn their inspiration from the
personal justice and compassion of a loving and faithful
God—the God and Father of our Lord Jesus Christ. Such
a message is created by experience, addressed to experience, and has no meaning outside of experience. And
because this idea works and other ideas of God derived
from metaphysics seem remote and ineffectual, many of the
most influential leaders of religious thought are indifferent
to any conception which does not bear directly upon the
Christian experience of to-day. We are therefore invited
to inquire as to the demands originating in Christian
experience which so far determines the content of our idea
of God.

XIV

The subjecting of the entire content of theology to
ethical standards is nowhere more significant than in its
influence upon the idea of God. Such a condition was
possible only in the later stages of Christian thought.
The traditional idea of God has been under a profound
double obsession; first, of Neo-Platonism with its doctrine
of an ultimate Reality utterly inaccessible to the human

reason; secondly, of Augustinianism, that to the will of God as absolute Sovereign is to be referred the arbitrary and irresponsible source both of God's action and man's obligation. This conception was further vitiated by two additional positions: that since the will of God was the sole source of right and wrong, the values of both might be reversed by a simple change in the divine will, and that while a portion of the divine will has been revealed to us, another, and possibly the most important, portion concerned with the divine decrees, remains hidden, known to God alone. As long as theologians by the aid of ecclesiastical authority could enforce such an idea of God, while it might measurably meet the need of the time,—it was the best they had, and any idea is better than none,—yet it would have to answer the challenge of the advancing moral consciousness. While it endured it occasioned many misgivings on the part of those who accepted it. Calvin confessed of one aspect of it, "I admit it is horrible!" In others it aroused only abhorrence; Wesley is reported as replying to a Calvinist, "Your God is my devil!" In the nature of things, it was permanently impossible that principles of conduct which were repugnant to men should be either attributed to God or tolerated in him. Purposes referred to him must be approved by the moral sense of men before they can be recognized as real in God and binding on the human will. For the ethical quest there is in the nature of God no unexplored remainder which, if reached, might yield up something irreconcilable with what we know of him. "God is light, and in him is no darkness at all."

The tendency under consideration is at present twofold. (1) To shift attention from the periphery to the center in the conception of God. Discussion of the natural attributes, so-called, such as wisdom and power, has given place to exposition of the moral qualities of goodness and love. If any conflict arises between omnipotence and goodness, the tension is resolved (as by John Stuart Mill) by the denial of unqualified omnipotence and subordination of it to goodness. (2) To ethicize the character of God to correspond with the advancing moral ideals of men. It is no longer possible to find a sanction for any form of social injustice which is obnoxious to the highest moral ideal by referring it to the divine will. A further tendency is powerfully operative, namely, to disentangle the purpose of God from all complicity with evil as such. He does not cause it; he does not will it as means to an end; he is forever against it and is forever committed to its overthrow. If evil is everlasting, even as is the good, yet in no sense and at no time may the idea of God be opened out so as to include evil in the slightest degree.

To make still more evident the ethical test to which the idea of God is subjected, we have only to remind ourselves of the efficacy of the criticism to which the historical doctrines of Christianity have been subjected; the doctrine of original sin according to which God accounted all men who were descended from Adam by natural generation guilty and liable to eternal death by reason of Adam's sin; the doctrine of an expiatory atonement, in which Christ assumed the guilt and punishment due to all or a portion of men for their sins; the doctrine of election according to which, out of his mere good pleasure, God from eternity chose some to everlasting life and reprobated or passed over others, thus dooming them to endless punishment; the doctrine of regeneration according to which, by almighty power, God miraculously recreates the governing disposition holy. These and other doctrines have as their chief significance the light which they throw on the conception of God. Christian thought has, how-

ever, taken all of these doctrines out of the region of pure
sovereignty, of mechanical substitution, of arbitrary
power, and required that they conform to the facts of
human experience and to ideals which alone make ethical
action possible. To the criticism, that to ethicize the
meaning of Christianity is to rob it of redemptive elements, and that to ethicize the character and action of
God is to strip him of his unique and irresponsible arbitrariness, it is to be replied, first, that the essential notion
of redemption is neither mysterious nor magical, but
ethical, and secondly, that justice and truth, goodness
and mercy have no other meaning with reference to God
than they have when applied to other moral beings.
Finally, since the characteristic idea of God in each
period registers the social ideal of that period, it is to
be expected that the profound changes through which the
world is passing, compelling new and hitherto undreamed-
of ideals, will necessitate corresponding changes in the
conception of God. As no one can forecast the form of
the new social order, so no one can measure the degree to
which the idea of God will experience modification and
enrichment. One may, however, safely assume that in the
immediate future the idea of God will be subject to more
radical change than it has undergone in any equal length
of time in the entire history of religious thought, and that
this change will in part take place in the ethical content
of its meaning.

XV

Various literary treatments of the idea of God bring to
expression the popular mood. Hitherto when the idea of
God has appeared in fiction, it has been in a purely formal
way. God has been brought in as a sort of figure-head

to give dignity to the story, to reinforce a moral situation, to lend atmosphere to the development of a plot, a sign-manual to indicate that the entire movement takes place in a Christian rather than a pagan environment; as the portrait of Washington, which we recognize as we pass it in the reception hall, shows that we are good Americans. Now, however, he who with silent voice and immobile features, but with benign and far-seeing eyes, has so long looked down upon us, has joined us in all the experiences of our life, not as a remote and detached beholder of our affairs, but one with us in the storm and stress of existence. Two instances may be adduced. In *Jean Christophe*,[1] Rolland says, "God was not to him the impassive Creator. . . . God was fighting. God was suffering. Fighting and suffering with all who fight and for all who suffer. For God was Life, the drop of light fallen into the darkness, spreading out, reaching out, drinking up the night. But the night was limitless and the divine struggle will never cease, . . . and none can know how it will end." H. G. Wells [2] declares that theologians have made extravagant claims for God, as, for example, that he is all-powerful, "but the common sense of men knows better. . . . It is not fair to say that he causes all things now. . . . God is not absolute; God is finite. A finite God who struggles in his great and comprehensive way as we struggle in our weak and silly way—who is with us—that is the essence of all religion."

While these are the most outstanding instances in recent fiction of a new conception of God, their significance lies less in their present form than in the fact that they herald the advent of a new day. Such writers are not to be

[1] Vol. III, p. 338.
[2] *Mr. Britling Sees It Through,* p. 406.

charged with levity or irreverence, or with simply exploiting a notion which by reason of its startling novelty will create a market for their books and furnish a fresh theme for the threadbare conversation of an afternoon tea. If the metaphysicians and theologians have no other God than one who is incapable of participating in human affairs—an abstract Deity, a logical formula, isolated and dwelling in Epicurean felicity—then those to whom the seething emotions and desperate struggles of our world are real will reinterpret God in terms of human need. If God is so defined that his existence and action make no practical difference to men, it is high time to ignore him altogether, as is even now the case with those to whom the traditional God means nothing, or else to seek some new conception which shall show him as really one with us in the experiences of our human lot. Moreover, when an idea, which has in one form become to a great extent inoperative, is presented in another form capable of functioning in new and more vital ways, those who are responsible for the time-worn idea are called upon to incorporate the newer meaning into their doctrine. Particularly is this true of an idea which, like Plato's idea of God, for fifteen hundred years dwelt undisturbed in the ethereal realms of speculative theology, but which has now descended to earth to take up its abode with men, to aid them in the creation and development of personal and social well-being. It is one thing when the idea of God is regarded as the possession of scholars, to be elaborated in learned treatises, to be read and understood by those only who have been trained in great universities; it is another and very different thing when an idea of God is presented in popular fiction which, reaching hundreds of thousands of readers, makes God for the first time of like nature with us, intelligible, sympathetic, companionable.

XVI

The new social emphasis in religion necessitates a redefinition of God. This arises from several points of view:

(1) To make the gospel real in settlement-work, house-to-house visitation, ministering to the sick, rescuing the fallen, caring for children, and other forms of approach to the hearts of men. Where God is indeed redeemer, comforter, and guide, he must be presented not only as one who knows the most intimate sins and sorrows and baffled hopes, but also as forgiving, soothing, and tenderly leading those who trust in him. This condition cannot, however, be permanently met by either of two methods. On the one hand, by presenting the God of the Nicene or Athanasian creed, or by defining him as an "immaterial substance, infinite, eternal, unchangeable in his being, wisdom, power, holiness, justice, goodness and truth." Such a being may answer the needs of theologians to whom his supreme quality is his aloofness and unlikeness to men, who are satisfied if he is so far away that even his very existence may be dispensed with and neither the virtue nor the happiness of men be seriously affected thereby. On the other hand, they are doomed to disappointment who expect that Christ can permanently take the place formerly occupied by God in religion,—the theologians having removed God to an inaccessible distance from men. This makes of Christ a kind of *interim* God, the outcome of which will be that either God will become practically disregarded, since he has no immediate contact with men, —in any case, he will have nothing of which men are in need,—or, since Christ can by no utmost stretch of reason or of faith take the ultimate place of God, a new definition of God will have to be suggested which will

reveal him as capable of the same real relation to men which Jesus realized in his own person.

(2) Religious education is in exigent need of a restatement of the idea of God. For the most part its subjects are young people, or, if the persons are mature, the character of the need is not changed. Many of these are in high school and college, with some training in science and some understanding of the modern view of the world. Few of them are versed in the subtleties of metaphysics, they know little and care less for the history of the traditional doctrine of God. What is required is some conception of God which shall make him real, attractive, and helpful to boys and girls, to youth as they cross the threshold of responsibility and self-realization, to men and women in the varied tasks of mature years, and which shall continue with them as they draw near to the end and the Silence. The historic creeds do not answer here; too many human events have happened since these great statements were drawn up. We do not think as their authors did concerning the Scriptures, the world, and man. Their philosophy is not ours. We care more for the concrete than for the abstract. We have far less faith in definitions than they had. We want no Deity who can be snugly imprisoned in cast-iron formulas and imposed by any body of men. Nor for religious education can we tolerate an idea of God which is belied by the highest intelligence of the age, inconsistent with every or even any science, from which in later years, if one will think in terms of modern thought, one frees himself only by a violent wrench.

(3) A further demand in this direction comes from the democratic consciousness which is fast spreading throughout the world. Two opposite and extreme types of social life—the autocratic and the democratic—have ever pro-

vided a favorable soil for the development of corresponding conceptions of God—kingship and paternity, sovereignty and love, transcendence and immanence. It will be impossible to preserve the absolute and irresponsible sovereignty of God when earthly kings have been deposed. The Scriptures speak of the casting down of kings and potentates that God alone may be exalted, but if earthly thrones disappear the throne in heaven will also pass away. Even Fatherhood, if it represents simply a paternal, however benevolent, instead of an all-pervading ministry of love, will cease to represent God to the democratic society. The analogy of Fatherhood is more significant as we discover another application. The father is father of the children, not that there may forever remain a gulf between him and them, nor are children born in order that they may forever be implicit subjects of the father's will, but rather that the relation of superiority and subordination may give place to intelligent, sympathetic, and complete mutuality. Jesus offers a suggestion which needs only to be carried into the relation of God and men: "No longer do I call you servants; for the servant knoweth not what his lord doeth; but I have called you friends; for all things which I have heard from my Father I have made known unto you."

We need constantly to remind ourselves that the principle of authority and the source of obligation are not wholly external, but partly and inalienably within—in the very nature of the moral consciousness and the moral ideal. The fear lest the basis of virtue would be removed or at least imperiled if the democratic were to supplant the autocratic relation of God to man is therefore groundless. Indeed, in no other than this conception can we find so rich a field for the culture of all individual and social good. If, however, one prefers an ethical to a political

term with which to characterize this relation, he may substitute "friendship" for "democracy" and all the values
will be equally conserved.   The aim is not to degrade God
to an unworthy plane so that he may share the Augus-
tinian limitations and defects of human nature, but to
maintain that man belongs to the divine type and is a
member of a commonwealth of which God is the first and
greatest, but whose priority and greatness only pledge
him the more to ministry and service.

XVII

The War has necessitated reconsideration and revision
of the idea of God.   Precisely what form the idea will
assume as a result of the War it is too early to predict.
Doubtless the change will take several directions.   Already,
however, many suggestions have been offered.   Some are
seriously advocating the notion that for two thousand
years God has been waiting for just this cataclysm of the
nations in order to bring to an end a world which has
grown old in sin and ripe for destruction.   Others have
advanced the view that God had no part in bringing on
the War; it is inconceivable that a Being of perfect love
could plunge a world into agony so monstrous and immeasurable.   Still others, feeling themselves obliged to choose
between goodness and omnipotence, have preferred to
regard the love of God as boundless, but to limit his
power: he would have prevented the cruelty, the blood-
shed, and the nameless horrors of the War, but he could
not.   There are others who are neither timid nor squeam-
ish, and are not afraid that God will be dishonored or
discredited if he is conceived of as a "Man of War," taking the necessary steps to bring about his ends, not with-

holding himself from even the "tumult and the shouting."
Once more there are those who have no theory as to the
agency of God relative to the War, but who find ample
scope for his action in guiding after-War conditions, in
directing the thoughts of men to just understanding of
the basis of national well-being, and in instilling into their
hearts a spirit of brotherhood and co-operation; and in
addition to this broader field, in countless ways inspiring
to individual and social ministry for those who have suffered and lost in the awful fortunes of war.

We cannot forecast the exact changes which will come
over the idea of God from this cause, yet several points
are clear. Some persons will steadfastly oppose any
modification of the traditional conception, insisting that
the War has served only to confirm all their previous
notions. Others will seriously attempt a readjustment
of their most cherished theories, with the aim of bringing
God into yet more intimate contact and agency with the
greatest social movement in history, of enlarging their
thought of him, and of reaching a basis of deeper confidence in the Living God. Already the many endeavors to
find a place for God in these tremendous events, even if
they are but partially successful, promise much for a
restatement of the meaning of God under present-day
conditions.

XVIII

The arguments for the being of God have now for
more than a century been subjected to searching criticism, with the result that in their commonly approved
form they bear little resemblance to the traditional statement of them. These will later receive suitable attention;
here the aim is only to suggest the influence which their
changed value has on the idea of God. If we limit our

reference to two of these arguments—the cosmological and the teleological—it is evident that so far as the idea of God is conditioned or defined by these, it cannot fail of being affected to the degree that they are discredited or transformed. If, for example, God is regarded as absolute Creator, on the ground that the cosmological argument leads to the First Cause in that sense, and it is shown that the argument is invalid when so conducted, and when God is conceived of as almighty Designer, on the ground that the argument for design proves universal contrivance in finite things, and it becomes evident that this argument is unsound, since the facts available do not warrant this inference, then, so far as the idea of God is dependent upon either or both of these conclusions, it must undergo modification. That these arguments may receive restatement is no doubt true, but in that case they will represent a different conception of the Supreme Reality. Other arguments, as the moral and the *consensus gentium*, have not justified the inferences drawn from them. If they are to be of service in our day, they must be redefined, with the result that a different God from the traditional one will emerge from the process. Moreover, if the theistic arguments no longer command assent from modern scholars, the idea of God to which they were supposed to lead no longer functions in the present-day religious needs of men. If, therefore, the newer rational approach to God is not more successful than that of former times, it would be better for us to ignore it altogether.

XIX

Another conception of God, which is not indeed the most fundamental, but which has occasioned much controversy, is expressed in the doctrine of the Trinity. This found dogmatic statement in the Nicene and later in the Athanasian formula. Although this is held to be binding in the larger portion of the Christian church, yet it has never received the undivided sanction of Christendom. The subject has provoked periodic criticism, many modifications have been proposed, and one may sum up the present situation as follows: (1) The being of God, if it is to have any meaning for either experience or thought, must be conceived as unity; never was this point of view more securely fixed for the definition of God. (2) Futile is the attempt to distinguish between Trinity and Triunity, on the ground that Trinity describes the self-manifestation, while Triunity refers to the inner and essential being, of God. (3) Schleiermacher's contention that the Trinity is the threefold way in which we become aware of the divine in our experience of redemption blazed the path for modern interpreters of this doctrine. (4) It is extremely significant that recent statements of the doctrine, differing as they do radically from the ancient formulas, are not controverted from the traditional side. This fact may be variously accounted for. The church may have shifted from the metaphysics of the Trinity to other subjects regarded as more vital to Christian experience. Many persons may have Sabellianized their view without being aware of the fact, and hence they do not feel the same repugnance to the modern presentations which they might otherwise feel. Moreover, since those who interpret this doctrine are yet careful to maintain the religious and spiritual values of the ancient formula, they are still within the spiritual fellowship of those from whom they differ in the phrasing of their faith. Unquestionably this doctrine has not received its final form; much is yet to be expected from a different logic, a different view of the world, and a different conception of experience.

II. HISTORICAL SKETCH OF THE IDEA OF GOD

I

In our survey of the history of the idea of God we are to consider only the high lights of its development, with the aim of ascertaining the principles which have guided the process and the contributions made by successive thinkers to the permanent meaning of the Reality. If we begin with the conception of the Hebrew prophets, this is not because they alone had a thought of God which arose out of their experience and was compelling, but because they were the most direct source from which the first Christian notion of God was derived.

II

At the outset attention is directed to two broad streams of tendency which flowed on for a time separately and then gradually merged in a common stream. Each appears to have originated in a different racial characteristic and to have satisfied a need destined to be complementary to the other. I refer to the Semitic quality of which the Hebrew prophets are the highest exponents, and the Aryan, which is for our purpose most fully realized in the Greek philosophers.

The Semitic idea of God is that of a Being in action. It took its rise in the variety and stress of experience: God disclosed himself in what he did. Knowledge of him was derived solely from his action. The Jewish religion developed under circumstances which necessitated belief in a God whose nature and relation to his people and the world were supremely ethical. The Jewish people had to believe this of their God. Their experience was attributed to a concept of God which was fundamentally ethical; Jahweh had chosen them; his relation to them was therefore not natural but ethical. In their passage from a nomadic existence through an agricultural stage to the complex conditions of a city and a state, with the necessity of subduing enemies and the organization of a unified social consciousness, they made increasing demands on the ethical character of their God. Their geographical location, their political exigencies, their experience in exile and afterward, intensified and defined to their consciousness practical needs which centered in their God. At first they did not know whether he would prove stronger than the gods of neighboring peoples, whether he would turn out to be greater than all gods, whether he would become the God of the whole earth who made and ruled all. Nor did they know until long afterward that their storm-god who became their tribal- and war-god was to disclose a spirit of impartial justice and a heart more tender than the heart of any mother. All the qualities of their God which underwent change were every single one ethical. The two matters on which more than on all else the welfare and progress of the world depend—sexual purity and social justice—were associated with a God who would ultimately tolerate neither the abominations of the Gentiles nor the inhumanity which violated the indefeasible rights of human life. Accordingly, as we receive the idea

of God from the hands of the prophets he is a self-conscious, perfectly free person; independent of the world,
yet absolute ruler of it; the eternal sovereign of men; the
alone Supreme in power, holiness, righteousness, wisdom,
love. The earlier polytheistic background has disappeared
and there has emerged an ethical monotheism.

At a period nearly parallel with this development of the
idea of God among the Hebrews, a similar process
appeared in Greek thought. Here, however, while the
ethical interest was by no means absent, attention was
concentrated upon the metaphysical properties of God.
The Aryan type of thought was essentially speculative.
Already both in Persia and in Greece, where Aryan
thought attained characteristic expression, the divine had
been conceived of in terms of essence rather than of action.
In Greece the conception of God reached its spiritual
summit in Plato and Aristotle. For Plato the world was
divided into two parts, the ideal and the actual. The
ideal or intelligible world is the world of ideas which are
immaterial, eternal, changeless, independent, self-existent,
and perfect. The highest idea is the absolute Good, that
is, God, supreme in the ideal as the sun is in the visible
world, immeasurably transcending all other reality in
value. The Good belongs to a higher category than personality; instead of being unreal, since God is an Idea,
he is the highest and only perfect Reality. In God is
accordingly found the meaning and purposive end of the
world.

To Aristotle God is pure intelligence, pure activity,
himself unmoved yet the prime mover of the visible world.
He is not creator "in the beginning," for the world equally
with God is self-existent and eternal. Although he has no
inwardly active relation to the world, yet he is the final
cause of all the motion in the world, precisely as the beau-

tiful and desirable attract, while he himself remains completely wrapped up in the contemplation of his own essential rational being. Now for the first time in human thought a metaphysical monism is established. Not merely as in Plato is God immateriality; he is pure spirituality or consciousness. Moreover, he is not only absolutely transcendent, but perfectly blessed.

In these two greatest of the Greek thinkers God is conceived of as purely rational. He does not rise out of the storm and stress of experience. He is not primarily ethical, even though in Plato he is called the perfect Good; indeed, the conditions of ethical being are in part denied to him.

A comparison of the Greek with the Hebrew idea of God reveals radically contrasting features—one static, the other dynamic; one ideal, the other historical; one metaphysical, the other ethical; one impersonal or superpersonal, the other intensely personal; one that of an abstract, the other that of a Living God.

The doctrine that the immaterial and the spiritual was the only reality failed to find its verification in further experience, unless indeed one portion of experience was to be resolved into an illusion. Accordingly, a type of thought arose which aimed to meet the new demand. The Stoics found in the material world the only reality, a position which involved a new definition of the material world. Instead of following Democritus in his simple atomic theory of all existence, the Stoics conceived of substance as neither pure matter nor pure mind, but as essentially dynamic. If Stoicism is to be referred to a Semitic origin, then its profound affinity with the volitional quality of the God of the Hebrews is explicable. The earlier dualism of Greek thought has disappeared; the universe has become a living being. God is conceived of as seminal reason, cosmic reason, universal law, destiny, providence.   Thus we are introduced to a thorough-going pantheism.   With Stoicism begins that long development of the idea of God in which "substance" plays a characteristic and consistent part.

The Epicurean theology marks an advance on the doctrine of Aristotle.   The gods exist indeed in complete isolation from the world and men; they

> "haunt
> The lucid interspace of world and world
> Where never creeps a cloud, or moves a wind,
> Or ever falls the least white star of snow,
> Nor ever lowest roll of thunder moans,
> Nor sound of human sorrow mounts to mar
> Their sacred everlasting calm." [1]

They are, however, endowed not only with self-consciousness, but with felicity.   An emotional quality now takes precedence as compared with Plato's rational principle; the rational principle is indeed present, but it is touched with emotion.   For the first time in religious thought happiness claims its right in an ideal experience.   The claim may be one-sided, and the gods thus described wholly self-centered, but humanity has learned its lesson. Henceforth no idea of God will be complete which lacks the property of joy.

III

Already in the New Testament period the Christian idea of God had been profoundly indebted not only to the Hebrew, but almost more to the Greek conception.   This

---

[1] Tennyson, *Lucretius.*

union of Hebrew and Greek thought which began to appear in several writings of the Old Testament and in the Apocrypha is still more significant in the New Testament. This is evident from several facts, such as emphasis on the transcendence of God, the Logos doctrine, and the beginning of the doctrine of the Spirit of God as a distinct subsistence. Later in the early church Fathers and the Apologists this coalescence became still more impressive. It is to be remembered that the idea of God developed for the most part on Greek soil, that its chief exponents had been trained in Greek philosophy, that the idea had to justify itself to the Greek consciousness, since it was here that Christianity was making its first great conquest; and it is not surprising that the Greek mind had something to offer to what had already been found true in Christian belief. In the situation created by the most intimate contact of Christianity with the Greek spirit, theologians were confronted by serious tasks: to maintain and develop the ethical monotheism of the Old and New Testaments against polytheism; to identify the God of revelation with the absolutely transcendent Being of Platonist and Neo-Platonist speculative thought; to investigate the inner nature of God with reference to its essential unity, to the Logos as the eternal revealing principle, and to its self-communicating activity. To effect this aim there were brought into play the highest categories of Greek thought.

At no time in the history of the Christian church has the doctrine of God been in so precarious a position as in the centuries preceding Augustine. Four great contemporary movements, all originating in the same general motive, threatened each in its own way to rob Christianity of the God whom its faith had enshrined as the God and Father of Jesus Christ—Mithraism, Gnosticism, Neo-Pla-

tonism, and Manichaeism. Each of these was primarily a
product of the Aryan genius, and each thrust the ultimate
idea of God into a region inaccessible to experience, where
even the possibility of ethical definition was excluded. In
the background of all of these was a common feeling, the
need of redemption. Never has the opposition between the
sensuous and the spiritual, between matter and mind, between the actual and the ideal, been sharpened to a more
radical contrast and contradiction than in the circles in
which these religions originated. The soul, weighted down
by the material, enslaved by the senses, fettered by the
flesh, and longing for deliverance, could be satisfied by
nothing less than release from earth and elevation to
its celestial home.   Mysticism, mythology, speculation,
fantastic gropings after incongruous elements, coupled
with a deep sincerity of purpose, characterized all these
movements of the human spirit.   In these faiths, however,
the divine, the world, man, and redemption, while marked
by many common features belonging to them and Christianity, were after all different from what was essential
to Christianity.   On the absorption or disappearance of
these forms of religion depended the continued existence
of the Christian faith.   It would have been a calamity if
any one of these or a fusion of two or more of them had
displaced Christianity as a religion of redemption.   It
was a perilous moment for the idea of God when the
Hebrew people passed from the nomadic to the agricultural stage, and again from the life of the fields to that
of the city, but none of these transitions was fraught with
the danger which lay in wait for it as it found itself
plunged into the welter of Greek speculative thought and
oriental mysticism.   Among the "ifs of history" one is
appalled as he contemplates the possible consequences of
the defeat of Christianity by one of these faiths, as, for

example, Mithraism. "The crisis was one the gravity of which it would be difficult to over-estimate. There have been crises since in the history of Christianity, but there is none which equals in its importance this, upon the issue of which it depended for all time, whether Christianity should be regarded as a body of revealed doctrine, or as the *caput mortuum* of a hundred philosophies—whether the basis of Christianity should be a definite and definitely interpreted creed, or a chaos of speculations." [1]

The advocates of the Christian idea of God have been reproached—and not without justification—for the mythological ingredients of their theology: mysticism in which feeling and vague aspiration sometimes crowded out rational judgment; sacramentalism which endowed selected objects and many rites with efficacious virtue; speculation by which they incorporated incongruous Greek ideas into the very substance of their thought; but when one has acknowledged the full force of these and other allegations, it yet remains true that, in comparison with the representatives of the other faiths, their very extravagances are convincing proof of their fundamental sanity. Instead of shivering the idea of God into irridescent fragments of speculative fancy, their last word concerning him was that of ethical personality. The world under control of demonic powers, malign and hostile to man, was the work of God and therefore subject to his sovereign will. Man in spite of his subjection to these destructive powers was yet free and capable of immortality through reception of the nature of God. And Christianity, instead of being a purely speculative, or mythological, or even simply an ethical, religion, was a religion of redemption, traced to a definite historical person, in whom God had

---

[1] Hatch, *Organization of the Early Christian Church,* p. 96.

taken up human nature into union with himself, in whom therefore he had come to men with forgiveness of sins and the promise and power of eternal life. However far it might wander from the simplicity of its founder's spirit and aim, it possessed, as did none of the other faiths, in the life and purpose of its founder, a principle of renewal.

Christianity was fortunate also in the type of men who became its advocates in this early day. They felt and rightly felt that the question of supreme moment was the idea of God, and upon this they concentrated the vast energy of their thought. As a result of the long debate, certain aspects of the Christian idea of God received statement which with comparatively little change have remained in force for more than a thousand years. The general results may be summarized. (1) The mythological elements which still clung to the Aryan ideas of God were for the most part done away; if there still lingered traces of this, even in the doctrine of the Trinity and the person of Christ, the writers were not themselves conscious of it. (2) The tension between the God of the Old Testament and the God of the New Testament which had been alleged by the Gnostics was relieved; instead of conceiving of the God of the Old Testament as a being below the supreme God, vengeful or even just, and the God of the New Testament as the highest and true God, merciful and just, they set upon a secure foundation the unity of God in his historical action over the chosen people, the Christian church, and the world. (3) The absoluteness of God which had from several directions been threatened was guarded from any suggestion of limitation; in his essential being he existed utterly apart from space and time, both of which were due to his creative action; even as these began by the divine will, so by the same will they might cease to be.

The Gnostics had referred the origination of the world to a process in the ultimate background of the divine nature; the Neo-Platonists had described it as an overflowing or as a streaming forth from the primordial inexpressible One. According to both, this process took its rise in the inner eternal nature of the Source of all, and hence in sheer necessity. On the other hand, early Christian writers, even when they held that the act of creation was eternal, maintained that it originated in the divine will and that this will was free. Thus the dualism which had shadowed Neo-Platonism and Manichaeism, setting up an eternal antithesis between God and the world, between God and evil, disappeared by the reduction of one of these terms—the utter dependence of the world and evil on God. God alone was real. The world was created. Sin originated with man. Evil had no metaphysical existence; and even if it is acknowledged as henceforth unending, it is wholly within the power of God; he can abolish it and the world in which it appears at any instant, if he so wills.

The pure spirituality of God was not, however, the only form of conceiving of him at this time. Tertullian presented God as substantial. Without body, members, form, and beauty there would be no God; hence no prayer and no worship, since these are not possible except toward concrete personality. The corporeality is not that of human beings; and if human qualities are attributed to God, they are such only in surpassing degree. Herein Tertullian discloses his affinity with Jewish anthropomorphism and with Stoicism. The theory of God as substantial appears to be very congenial to the human mind. Theologians have never for any length of time been able to free themselves from this point of view. The pure spirituality of God is too abstract a notion to appeal to any but the most abstruse metaphysical thinkers. It can point to no analogies, for in the entire circuit of our experience there is no mind without embodiment. Moreover, there would be nothing to quicken the imagination. Faith and love cling only to the concrete. For such reasons as these the Hebrews never rose to the conception of God as purely spiritual. Later we shall see how the feeling of Tertullian has haunted and influenced theologians in succeeding periods.

At this time little attempt was made to find God in experience. The interest was apologetic, to clear the idea of God from misapprehensions which Christians were accused of holding, and to show that this idea embraced all that was of worth in the Greek thought of the divine. They aimed also to convince their countrymen of the truth of Christianity; and since this centered in the idea of God, it was perfectly natural for the church Fathers to seek to make this idea at home in the highest reaches of Greek speculation.

IV

In Augustine the tendencies culminated which had been active in the church since its beginning. In general, these may be reduced to two—the rational and the empirical. He had first of all been profoundly indebted to a series of religious philosophies. In his *Confessions* he relates the stages through which he passed in maturing his Christian ideas. First, Manichaeism in which God, conceived of as substantial light, was the God in absolute distinction and separation from darkness or evil and from the material world. Later, in Neo-Platonism he found a point of view for conserving two interests—the Logos doctrine of the New Testament—the divine principle of revelation,

and, with the Logos as a mediating principle between God
and the world, a pure and perfect Being inaccessible alike
to experience and to thought. Apart from his relation
to the world, God is to an incomparable degree the Absolute One, Simple Being, as distinguished from the manifold and changing existences of the phenomenal world.[1]
This position involved certain elements which are perhaps
not susceptible of complete reconciliation. On the one
hand, he affirms not what God is, but what he is not [2]—
a fact which should be emphasized but not over-empha-
sized. Augustine is not the only sinner in this regard,
for he shares with nearly all the great theologians this
contradictory attitude. On the other hand, God is *essentia*,
that is, he is the immanent reality in all existence.[3] His
knowledge is an eternal fullness, self-identical, an intuition
of the eternally present, in no way conditioned by the
finite which exists only because God knows it. He is the
highest good and self-contained. Augustine turned from
Manichaeism because it found the origin of evil in an ultimate and eternal dualism, but he retained its conception
of the immeasurable transcendence of God. Neo-Platonism appealed to him by reason of its doctrine of the
infinite elevation of God above the world and its doctrine
of the over-soul by which the inaccessible God communicates his Being to the world. Although both Manichaeism
and Neo-Platonism were unsatisfactory as a philosophy
of life, yet their fundamental ideas were preserved in his
Christian doctrine of God.

Augustine was also deeply indebted to Dionysius the
Areopagite for contrasting elements in his conception of
God. In Dionysius for the first time the attempt was

---

[1] *De Civitate Dei*, 11, 12. *De trin.* 6:4-6.
[2] *De trin.* 5:2.
[3] *Ibid.* 5:2.

made to blend a fully developed Neo-Platonism with Christianity. Augustine was no less a mystic than was Dionysius, but in contrast to the Areopagite he sought in experience the secret of the Eternal. The nature of Augustine was one of extreme richness; while others might be content with a mystic philosophy whose roots pushed deep into the soil of rationalism, he could rest only when the claims of his heart were satisfied. Accordingly, his experience provided the other source of his idea of God. One might indeed say that among Christian theologians before Augustine there had never been any immediate experience of God. St. Paul's experience had been with the "risen Christ." With Augustine, however, "grace" took the place of Christ. God was his alter-ego, his other and completing self, who searched and to whom at the same time he laid bare the inmost secrets of his soul. God was his better self before whom he poured out his most intimate confessions and his penitential tears. He carried on an inner dialogue between himself and his ideal of truth and purity, which ever and again blinded him by the ineffable splendor of its beauty and grace. The significance of this aspect of Augustine's idea of God cannot be overestimated. Instead of continuing as an object of speculative regard, however this might minister to a theory of redemption, God comes to live with him, thinks in his thoughts, and shares his changing emotions. For him the question of the prophet receives its satisfying answer: "Will God verily dwell with men on the earth?"

Such was the energy of Augustine's experience of God that it has been continuously influential in all later generations. It has made itself felt in the highest degree in those who have sought perfect union with God as the goal of long discipline, in those who have found here and now in communion with God the fruition of their longings; and even the common man has a new courage as he feels:

"No distant Lord have I
Loving afar to be;
Made flesh for me, he cannot rest
Until he rests in me."

Such an idea of God as that of Augustine is not without its dangers which have not seldom been realized. (1) It tends in an excessive degree to individualize God and the relation of the soul to him. (2) It tends also to encourage a type of experience in which one detaches himself from the social group that he may the more uninterruptedly "enjoy his religion." That this is not, however, an inevitable consequence of the idea in question may be seen in Augustine himself, a man of the most prodigious social activity both as writer and as administrator of great affairs, in St. Bernard, St. Francis of Assisi, St. Theresa, Luther, John Wesley, and Schleiermacher.

Augustine attempted no reconciliation of the opposite poles of his conception of God—the God afar off and the God who was near. In some moods he took refuge in one, in very different moods he found strength in the other, aspect. It may be questioned whether he was aware of the inner incompatibility of the two points of view. Nor are we in position to imagine in what way he would have sought an adjustment, if the problem had presented itself. In any case, no one has ever set forth these two aspects of the idea of God—whether contrasting or complementary—with such energy of conviction as this great Father of speculation and experience. Partly for this reason and partly on account of the conditions of thought for more than fourteen hundred years afterward, the greater theologians followed in his steps, yet mostly in the mystic and speculative rather than the experimental path.

V

For more than a thousand years, however, no one added to Augustine's thought of God.   In the ninth century John Scotus Erigena, in the twelfth century Bernard of Clairvaux and Hugo and Richard of St. Victor, in the thirteenth century Thomas Aquinas, in the fourteenth century Meister Eckhart, and in the seventeenth century the Cambridge Platonists did no more than by the aid of the reigning philosophy—Neo-Platonist, Aristotelian, or Platonist—to unfold the mystic or speculative side of Augustine's conception.   God is presented as incomprehensible and ineffable, the Absolute Mystery, in which all affirmations and counter affirmations are annulled and reconciled;[1] or, since man's intelligence is his highest prerogative, he may with Aristotle regard God as pure thought, or with the Neo-Platonists as pure Being, the ineffable Absolute, utterly transcending human knowledge: one may not know what God is but only what he is not, or one may deny to the Godhead even the highest categories and yet maintain that the essence both of the world and of the soul is God.

In general two paths led to the idea of God.   The first was the speculative, depending on a theory of knowledge, the Aristotelian logic, and a peculiar dialectic developed by the Western mind.   The second was the contemplative, which alone promised the highest satisfaction to the heart's desire to know God; at the end of a severe dis-

---

[1] Erigena.

ciplinary process thought is transcended, effort laid to rest, and in love the soul is united to God; or again not a logical conception but an intuitive vision of God crowns the endeavor to know him; or once more the soul having withdrawn from all outward things and from sense-perception into its inmost self, lets the absolute Deity which is its true essence become all. Plainly this is mysticism. Whatever mysticism is,—and no two definitions agree,— it witnesses to an indestructible conviction that there is such an affinity between the soul of man and the ultimate reality of the world that not by discursive thought but by an immediateness of consciousness the soul becomes aware of God or feels its oneness with him.

Two other aspects of the idea of God appeared during these centuries, both of which were a revival of Augustine's conception. One of these (Duns Scotus) found in the divine will the final truth of his being. Thus attention was turned wholly aside from a doctrine of God which had prevailed since Tertullian, from God as infinite substance to God as purely dynamic, conceived as force or will. This conception has its root in Augustine's theory of predestination, echoing a bold suggestion of St. Paul, that will in God may be both ultimate and arbitrary. Such a view involved serious consequences for both the present and the future idea of God, and for the meaning of his relation to a world of moral beings. If the primacy of will in God is absolute, then the rational either wholly disappears or is subordinate to the volitional element, and his will becomes the only source of truth and justice and all ideals. Another more favorable consequence would be that the defining characteristic of the being of God is not a static changelessness, but activity. No self-contemplative felicity, no fullness of being, however this is described, but energetic purposiveness, an eternal will of good is the essential nature of God.   Later generations will more fully define this will and its relation to the world, both of things and of men, but a note has been struck which is destined to dominate the idea of God.

The other aspect referred to has its bearing on the relation of God to experience. From this point of view the speculative quest was ignored. What God might be for the soul's daily needs was alone considered.   St. Francis of Assisi, St. Bernard of Clairvaux, St. Catherine of Siena, and St. Theresa are only instances of those at this time to whom God was more real than their own intensely living selves. They offered no criticism of the idea of the inner being of God as transcendent and unapproachable,—this in common with others of their day they acknowledged,—but this aspect of God was not their chief interest. And we must not place it to their discredit that, instead of resting content with speculating on God as others had done, they found their supreme satisfaction in the most intimate converse with him, more intimate, more constant, tender, and affectionate indeed than with any earthly friend. If God is one who enters into communion with men, who with unwearied and inspiring sympathy follows them in the vicissitudes of their experience, to whom they may pour out the most trivial no less than the most serious concerns of their hearts, then the future of piety is safe, and religion as an experience may renew itself with each new generation of those who seek God.

VI

For several hundred years until Spinoza, no distinctive feature was added to the idea of God. Luther, Calvin, and Zwingli, each from a different angle and with varying shades of emphasis, reproduced only Augustine's point of view. With Spinoza, however, a new cycle began. Not that his conception was wholly new. He derived from Neo-Platonism a transcendent element, from Neo-Platonism, the Stoics, and Bruno a pantheistic trend, and from Descartes his mathematical impulse. God is absolute Substance, self-existent, all-inclusive, hence defined by nothing outside of himself. Since all existence known to us is either extension or thought, and since neither of these is complete in itself, each has to be referred to an infinite existence of which it is an essential attribute. Beyond these we may assume the existence of an infinite number of attributes in the All-Real Being, unknown indeed to us. The attributes of extension and thought appear in an infinite variety of finite forms, and they have no existence outside of these forms. God is thus the immanent causal essence in all things. There is no God apart from the phenomenal world, and no world apart from God. God and Nature are interchangeable terms. He is the active principle of all change (*natura naturans*), and he is the changing forms in which this active principle embodies itself (*natura naturata*). If one asks, What God is? all the well known definitions except self-existence fall away, and we are face to face with unrelieved pantheism. God is free, since there is no reality outside of him to limit or constrain, but at the same time he is necessitated by his essential nature. In the Deity is no unified self-consciousness, no discursive intelligence, no purposive will. Since man is a phase of God, he has both a transient and an eternal aspect,—transient, so far as he appears in ever changing modes; eternal, as embodying the dual elements of extension and thought. The reality of man is God.

Leibnitz's doctrine of God occupies a point of view

diametrically opposed to that of Spinoza. First of all, he substitutes Force for Substance, or rather interprets substance in terms of force. This is true not only of God, but of the universe,—all becomes spiritual and dynamic. Whereas Descartes had divided reality into three elements, God as the most perfect Substance, and the world as finite substance consisting of extension and thought arbitrarily connected by omnipotence, and Spinoza had conceived of existence and thought as attributes of the one Substance, Leibnitz held that, since all reality is force, even bodies no less than minds are immaterial and illocal. Thus the universe is composed of an infinite number of monads which owe their existence to the central creative Monad or God. This highest Monad, an infinite and eternal Being, existing apart from the world, is pure and perfect intelligence and activity. Such is the nature of his consciousness that before the creation of this universe he presented to himself an infinite number of possible worlds; among all of these as possible, some degree of evil, both metaphysical and moral, was unavoidable. Although he was free to create or not to create, yet such was his wisdom and goodness that if he saw fit to create, he could not but choose to give actuality to that universe which contained the least evil, that is, the best of all possible worlds. In his creative activity, God made the finite monads each absolutely independent of all others, and yet at the same time so interrelated from the point of view of mechanism and teleology that together they form a perfect correspondence of activity, so revealing a pre-established harmony. Now for the first time in the idea of God and the world we pass from monism and dualism to a vital pluralism.

VII

Until the last third of the eighteenth century philosophers and theologians had not seriously questioned whether the human reason was competent to arrive at the truth concerning God. The many diverse views and the endless controversies respecting the idea of God suggested neither discouragement nor hesitancy in the unwearied quest for reality. With Hume and Kant, however,—with each for a different reason,—began an attitude of mind which has influenced much thinking until the present hour. Hume, who applied the psychological and historical test to the meaning of religion, is unable to reach a conclusion concerning the being of God with which he is satisfied; and Kant, in his divorce of the theoretical from the practical reason, allows the practical reason the only valid word concerning God. In response to the rational demand one may indeed posit a reality to which may be assigned "necessity, infinity, extra-mundane existence, freedom from limitations of time and space," but since this postulate transcends all experience, it is insusceptible of proof or disproof. In answer to the moral demand one may postulate a God who guarantees the validity of the highest good, and is therefore the kind of being who will crown our endeavors with happiness. In this way he opened the door to the conception of God as a being inconceivable to thought, but an object to which we yield ourselves in faith and self-surrender.

This general point of view has determined the idea of God as presented by many influential writers; in Great Britain by Hamilton, Mansel, Spencer, Matthew Arnold, John Henry Newman, and Balfour; in America by Horace Bushnell. Each of these thinkers has his own reasoning by which he explained and justified his peculiar way of approach to the idea of God. Hamilton held that while the Infinite cannot be known, on account of the relativity of knowledge and the philosophy of the unconditioned, yet it "is, must, and ought to be *believed*." Mansel contended that the human. mind, in virtue of its constitution, involves itself in contradiction whenever it ventures to speculate concerning the Infinite, the Absolute, and Personality as applied to God. We are therefore thrown back upon supernatural revelation for the source of our knowledge concerning all that relates to God,—a revelation addressed to faith. Accordingly, there is no rational standard for a criticism of the traditional, or, for that matter, any notion of God. An attitude not unlike that of Mansel was advocated by John Henry Newman.

Herbert Spencer sought a middle path in which to reconcile the conflicting interests of several tendencies, as, for example, the Positive Philosophy of August Comte, according to which, since phenomena alone can be known, the question of an Absolute may be altogether ignored; the philosophy of Hamilton in which the relativity of knowledge was coupled with certainty concerning the reality of the Absolute and Unconditioned; the evolutionary view of science in which the organic world is conceived of as developing according to law—the method of creation; and current theories according to which both God and the world are equally real to thought. For Spencer the idea of the "Ultimate Reality" was an "absolute datum of consciousness." We cannot, however, know this Ultimate Reality, since to know is to limit and thus to separate what is known from the Unlimited and Unknowable. This agnosticism is qualified by affirming the reality of a First Cause, a Power present in all things, an Infinite and Eternal Energy from which all things proceed, of the same nature as that which wells up in consciousness.

When all is said, we are in the presence of an Eternal Mystery before which our true attitude is that of reverence and awe. The implications of Spencer's doctrine were developed by John Fiske in a clear and consistent theism.

Matthew Arnold adopted the general view of Hamilton and Mansel concerning the unknowableness of God as the Ultimate Reality. He sought to conserve the religious value of God by two considerations: (1) Our apprehensions of reality are embodied not in terms of exact knowledge, but of poetry and eloquence. The term God does not submit itself to a logical formula, but is poetic and literary and is thus sufficient for our practical needs.[1] (2) For the personality of God he substituted the memorable phrase, "An enduring Power, not ourselves, that makes for righteousness."[2]

Rising out of the same general background are the views of two widely influential writers, Ritschl and Sabatier. Ritschl excluded metaphyiscs from theology, and with this went his rejection of speculative theism. Moreover, ecclesiastical dogma, a mixture of theology and Greek metaphysics, must undergo a sifting in which all cosmological speculation is swept away. The only values which are enshrined in religious knowledge relate to pleasure and pain and find their meaning not in looking backward to causation, but forward to purpose. Accordingly, as Kant observed, the idea of God belongs to the region of practical faith rather than of theoretical knowledge; and the content of the idea will be perfectly expressed in that of a loving Will revealed in the reciprocal relations between Christ and God, by which those who trust in him

---

[1] *Literature and Dogma*, p. 11.
[2] *Ibid.*, p. 52.

are assured of spiritual dominion over the world and a perfect moral fellowship in his kingdom as the highest good. For Sabatier our knowledge of God is concerned neither with metaphysics nor with cosmology, but only with his will so far as related to us. We are in no uncertainty as to the meaning of God which answers to the need of our hearts. The inner contradictions of our being, the devastating threat of the external world, and the conflict of the self with the world, waken in the consciousness that which solves the discord in a final harmony. If human life is to eventuate in personality, then God must be the inevitable postulate of man's moral and spiritual ideal.

As long ago as 1848 Horace Bushnell had been engaged on essentially the same problem and he arrived at the same general result. By a theory of language instead of by a theory of knowledge he emancipates his thought of God from metaphysics. The gospel is a gift to the imagination. The idea of God which rises from one's religious experience is so defined as to meet the demands of that experience. If Bushnell had been familiar with the philosophy of Kant, it is more than doubtful if he would have adopted it in preference to his own method, as pointing the way to his conclusion. The Absolute as such had no meaning for him; only as it came into some instrumental relation to us could we become interested. He therefore conceived of representative forms standing out, as it were, from the Absolute—the *dramatis personae* of revelation, conveying to us as far as possible the infinite in finite terms. The Son bodies God forth in the creation and government of the world and at last as incarnate in human form. As thus incarnate he calls out and sets over himself in celestial exaltation the Father, impersonated in lively convertible form. To complete this representation of God, the Spirit is conceived of as acting within us under conditions of space and time. The key therefore to the idea of God as revealed is found in the "instrumental Trinity," the incarnation, and the Spirit as permanently operative in the life of man.

VIII

The idea of God as deriving its meaning from social experience has been greatly reinforced by the psychology of religion. The history of religion shows that this idea has developed in correspondence with such experiences. Hoeffding made it clear that the psychological notion of God took its rise in the feeling of the conservation of value, to which Professors Irving King and Edward Scribner Ames have added that it answers to the consciousness of the highest social values. The idea of God detached from social experiences in which it gets its only meaning and reduced to metaphysical terms is a pale and worthless abstraction. Professor Ames likens an attempt of this sort to that of a child who seeks behind the mirror for the reality whose image he beholds. Where the consciousness of values increases, there the consciousness of God also increases. Not backward to a First Cause, nor outward to an abstract notion, but forward to the age-long process where social values come to richest expression, are we to look for development and culmination of the idea of God.

A position having certain points of affinity with that just mentioned is winning recognition. God is defined not as infinite Substance, nor as imperturbable Absolute, but in terms of progressive purpose. The antithesis proposed is—"The immutable Absolute or a God who

Strives." [1]   If with President Faunce God is conceived
of in terms of purpose, and one looks for this purpose
in the only place where it is revealed, several very suggestive inquiries are set on foot.   If the world is plastic
and growing, unfinished yet progressively realizing an
ideal, is the divine life itself more finished or complete
than its expression in finite forms?   Are not the limitations of time and space, the inertia and opaqueness of
matter, as real to God as to us?   Does not the conflict
of good and evil on the field of life, and especially in
the consciousness of man, disclose the fact that the world-
ground is itself not beyond good and evil, but is somehow
identified with these, in sympathy both with the struggle
for existence and the attainment of moral values?   If
God is the same yesterday, to-day, and forever, is this
because he is a changeless Absolute or a consistent and
changeless purpose, slowly but gradually and effectually
realizing itself in nature and human life?   And when
finally we confess, "I believe in God the Father Almighty,"
do we think of Cause and Substance and the Absolute,
or of a conscious Presence which pervades all with a good
will, a will which indeed outruns immediate realization,
but is nevertheless inextricably involved in the processes
of its fulfillment?   The meaning of God is thus identified
with the purpose and love disclosed in the world of
experience. [2]

On this subject, as on so many others pertaining to
religious experience, Professor James offers suggestions
which have the force of confessions of personal faith.
(1) He writes, "I myself believe that the evidence for
God lies primarily in inner personal experience." [3]   (2)

---

[1] Cf. H. W. Wright, *Am. Journal of Theology,* Vol. XI, pp. 128-130.
[2] Cf. W. H. P. Faunce, *What Does Christianity Mean?* pp. 51 ff.
[3] *Pragmatism,* p. 109.

He advocates the view of God as finite against the doctrine of the Absolute; the latter is "an improbable hypothesis." He thus criticises and repudiates the monism of Spinoza in which the many are dissolved in the One, and the later monism of the idealists in which the many exist indeed, but as objects of the eternal thought of the One. This idea of God is more consonant with the pluralistic panpsychic view of the universe into which we have been drawn; furthermore, it provides the only basis for maintaining the fact of the will as creative, of evil as not simply appearance, and of history as real. In addition, this doctrine means for God environment, time, and a history like our own. Finally, such a conception allies itself with the actual experience of men in relation to God; for however men have thought of God as great, and even as surpassing human comprehension, they have never regarded him as all-embracing, and have always affirmed an "other," an actual environment of some kind beside him.

III. PRESENT-DAY CONCEPTIONS
OF GOD

I

A COMPARISON of the traditional presentations of the idea of God discloses a singular sameness in the *a priori* method of approach and the conclusions reached. The same arguments for the divine existence appear and reappear, only varied with a somewhat different shading and perhaps order of treatment, with here and there an argument omitted which has been found valid by other thinkers. The same attributes are predicated of the divine nature, with practically the same names but with different classification and arrangement, and in general with unimportant differences of definition. Other and contrasting conceptions have indeed appeared, as, for example, by Spinoza and Hegel, but since these were "unorthodox" they have had little appreciable influence upon the official doctrine. Now, however, a new phenomenon has arisen. From a condition of almost complete rigidity the idea of God is becoming to a high degree plastic. Many innovating conceptions of God are not only put forth, but are receiving wide and serious consideration. In this it simply shares the movement which has overtaken all ideas. Various causes have conspired to this result: the loosening of the hold of dogma before the challenge of the historical spirit; the transference of a portion of authority from the outer to the inner court; the new view of the world with reference to matter and energy, space and time, and

the testimony of all the sciences; the new psychology in
its account of the nature and development of the religious
consciousness; the new social emphasis in which the center
of gravity is shifted from the autocratic to the democratic
ideal; finally, and perhaps more influential than all of
these interests, the desire to find some interpretation of
reality which shall approximately express the reaction of
experience to the infinite mystery of the world.

This condition is highly significant, although it may
not be possible to come at its full meaning. Yet several
conclusions are warranted: the traditional idea is inadequate; men are no longer content to have a God at second-
hand; only so far as he is real to their experience is any
idea of him valid; the fact that this idea has once more
assumed a fluid form holds the condition and promise of
a genuine development; finally, the idea of God is like
other ideas, perfectible, not in the sense that it will ever
be completely equivalent to its object, but that it is susceptible of endless growth and forever approximates, even
if it falls short of, its goal.

Already in orthodox circles great and even radical
diversity of interpretation of the idea of God has arisen
without calling in question the correctness of the views
themselves or the authors of them. That these views
concern the actions and attitude and not directly the
nature or character of God, is incidental. Any discussion
of God, except as it is based on his actual working, is
purely speculative; on the other hand, the character of
God must be inferred from his purposive activity. Here
the widest latitude of thought has prevailed and almost
every conceivable divergence of view is found. By one
class of thinkers predestination is defined as absolute and
final, by another as conditioned on foreknowledge. According to one view, the will of God determines human choice;

according to another, the initiative of choice is wholly within the human will. Theories of the relation of original sin to the divine judgment, of the relation of sin— "permission of sin"—to the divine will, of the imputation of the guilt of sin as related to the sin of Adam, have been broached with the greatest diversity of interpretation. The person of Christ has been presented in manifold conflicting forms: his essence as eternal; his twofold divine-human nature; his knowledge; his humiliation; his suffering; and many other items of his being and character have received the utmost variety of statement. Concerning the work of Christ or the atonement, the same difference of treatment is in evidence: a ransom paid to Satan; a satisfaction by the undeserved death of the God-man to the infinite honor of God injured by sin; satisfaction to the broken law and endangered government of God by a penal example in the death of his Son; the work of Christ a satisfaction to the justice of God through his endurance of the punishment of sin; the death of Christ a revelation of the good will of God to forgive sin. Regeneration is referred to the miraculous agency of God, in which the soul is instantaneously and passively renewed, or to the co-operative action of God and the soul, or to the normal awakening of the person to the Christian ideal under the influence of religious education. The kingdom of God is presented as a human historical development in which the divine will is progressively realized, or as awaiting a catastrophic event in which Christ will suddenly appear to usher in the millennium. The doctrine of the future life of souls issues in a trilemma—eternal punishment of the wicked and everlasting happiness of the saved, conditional immortality, universal restoration.

These and many other subjects have been thought out and formulated by theologians almost as if they were

self-contained and could stand alone; whereas none of
them has any meaning apart from its relation to the idea
of God. It seems, however, to be taken for granted by
each advocate of a particular theory that God will back
it up. But unless God is many-sided and self-contradictory—a house divided against itself—he can be depended
upon to carry out not more than one, and perhaps no
single one, of the programs outlined above. On the one
hand, it might be supposed that if the individual subjects,
as sin, the person and work of Christ, the beginning and
development of the Christian life, were investigated first
of all in the field of experience, this would lead to a conception of God whose actions were disclosed in that field.
But in all works on theology where these themes are
systematically unfolded, the doctrine of God occupies the
first section and has therefore been completed and left
behind before the other subjects are discussed. On the
other hand, while in all these presentations the doctrine of
God is practically the same, one is at a loss to account
for the very great dissimilarity of purposes and actions
attributed to him. The significance of these wide diversi-
ties of view among theologians lies, however, in a two-
fold direction: first, when they have unified their own
materials with reference to the will of God it is seen that
they are dealing with very different ideas of him; and
secondly, they have opened the door to all serious thinkers to seek for themselves such ideas of God, however
various these may be, as will best represent the meaning
of the world as reflected in experience.

Hitherto the idea of God has been to a great degree a
theme for accredited theologians, and their judgment has
been left unquestioned by all except theologians of a
different way of thinking. Whoever, outside of these
circles, ventured within their hallowed precincts, was

regarded with suspicion or condemned as an intruder into domains where only those had a right to think and speak who had been invested with the sacred mantle. Now, however, breaches appear in the walls, many of the ancient boundaries have disappeared, and incursions are freely made into these fields where the ultimate meaning of life is sought. The poets have, indeed, never been barred from the company of the prophets,—their word is only another form of the prophetic message. But to-day men with insight and aim equal to that of prophets and poets but without theological training or bias, are among the "seekers after God." They make no appeal to revelation as the source of their judgment. They bow to no ecclesiastical authority which would bind their inquiry. They are free-thinkers in the highest meaning of this term, subject to no compulsion but that of the truth as it authenticates itself in their own reverent consciousness. Never has interest in the idea of God been so widely distributed or found representatives among so great a variety of serious and thoughtful writers—physicists, biologists, philosophers, psychologists, students of comparative religion, novelists, historians, sociologists, and specialists in many other lines of human endeavor. The feeling shared by all of these is that the idea of God has too long been a subject of purely speculative interest. Ideas once associated with him were no doubt at that time vital and are still intelligible enough, but they are felt to be antiquated. They no longer function; they are worn out; for the present generation of thinking men they seem remote, ineffective, unmeaning.

This attitude of mind has recently become acute. The remainder of this chapter will be devoted to a presentation of some of the more recent endeavors to restate the idea of God in terms fitted to meet the needs of our own

time. Already in the latter half of the last century John
Stuart Mill and Matthew Arnold created uneasiness and
brought down upon themselves bitter reproach by representatives of the established order on account of their
suggested modifications of the customary doctrine of God,
—one, by setting goodness over against omnipotence, as
Epicurus and Hume had already done, by insisting that
goodness must be the same in God as in men, and by being
willing to be damned if such was to be the alternative for
his preference of intelligible goodness to an unlimited,
irresponsible, merciless power in God, the other, for bringing God down from inaccessible heights of dogmatic theology to the experience of living men—the "enduring
Power, not ourselves, that makes for righteousness."

II

In our generation Professor William James and later
H. G. Wells have done more than any other two writers
to liquify the idea of God and cause it to flow freely
again in the channels grooved deep by experience. Professor James' conception of God as finite has already
been described. He is dissatisfied with the traditional
static Absolute; he feels that it is impossible to establish
sympathetic relations with such an Absolute; the metaphysical properties attributed to God have neither intelligible nor practical meaning; the scholastic arguments are
unable to prove the truth of moral qualities in such a
being; the existence of this being could never be established; and even if his existence were established it could
make no possible difference in our experience;—all this
forced him to seek elsewhere than in metaphysics or traditional theology for an idea of God that would "work."

This he found in a God who is finite either in knowledge or in power, perhaps in both.[1]

According to Mr. Wells there are three aspects of reality to be considered in our approach to God. (1) The ultimate, unfathomable mystery of the world, which he designates as the "Veiled Being," with which we are in no way concerned. Whatever else it is, it is not the Absolute and Unconditioned, but whether it is simple or complex or divine is beyond our power to conceive. Whether God knows any more about this ultimate Being than we do is also uncertain. (2) A Life Force or Will to Live, disclosed in nature, proceeding in some inconceivable manner from the Veiled Being, thrusting itself forth into the myriad forms of existence, giving to each its distinctive quality—strength, agility, cunning, love, hate, greed, beauty, delight, weariness, disgust, and fear of death. Some have called this the Gnostic Demiurge, others the Dark God of the Manicheans, and still others Mother Nature. (3) In all this welter of experience we have become aware of a new reality. "God comes we know not whence into the conflict of life. He works in men and through men. He is a spirit, a single spirit, and a single person; he has begun and he will never end. He is the immortal part and leader of mankind. He has motives, he has characteristics, he has an aim. He is by our poor scales of measurement boundless love, boundless courage, boundless generosity. He is thought and steadfast will. He is our friend and brother and the light of the world. That briefly is the belief of the modern mind with regard to God." This knowledge of God is based entirely upon experience. "It has encountered God. It does not argue about God: it relates." This

---

[1] Cf. *A Pluralistic Universe*, pp. 311-312.

God is "neither all wise nor all powerful," nor is he the "Maker of heaven and earth." He "presents himself as finite." The doctrine of Mr. Wells is summed up in two opposite positions: first, complete agnosticism in the matter of God, the Creator, and, secondly, entire faith in the matter of God the Redeemer. God is thus conceived of "as a finite intelligence of boundless courage and limitless possibilities of growth and victory, who has pitted himself against death, who stands close to our inmost beings, ready to receive us and to use us, to rescue us from the chagrins of egotism and take us into his immortal adventure." We seem here to have a reality which began with the human race, growing with its growth, the ideal which gathers up into itself not only all the finer achievements of humanity but also all its unmeasured possibilities as well, "the underlying human memory, the increasing human will," the spirit in us which is forever urging to the realization to what is potential in us, which, since we are destined to an immortal existence, is therefore in itself everlasting. And because the values here are personal, involving all and more than the values of individual human lives, God is superlatively personal, yet not in the technical orthodox sense.[1]

A doctrine of God having some points of resemblance to and many more of difference from that of Mr. Wells is presented by Samuel Butler.[2] The world as we experience it is divided into "three great concentric phases of life": (1) The simple cell of the organism which is a perfect unit or person; (2) Each organism whether vegetable, animal, or human, is a living unit or person; (3) The totality of which organic existence as disclosed to us

[1] Cf. *God, The Invisible King.*
[2] *God the Known and God the Unknown.*

in evolution—animals, plants, and the human race—unite
to form the all-inclusive Person or God. Each of these
forms of existence has a dual phase, mind and body. The
cell is to some degree conscious, but knows little or
nothing of the larger organic unity of which it forms a
part. In like manner each of the larger units, whether
vegetable, animal or human, is only dimly aware of the
still larger unit or personality of God of which it is an
integral part. The consciousness of God transcends our
consciousness even as ours transcends that of the single
cell. Our God is a visible personality, inconceivably vast
yet limited, present in all tangible forms on the earth,
capable of waste and repair, of sensation, movement, and
memory, existing through immeasurable time, *quasi*-omni-
potent and *quasi*-allwise, growing as the outcome of all
past lives, with a moral government exercised through us.
This God is distinguished from the pantheistic and orthodox conception. The God of pantheism is impersonal.
The God of the orthodox is also rejected, since it too as
being purely spiritual is impersonal. Whether outside of
the God of our world and the Gods of other worlds there
is a fourth concentric phase, a still higher, more inclusive
unit or personality is unknown to us. Yet from consideration of the origin of matter, the primordial cell, and
the arrangements by which the earth is fitted for life, we
are drawn on to the supposition of a vaster Person behind
our God and the Gods of all other worlds, with soul and
body, knowing beforehand what he wanted, who called
our God and all others into existence. We are indeed
members of our God, but of the Unknown God we are
children.

In this exceedingly novel presentation Mr. Butler seeks
a reconciliation of many conflicting claims—the rights of
metaphysics, the findings of experience, the various strata

of scientific knowledge, the consciousness of values, the sense of mystery, the feeling of reverence which shades off into awe, with a somewhat vague reminder of the three-fold aspect of the official doctrine of God.

III

From the social point of view two very interesting and fruitful suggestions are offered. The first is by the lamented Professor Rauschenbusch, who proposes three requisites for a doctrine of God. (1) It must be free from despotic or aristocratic elements, in order that it may become democratized. (2) It must in no degree be implicated in the unjust sufferings arising from remediable social conditions, that is, love must be drawn into the foreground to furnish the principle for divine action. (3) Through the spread of a monotheistic faith, it must become the bond of racial unity; freedom, justice, and solidarity must be reflected in the conception of God.

A second presentation is by two writers of wide social experience. The new consciousness of the worth of the rational self, of the power of social solidarity, of evolution as the development of the inner principle of the world, the presentiment of the immeasurable possibilities which await realization in the cosmic movement of which man is a part,—these and other conditions are contributory to a fresh statement and solution of the problem of the world in terms of the social consciousness. From the point of view of developing humanity arises a new definition of the God-idea. This proceeds from a union of the scientific and the social interest. "This new spirit, forming itself as it were upon the restless sea of humanity, will, without doubt, determine the future sense of God. . . .

The deistic conception of an age now completely past, that God is some distant monarch, will fade into the darkness with the social system which gave it rise; and society as a federal union, in which each individual and every form of human association, shall find free and full scope for more abundant life, will be the large figure from which is projected the conception of God in whom we live and move and have our being." [1]

"It is accordingly this 'large figure' not simply of human but of cosmic society which is to yield our God of the future. It is the figure of myriad lives, and yet of one vast group life, in ceaseless activity. There is no place in the figure for an eternally perfect being, and no need; no need, for the vast society by its own inherent mass-dialetic—of struggle and adaptation, co-operation and conflict—is working out its own destiny; no place, for the society, democratic from end to end, can brook no such class distinction as that between a supreme being favored with eternal and absolute perfection and the mass of beings doomed to the lower ways of imperfect struggle. It is the large figure out of which is projected the conception of God *that is ourselves*, in whom and of whom we literally are; the God that, in every act and intention, we, *with all our countless fellows*, are realizing. Nor indeed is it a God, as idealistic absolutists would have it, in whom our imperfect actions vanish in perfection, but one in whom they are the means whereby out of an imperfect present, a less imperfect future is wrought. It is a God that in one respect is in the making, growing with the growth of the world; suffering and sinning and conquering with it; a God, in short, that *is* the world in the

---

[1] *Studies in Philosophy and Psychology*, by former students of Charles Edward Garman; R. A. Woods "Democracy a New Unfolding of Human Power," p. 98.

unity of its mass-life . . . a God *growing with the world.*" [1]

Here we have a mystical presentation, compounded of all the elements which constitute the complexity, the unity, the greatness, and the appeal of the developing social consciousness. One is reminded of Comte and his Religion of Humanity. Unquestionably this substitute for the official idea of God represents the only concept and aspiration which vast bodies of men and women set before themselves as a religion and to it yield the consuming devotion of their hearts. Provision is made for love: "Since the condition of mutuality or love is the highest condition which we are able to conceive, we may rightly say that God is love—not indeed a personal lover, but that deep-lying, ever persistent, ever growing tendency toward mutuality of life which is at once the foundation of our own existence and the promise of its consummate realization." [2]

IV

Turning from the social to the philosophical realm, attention is directed to an approach to the idea of God by way of the New Realism. This doctrine divides the real into values, non-values or the neutral, and evil. It is to be distinguished from the theory of the Absolute One, of whom the good and the evil are only differentiations; both good and evil are indeed actual, but evil is by its very nature transient and is destined to disappear in the Absolute One in whom all oppositions meet and are overcome. Why only the evil and not the good ultimately vanishes does not appear. Other advocates of this phil-

[1] *Hibbert Journal*: H. A. Overstreet, "The Democratic Conception
[2] *Hibbert Journal, Idem,* Vol. XIII, p. 171.
of God," Vol. XI, pp. 409-410.

osophy of the Absolute hold that evil is good in the making, and that this claim is in accord with the theory of evolution, to the effect that whatever is a means or is incidental to the good is itself a good. The New Realism, however, rejects this for two reasons: (1) it is rationally inconclusive, since there may be some irreducible evils; (2) men actually fight the evil as such, and this would not be the case if it were either a phase of the good or transformable into the good. Accordingly, evil is not a value but is radically opposed thereto. In the definition of God therefore we do not include evil and ugliness, nor what is neutral in respect to value, but only values. God is the sum of values—truth, goodness, beauty, justice—both as these are eternal "in a heaven by themselves" and as they are the efficient cause of the same qualities, together with love and reverence and virtue, among men. In a word, God is Value. And it follows that if he is personal, he is more than personality, just as the social order among men is more than the personality of each individual member. He is also both transcendent and immanent: transcendent as truth and goodness and beauty subsist eternally in a world apart from space and time; immanent as these exist in our human social world in concrete forms of the divine ideals. Moreover, since God and nature belong to different realms of thought, he is supernatural, yet not as contradictory to nature. He is the power which works in and with men, giving light to their reason, purifying and exalting their emotional reaction to the ideal good, and empowering the will in every moral struggle and conquest. Here, then, is a renascence of the idealism of Plato which has haunted and inspired the yearning of men for more than two thousand years. According to the New Realism, not all that is real is ideal but all ideals are real: the supreme ideals are the supremely real. The particular concrete real which embodies the ideal, however it approximates perfection, never becomes identical with it but remains forever numerically distinct from, although forever kindred with, it. On the other hand, the perfect ideal abides in undimmed and matchless splendor through all human approaches to Truth, Goodness, Justice, and Beauty, to Love and Reverence.[1]

According to another exponent of the New Realism the universe is striving toward a not yet realized perfection. The ascent has been from pure space-time or matter through life and consciousness toward a goal which is not that of a personal God but a "quality of Deity." God does not yet exist, save as the universe is striving toward Deity. At present the highest development reached is religion: "the sentiment in us that we are caught in the movement of the world to a higher level of existence." But this is not the end; the movement registered in religion is striving to a still higher point in which the quality of Deity emerges. When this is reached the possessor of it, or God, will not be an individual, for he would then be finite. On the other hand, as the universe is infinite, so the perfection toward which it strives as its goal will be infinite and, as realized, the infinite actual God. Each stage of the ascent to perfection has presented two aspects,—one actual and persisting, the other ideal but ever passing into actuality, at last to become the perfect actual or God. Accordingly, God is to be conceived of not as the absolute Originator of the World nor as a present existing Reality whether immanent or transcendent or both, but as that to which the ideal energy of the

---

[1] Cf. E. G. Spaulding, *The New Rationalism.* R. B. Perry, *The New Realism.*

universe tends, a quality of perfection which is only another name for Deity.[1]

V

Another idea more in line with the common notion of
God as personal conceives of all existence as pervaded by
an active spiritual reality from which it receives its direction and meaning. This is to be distinguished from both
the theistic and the pantheistic view of the world,
although it may be in agreement with these at special
points. The position is that God is the immanent source
of all that is. All phenomena are caused by his will; all
laws are description of the constant methods of his working; creation is a continuous forth-putting of his energy
—his providence; gravitation is one of the forms of his
conservation of the universe. He is thus the Infinite
Spirit that dwells in the infinite universe. "In him we
live and move and have our being." Various designations
may be given to him according as different aspects of his
being are presented, in this following the Hebrew people
in the successive but always incomplete names by which
they described their many-sided experience of God. Not
inappropriate therefore as names of God will be: "the
Infinite and Eternal Energy from which all things proceed," "Vital Force," which is the principle of creative
evolution, "Father," of the Christian Scriptures and of
Christian experience, and the less specific term "God,"
which since it lacks a fixed *a priori* connotation may embrace a wide variety of suggestive meanings. This Being
pervades the entire world as the spirit pervades the body.

[1] Cf. *Space, Time and Deity:* the Gifford Lectures, 1916-1918, by
S. Alexander, Vol. II, p. 361.

So immediate is his action throughout the universe that there is no room for second causes. Accordingly, there are no hierarchies of being as intermediaries between God and the world, and especially between God and men. Personality is not to be refused to him on the ground of anthropomorphism. We cannot escape interpreting reality in terms of the human consciousness, the highest in terms of the highest. Personality is our most significant category and represents the supreme quality of the worthiest life that we know. There may indeed be qualities in God higher than any in man, but at least the highest that belongs to man is not alien to him. However, the chief point is the immanent and pervasive energy of the divine in our world. Its distinction from the traditional doctrine of God is its rejection of any form of transcendence: God has no life apart from the world, hence no place is found for an essential Trinity with an "inter-trinitarian procession" of Father, Son, and Holy Spirit, existing before and apart from the creation, eternal. We know and can know of no activity in God other or greater than that which is manifest in the phenomenal universe. Since there is no divine transcendence, there is no mediation between God and the world and especially men. The traditional doctrine of the Spirit as immanent, permeating, and active in all existences according to their rank in the scale of being corresponds more nearly to the view under consideration. Yet the divergences of one from the other are so many and serious that neither party would accept the implication of the other. It differs not less from the common theistic position, since in addition to immanence this involves transcendence. The difficulty of reconciling these two points of view, which has always beset the traditional theist, is therefore wholly relieved. It may be alleged that this is accomplished by resort to violent surgery—the elimination of an essential property in God; but according to this doctrine no loss is to be feared: such a property has never existed. Moreover, the gains from this conception far overbalance the losses, for from the region of the transcendent has arisen most of the confusion of thought, the insoluble mysteries, and the distracting divisions of theological controversy.[1]

VI

In unconfessed, perhaps unrecognized, alliance with the position just described are two others which at first view appear dissimilar not only with it but also with each other. According to one of these the place of God in the world is taken by Christ. The Trinitarian formula is indeed applied to God,—he is Father, Son, and Holy Spirit,—but the terms seem remote and unreal. "The Father by himself is the divine nature, latent, unexpressed, and unrevealed": he is therefore so far as experience is concerned a negligible quantity. The Holy Spirit the "incarnate Christ now made omnipresent and omnipotent." Again but for some vague and valueless theological reference, the Holy Spirit as possessing a distinct subsistence, may be wholly ignored; we know him only as the Spirit of the incarnate Christ. The living God whom we see in nature, in whom we live and move and have our being, is none other than the Christ: he is the immanent and revealed God. In this presentation God as Father is entirely beyond our reach; he is all the same to us as if non-existent. The Holy Spirit is so far identified with

---

[1] Cf. Joseph Le Conte, *Evolution and Its Relation to Religious Thought.* Charles W. Eliot, *The Durable Satisfactions of Life,* pp. 157 ff.

Christ both as incarnate and as present and active among men that he seems to be only another name for a function already completely absorbed by Christ. Whether in creation or redemption, therefore, Jesus Christ is the only God we know. He is the originator and upholder of the universe. "The system of forces which we call the physical universe is the immediate product of the mind and will of God in exercise, Christ is the creator and upholder of the universe." Furthermore, the attraction of gravitation and the medium of knowledge are only other names for Christ; he is also the principle of induction. The universe with all its law and rationality *is* Christ, and it follows that he is the principle of evolution. To add that, notwithstanding the omnipresence of Christ in the world as the sole divine spirit and power in it, he is *before* and *above* it, contributes nothing that can function in our experience. The only God known to us is Christ, and the only Christ known to us is in the world; beyond this brief summary all affirmations are speculative.

According to the second position, the place of God and the essential Christ is taken by God the Holy Spirit. The idea of God as Father, as guardian, hence as external, as above and separate from us and of his kingdom as in heaven, is relinquished. We are to think of "an internal Spirit working within us—a constraining, immanent influence, a vital, propelling impulse vibrating through us all, expressing itself and fulfilling its purpose through us, and uniting us together in one vast spiritual unity." [1]

VII

There are many writers to whom the customary doctrine of God is a jargon of unmeaning metaphysical

[1] Sir Francis Younghusband, *A Review of Religion.*

terms, who are, however, unwilling to dispense with the word "God." For them it carries precious values without which our lives would be hopelessly impoverished. These values have for so long been associated with the word that if it were surrendered its disappearance would jeopardize the very interests which have been embraced and symbolized by it. Ernest Renan, confronted with this dilemma, himself having no sympathy with the contents of the orthodox dogma, said that "The word God being respected by humanity, having for it a long acquired right, and having been employed in all beautiful poetry, to abandon it would overthrow all habits of language. . . . Tell the simple to pass their lives in aspiration after truth, and beauty, and moral goodness; and your words will be meaningless to them. Tell them to love God; and they will understand you perfectly. . . . Under one form or another God will always be the sum of our supersensible needs, *the category of the ideal.*" [1]

In harmony with this suggestion, the late George Burman Foster says, "The word God is a symbol to designate the universe in its ideal forming capacity." And a modern Platonist, whose vision of "the infinite mystery" kindles the same exalted mood as burned in the reverent spirit of the great idealist, refers to "the good that is only another name for God." [2]

Such an idea of God is in general the one presented by leaders of the Society of Ethical Culture. Its aim is (1) to enshrine moral ideals and tendencies as objects of supreme reverence; (2) because of this to protest jealously against the deification of superhuman powers. The question whether the God of traditional theology exists

<hr/>

[1] *The Poetry of the Celtic Races, and Other Studies,* by Ernest Renan, pp. 136-137.
[2] George A. Gordon, *Aspects of the Infinite Mystery,* p. 49.

is without interest.   Even if the existence of such a God were to be proved, no use could be made of this result in their religious services.   According to Felix Adler, while we must affirm an Ultimate Reality, we can know only this of it, that it is the cause of the spiritual perfection which is the flying goal of our hope.[1]   We need, therefore, to substitute Humanity for Divinity; not humanity as it is, but as slowly transformed.   The ideal is social, not of one Infinite Being but an infinitude of beings, in increasing organic unity, permeated by the same spirit, raised to the highest conceivable power.   The moral ideal is that of a "multiple God," a "commonwealth of spirits," therefore democratic.   Another very suggestive writer says that "to ask is there a God, is to ask whether there be in very fact any source from which supreme blessings will be gained if one attends steadfastly and reverently to it."   He maintains that "any object toward which steadfast attention is turned, in order to derive the greatest blessings, is a God."   He believes, too, that the social ideal is such an object.[2]   Still another representative of the Society of Ethical Culture defines God as the totality of good in the world.[3]   This means first that God is the moral idea in which all actual and possible personal values are integrated; secondly, he is the desire to seek this good for the sake of the blessedness it offers; and thirdly, he is whatever in any degree satisfies the ideal demands of our personal and social life.   The reality may be designated by many names and symbolized as it has been in the entire religious experience of men by the widest variety of idealized objective

---

[1] *The Religion of Duty,* p. 27.

[2] Stanton Coit, *The Soul of America,* pp. 191, 200. Cf. *The Ethical Movement; Its Aims and Principles,* p. 190.

[3] Horace J. Bridges, *The Religion of Experience,* p. 71.

forms—customs, institutions, laws, and worship. The essential thing is the values which have been distilled in the experience of the race, which men cherish as the highest they know, particularly those which are common to them in their ideal social relations. Goethe sums up this attitude in the often quoted words:

> "Im Innern ist ein Universum auch,
> Daher der Völker löblicher Gebrauch,
> Dass jeglicher das Beste, was er kennt,
> Er Gott, ja seinen Gott benennt,
> Ihm Himmel und Erden Übergiebt,
> Ihn fürchtet und womöglich liebt." [1]

It is claimed that this substitution of the ideal social interests of humanity for the God-idea of the past in no way lessens the impulse to sympathy and service in relation to one's fellowmen, and thus to the attainment of personal virtue; on the contrary, it enriches and intensifies it, since interest is not drawn off to a superhuman object but is wholly concentrated on that which absorbs all its energy and love. The ideal to which society devotes itself, instead of being separated from the immediate object of its endeavor, is within humanity and inseparable from it.

The cleft thus suggested between the idea of God in Ethical Culture and that of Christian tradition is not, however, as deep as it appears to be. With few exceptions the immanence of God has been a cardinal article

---

[1] "Within us all a universe doth dwell;
And hence each people's usage laudable,
That every one the Best that meets his eyes
As God, yea, e'en *his* God doth recognize;
To him both earth and heaven surrenders he
Fears him and loves him too, if that may be."

of faith in the church, and this has become vivid and vitalized by the doctrine of the Living Christ and the Holy Spirit as the indwelling presence of God.   In this way the transcendent, absentee aspect of God has been at least relieved, if not completely overcome.   The aim has been to live the life of God under human conditions, that is, to incarnate the spirit of Christ in the personal consciousness, and to realize the spirit of God in the social aims and co-operation of the Christian community.   The social ideals of the Christian church have indeed not always been as worthy as those of the Societies of Ethical Culture.   With this admission, we must, however, add: (1) the past social ideals of the church were inferior to the developed ideals of the church to-day; (2) the highest social ideals of the church are to-day in no degree inferior to those of the Ethical Societies; (3) Ethical Societies are themselves indebted to the evolution of social ideals in the church for the content of their principles and aims; (4) the church and the Societies of Ethical Culture draw their inspiration from essentially the same source; it is a question partly of names and partly of method.   If, on the one hand, the Ethical Societies ignore a God who is wholly transcendent, on the other hand, the church more often conceives of its God in terms of the personal and social ideal, immanent in all the spiritual movements of men.   And both may with one accord confess that God is "the Real Being from whom the highest conceivable good is derived if we attend to him."

There is a large group of writers—men of high seriousness of purpose—to whom the dogmatic formulas of the creeds are felt to be an inadequate expression of the Supreme Reality of the world: scientists, as Huxley and Clifford, who in utmost seriousness bowed down before the inviolable sacredness of the order of nature; socialists,

as Robert Blatchford, concerned with the needs of struggling masses; naturalists, as John Burroughs, who find
in nature the revelation of ideal values; philosophical
students of human experience, as Overstreet, who look to
democracy in its social and cosmic development for the
emergence of the divine. It would be an abuse both of
language and of understanding to call these men atheists,
skeptics, or even unbelievers. Beyond question, if the
Athanasian propositions are authoritative and final, such
men are to be condemned. Who would, however, be willing to judge them by such a standard? Here it suffices
to say that to none of these men is the individual the
highest reality of the world; to all of them single facts
and personal experiences are elements in a larger whole
which is in process of unfolding in the ordered course of
the world-evolution. Most men who occupy relatively the
same position as the writers just referred to are willing
that the term God should be interchanged with other
terms as "tendency in the universe," or "nature," or
"Absolute," or even itself given up, provided only that its
value for life is retained. By whatsoever name men designate this value, "it is something not themselves and greater
than themselves, something which by its very existence
makes everything supremely worth while, overrides and
subsumes evil, intensifies and makes omnipresent Good,
and concentrates and satisfies in itself those ideal impulses
that otherwise would be tortured and broken about an
imperfect self." [1]   Even though the customary conception,
and especially the name of God, is given up and others
substituted, as the "Unknown and Unknowable," "the
Power, not ourselves, that makes for righteousness," or
"Nature," all phrases leave much to be desired if they

---

[1] G. Lowes Dickinson, *Religion: A Criticism and a Forecast.*

"fail to include the most essential quality of the conception they attempt to express, namely its awful and mysterious majesty. It cannot be doubted that the one English word for that conception must ever be—God." [1]

VIII

In Christian Science the term "God" represents a conception which has little in common with other modern ideas of God. Christian Science employs many words as definition or rather as synonyms of God—Principle, Mind, Spirit, Truth, Love. It teaches that there is but one Being, incorporeal, omnipotent, omnipresent, omniscient, infinite and absolute substance. God is the only Mind. All true or real life is a spiritual expression of God, and is therefore perfect as God is perfect. Man is in no sense material, nor is he composed of material elements, as blood, brains, bones, or other physical properties; on the contrary, he is spiritual and perfect, the image of Love. He is eternal and has no mind separate from God of which he is the expression. Since God is the principle of man, and man is the idea of God, man cannot sin. Since God is omnipotent, God can effectuate only that which is perfect; accordingly he cannot create an imperfect world, nor can he engender in man freedom to sin. The perfection of God makes it impossible for him to be a party to the sin, sickness, suffering, and death of the material or unreal world. Since God is omniscient, he can know only the perfect; the material world, being imperfect, cannot be known by him as we know it. He could be conscious of the unreal and temporal, of sin and

[1] Richard Le Gallienne, *The Religion of a Literary Man.*

sorrow, of suffering and death only if he himself became sinful and finite, that is, if he possessed the imperfect human consciousness by which he might misrepresent to himself our spiritual creation as material.

We do not inquire concerning the immediate historical genesis of Christian Science, or the personal sources responsible for its beginnings. Far more valuable to us is an analysis of the content of its idea of God as related to the idea of God in idealistic systems of thought. The fundamental principle here is unquestionably pantheistic: "God is all in all"; "All in all is God." It is not the ultimate pantheism of Paul, nor is it the unqualified pantheism of Spinoza: evil is no part of the necessary, although free, self-expression of the Infinite. It is a purely spiritual pantheism. All reality is spiritual, and all spiritual reality is God. This may be defined in part as metaphysical, but still more as an ethical idealism.

The theology of Christian Science has interesting affinities with the philosophy of Plato and Aristotle. It draws from Plato a part of its metaphysics and ethics. The only reality is ideal. The ideal is eternal. All that exists is real, so far as it partakes of or is a revelation of the Absolute and Changeless Eternal. This reality is Intelligence or Mind. It is Thought in the highest degree, indeed, Absolute Thought, which transcends and therefore eludes exhaustive logical definition. All human souls, so far as they are pure intelligence, are eternal and in idea are perfect, however for the period of their earthly existence they may be under the delusion of sense. The absolute reality is not merely intelligence but the absolute Good. For man the ideal good is won partly through an insight into the pure, incorruptible essence of the human soul, akin to God, thrust for a brief space into the evanescent unreality of earthly existence, and partly by making the ideal good of eternity the supreme and only good of mortal life. There is a tendency in the Socratic direction to identify knowledge and virtue, and this appears to be as true for God as for men.

Its affinity with Aristotle's conception appears in its relation to his designating term for God as pure intelligence. The Supreme Being is utterly self-contained and self-sufficient, without sensations, perceptions, appetites, or feelings which take the form of will. Since his knowledge is concerned only with the perfect, he knows nothing of the finite world which exists outside of himself. His intelligence, being infinite, is directed only to the infinite and absolute reality, namely, himself. Thus his life is that of pure self-contemplation. As far as God is concerned, our finite world and all its imperfection is the same as if it were non-existent. There is indeed this variation from Aristotle, that whereas in Aristotle the divine intelligence is oblivious of all outside of itself, in Christian Science God's knowledge embraces man, since man is perfect; the difference is, however, more apparent than real, for, according to Christian Science, man is not a part of the finite world, and hence imperfect and unreal, but as a self-manifestation of God is perfect and necessarily included in the divine self-consciousness.

When Christian Science presents "mercy" among the attributes of God, one sees that it has not completely freed itself from a use of terms to which it can assign no meaning. It holds, on the one hand, that man is incapable of sin and suffering, and on the other hand, that to God sin and suffering are absolutely non-existent. But "mercy" is meaningless apart from ill-desert or suffering in man and apart from God who both knows and has compassion on human misery and sin.

One looks in vain in the Christian Science conception of

God for any point of union between it and the teaching of Jesus; the two have nothing in common except the name "God." The utmost contrast drives them hopelessly apart. If one is true, the other is false. It would be a misstatement to say that the Christian Science idea of God is a development of the Christian idea; its essence is Greek rather than Hebrew. It is no less repugnant to Jewish than to Christian theology. The Greek conception of God with which this idea has the closest affinity, was never permanently influential in the religious life of Greece and Rome, nor had it power to maintain itself as an idea by itself; whatever permanence it enjoyed was derived from its alliance with vital elements of the Christian faith. One may discover the secret of Christian Science in its optimistic ignoring of the privations which disturb and darken human joy, in its inculcation of the Stoic attitude toward pain and death, coupled with the conviction that goodness is the essential heart of things, and that all evils are superficial and temporary and yield to mental suggestion, but these all grow out of its peculiar idea of God.

IX

An interesting side-light is thrown on the present attitude of a goodly number of educated men in a report of Professor Leuba of a *questionnaire* on "The Belief in God and Immortality." He attempts no complete exposition of the term "God." It fully satisfies his purpose to say that it "designates beings with whom can be maintained the relations implied in all historical religions in which a God or gods are worshipped, i. e., direct and affective relations. A personal God as here understood is therefore not necessarily an anthropomorphic but certainly an *anthropopathic* being." He addressed his questions to a carefully selected list of scientific men and received replies from a majority of these. Dividing the respondents into two groups of lesser and greater eminence, he tabulates affirmative replies as follows: from scientists, 48.2 per cent of the first and 31.6 per cent of the second rank; from sociologists, 29.2 per cent of the lesser, and 19.4 per cent of the greater eminence; from psychologists 32.1 per cent of the lesser, 13.2 per cent of the greater. This part of the inquiry, limiting reference to belief in God as personal, from whom answers to prayers may be expected, was in many respects neither so conclusive nor so significant as would at first appear. While the investigation uncovers a very suggestive condition—in its lowest terms, an aloofness from, if not positive rejection of, the traditional idea of God, yet one may not without further ado label all those who replied in the negative as atheists. For there are many who regard God as personal but have long since ceased to believe in objective answers to prayer. Again, there is an increasing number of thoughtful men who avow belief in God, yet maintain that not personality but super-personality or some less anthropomorphic term should be applied to the Reality of realities. Moreover, Professor Leuba explains that one reason why some of those addressed declined to reply was their misconception of his aim, and he adds that instead of preparing statistics on philosophic opinions about God and his relation to nature and to men, his "sole interest was to find out how many of those accepted a particular conception of God and his relation to men." As compared with the traditional belief in God as final, the result of this *questionnaire* seems very disconcerting. And yet it is not disquieting. When one considers the seriousness of scientific men, the reverence for reality wherever it presents itself to their experience, their absorption in the field of their investigation, their unwillingness to express a judgment on matters which lie beyond their special task, and finally the fact that professed theologians differ radically on the very subjects under discussion, one is not surprised that the men inquired of returned so many negative replies to the question "concerning a particular conception of God."

IV. THE THEISTIC ARGUMENTS—IN GENERAL

I

No SINGLE aspect of the idea of God has passed through as many vicissitudes as have the so-called theistic arguments. A survey of the principal stages which have marked the changing affirmations and points of view will make this statement clear. We may conveniently divide these into several periods, marked by general characteristics: the ancient—partly naïve and partly reasoned, the medieval, the late XVIII century (English), the revolution introduced by Kant, and the more recent views springing from the doctrine of evolution, the psychology of religion, and other present-day methods of interpreting reality. The arguments commonly adduced in proof of the being or nature of God are the cosmological, the teleological, and the ontological; these have been supplemented by several others, as the historical, the *consensus gentium,* and the moral.

II

In the first period our attention is drawn to two types of thought—the simple intuitive views of the Hebrews, and the highly speculative position of the Greeks. Everywhere in Hebrew thought the existence of their God was taken for granted. The apparent arguments put forth by their great prophets never formed a basis for their belief, but were instead a confirmation, a beau-

tiful and fitting confirmation of a conviction already
established beyond the possibility of shaking. The question whether he who formed the organs by which we are in
contact with the world should not himself possess the
same, carried its own self-evident answer. And long afterward the apostle whose thought was tinged with contemporary idealism beheld in all visible things a manifestation
of the unseen divine reality. Nothing was, however, further from their intention than to support by argument
what seemed to them self-evident, and therefore convincing and incontrovertible. The being who was thus
revealed was indeed not one of pure spirituality, but this
fact does not in any way alter the force of our contention. The world was the purposive disclosure of a
rational will, to be interpreted through human qualities,
or where these failed, through God's specific self-revela-
tion, and if this was lacking the appeal was made to faith
in the unsearchable riches of the divine will. Paul might
argue concerning other questions, as for example the
institutions of the Jewish church, but he shared with all
others the unshakable assurance of the being of God. He
had therefore need of no formal argument to establish
the existence of God.

For the two great thinkers of Greece the idea of God
was the postulate of their interpretation of the world.
The changing aspects of the world, its incompleteness, its
dramatic tendency toward something other and higher
than itself became intelligible only in the light of a perfect reality of which all finite things were but partial suggestions. They approached this idea from different
angles, and their conception of God both as to his nature
and as to his relation to the world was not identical, but
this in no way invalidates the fundamental fact that for
both of them equally the meaning of the world was to be

sought not in itself but in God. It is not so much an argument from effect to cause, from thought to being, from
ends perceived to a purposeful intelligence, as that in the
very structure of their thought was the implication of
God. The world as they regarded it was conceived somewhat as follows: its ideal destination according to Plato
involved that what was real in it must be disengaged from
the sensuous aspect and rise into the supersensible sphere,
there perfectly to realize its end in union with the absolute good or God; according to Aristotle it was to strive
after and become like God, but since it was forever separated from him by an impassable gulf, it could never
become one with him.

In his analysis of consciousness Plato laid bare two
ultimate forms of thought, one dealing with abstract conceptions, the other with necessary, eternal ideas. Since
these ideas constitute the characterstic nature of the
soul, it is evident that the soul is of the same essence with
absolute truth, absolute beauty, absolute good or God.
In one sense he who seeks God goes outside of himself,
but in anther and truer sense he finds God within. This
can hardly be called an argument for the being of God;
it is rather an intuition, an analysis, and an evaluation of
the eternal and absolute quality of mind. He employs
the vehicle of mythology to convey his meaning, but even
so the meaning is clear,—all that is real in the soul is to
be referred to God, not indeed as static but as dynamic,
and as partaking of the truth and goodness of God. Thus
the argument from cause has validity, although not in the
form which arose later. Since thought is central in the
world, the highest Idea or God is the starting-point of all
our interpretation of the world—"the light of all our
seeing."

In Aristotle the theistic argument took two forms: one
based on the gradual perfection of ends in nature, the
other derived from an analysis of motion—the argument
of the Prime Mover. According to the latter argument
the world is self-existent and is characterized by eternal
motion. Motion involves both something mobile and an
immobile Prime Mover; or otherwise stated, it involves
both potentiality—a possibility of becoming—and a
reality to which neither change nor addition is to be
alleged to make it complete. The potentiality of the
world expresses itself in striving after and realizing ideal
ends, but since these are not immanent in the world but
only perfectly realized in God, one who would explain the
world must affirm a Being who perfectly and eternally is
what the world eternally aims to become; a Being infinitely self-contained and self-sufficient, an absolute self-
consciousness, of supreme felicity, the cause of the world
not as efficiently originating it but attracting it as simple
beauty attracts its object for which the world has inherent fitness. Accordingly, the world, although self-existent, is not self-sufficient: its ends are not from itself but
from God. It matters not to the argument that God is
wholly absorbed in the felicity of his own self-conscious
intelligence and knows nothing of the world, or, on the
other hand, that the world can come into no reciprocal
relation with God. The principle is that the imperfect
is conditioned by the perfect, all becoming presupposes
the complete, and striving toward the ideal would be pursuit after a phantom unless the ideal was already actual.
If therefore the world is to have meaning, this is to be
found not in itself but in God. This is the course of
the various well known forms of the argument for the
existence of God from the incompleteness and contingency
of the world. By Christian writers it was, however, as will

later appear, set in a very different frame from that of
Aristotle.

III

Anselm, who is the earliest of the great thinkers of
the church to construct formal arguments for the existence of God, proposes two ways of approach. In the first
he maintains that the most universal is the most real
being (*ens realissimum*) and the most real is the most
perfect being (*ens perfectissimum*). All finite greatness
and goodness are such by reason of partaking of absolute greatness and goodness. He, however, than whom
nothing greater can be thought is such not by participa-
tion in anything else but in himself *per se*. The cause of
existing things is therefore not in themselves—they can
be thought as non-existent,—but in a single cause which is
necessarily both self-existent and self-sufficient. This cosmological argument, derived from Platonic idealism, is
supplemented by the ontological argument which reasons
from thought to being. The idea of the greatest possible
or perfect being is universal. But this idea is not complete unless existence belongs essentially to it; otherwise
one could conceive of a still more perfect being, that is,
one who had metaphysical existence: an actually existing
being has more perfection than one existing only ideally.
To the objection that one might with equal cogency argue
from the idea to the existence of the Fabled Island, if
only perfection were attributed to it, Anselm had no satisfactory reply to offer. He failed to show the nature
of the necessity of this idea in consciousness and to prove
that necessary thought and absolute existence were bound
up together. For several centuries deep thinkers have
pondered the problem thus thrown out, feeling the attrac-

tion of it, unable to deny to it all validity, coupled with a secret hope that a solution somewhere awaits it.

Descartes added to the conception of Anselm an argument which involves two principles. First, the idea of God, that is, of a perfect being, could not arise in the human mind since the human mind is finite and imperfect; hence it must be referred to a perfect cause or God; therefore God exists. Secondly, the contingency of all finite things, since the reasons for their being do not lie in themselves, requires the assumption of a being whose ground of existence is in himself alone: self-existence is a necessary element of perfection, and therefore of God. The entire cogency of this argument lies not in the force of the inference from the idea of God to his existence, but *if* the existence of God is assumed, then naturally the quality of perfection follows.

IV

The first ominous warning with reference to the theistic arguments came from the philosopher who shares with Kant the distinction of blazing a new path for theistic thought, the end of which no one can foresee. Hume [1] in a posthumous work, allowed a certain validity to the cosmological argument. He affirms that the existence of Deity is plainly ascertained by reason. The inference as to the nature of this Being is from the order and design in nature, and is limited to the attributes of intelligence and design. "The cause or causes of order in the universe probably bear some remote analogy to human intelligence." This judgment is, however, qualified by the

---

[1] *Dialogues Concerning Natural Religion,* 1779.

alternative question whether the material universe as well as the mind may not be self-existent and contain the spring of order in itself. The present order of the world arising from long continued motion and transpositions is self-supporting and perhaps eternal; here each part is related to every other, the whole having the appearance of art or contrivance. This, if it could be established, would dispose of the ontological argument; it would also essentially change the idea of the nature of the Being whose existence Hume in common with all rational minds affirms.

Although he allowed that the existence of God was evident in the physical order, yet he was unable to attribute to him any moral qualities. From a consideration of the conduct of events in a supposed particular providence in human historical life, he reverses the well nigh universal judgment; for him the world, instead of being a sphere in which a purpose of good is disclosed, presents the spectacle of such conflict and confusion that no inference can be drawn concerning the divine justice, benevolence, mercy, and rectitude. Nor is relief to be sought in the choice between a being who is almighty but of limited goodness and one who is perfectly benevolent but of finite power. On an inductive survey of human life the only conclusion which is warranted by the facts is that God is entirely indifferent to moral values, whether of good or evil, even as he is indifferent to heat and cold, to drought and moisture. Aristotle had already presented the idea of God as one who is wholly oblivious of both the physical and the moral world, the Epicureans had isolated their gods in a region wholly withdrawn from the world of men.

Augustine and Calvin, making God the predestinating cause of sin as well as of goodness, had at the same time shown that evil and good were alike necessary to God, since both were rooted in the divine will. Spinoza conceived of particular forms of good and evil as evanescent but equally necessary forms of the Absolute. Hume infers a God of boundless wisdom and infinite and unvarying power, but finds no warrant for attributing to him any moral purpose or interest in human virtue. Whatever meaning therefore the idea of God may have, it "affords no inference that affects human life, or can be the source of any action or forbearance." In this connection two other suggestions of Hume from a very different point of view must not be passed by. (1) In his *Enquiry Concerning Human Understanding* he conceives of cause as a relation which the mind by reason of long association establishes between events, as heat and light; it is therefore purely subjective, limited to the phenomenal world, and incapable of metaphysical reference. The question as to the cause of the world lies beyond the power of the human understanding. (2) Since the world is "singular," that is, there is no other world with which to relate it, an attempt to connect the notion of cause with it is futile. Thus the cosmological argument loses its cogency. It may be a question which of these two general points of view represents Hume's final position.

V

Kant arrives at a position diametrically opposed to that of Hume in the *Dialogues*. Whereas Hume had affirmed the validity of the rational argument for the being of God but denied the force of the moral argument, Kant aimed to show the utter baselessness of the rational arguments—the traditional cosmological, ontological and teleological—and to frame a moral argument which would rest upon an impregnable foundation. By dividing the world into two wholly disparate sections—the noumenal and the phenomenal, by a critical theory of knowledge according to which phenomena alone fall within the scope of human understanding, while by the way of the speculative reason the ultimate reality remains both unknown and unknowable, he has made necessary a totally new approach to the idea of God. This is primarily subjective, through the pathway of experience. The starting point is a postulate which is proposed for verification. If at the outset the postulate appears arbitrary, it is not intended to remain so; indeed the aim is by moral endeavor to transform the assumption into an experience. "I *will* that there be a God, that my existence in this world be also an existence outside the chain of physical causes and in a pure world of the understanding, and lastly that my duration be endless." [1]   According to Kant we live in two worlds, one a causal order in which necessity rules, the events of which lie beyond man's causal power, since he, too, is a member of the chain, the other a sphere of ideal values which are wholly within the power of man to realize. In this latter sphere freedom is postulated as the indefeasible condition of virtue. A second condition is the duration of immortality in which freedom may attain virtue. But since the *summum bonum* includes happiness as well as virtue, since there is no ground in the moral law for happiness, and since happiness is dependent upon nature which takes no account of either man's power or his deserts, and is on this account beyond his reach, we have to add to the postulates of freedom and immortality the postulate of God as the necessary condition for the completion of the highest

---

[1] *Theory of Ethics*, p. 241, transl. by Abbott.

good.   Here is postulated a cause of nature in whom is found the principle of the harmony of nature with rational wills.   The action of this being involves intelligence, and his causality, will.   Accordingly, "the postulate of the *highest derived good* (the best world) is likewise the reality of a *highest original good*, that is to say, of the existence of God. . . . Thus it is morally necessary to assume the existence of God."

When therefore Kant says, "I will that there be a God, that my existence in this world be also an existence outside the chain of physical causes and in a pure world of the understanding, and lastly that my duration be endless," his position is in a high degree subjective, and he is giving expression to a supreme article of faith; at the same time he intends to offer an incontrovertible argument for the being of God.   He made his appeal to life, and in life rather than in the speculative reason would be found as he believed the vindication of the idea of God.   His argument is open to serious criticism, both for what it includes and for what it omits.   One might even maintain that with such a theory of virtue the conception of God was superfluous.   In spite of criticism, however, his argument opened the way to a new approach to the meaning of God, wherein such moral and religious values as he had no appreciation of have become central and decisive.   As a result the ancient metaphysical paths have been largely abandoned or else laid out anew, and the moral argument has become a populous thoroughfare to the interpretation of God.

VI

The influence of Kant's criticism of the theistic arguments may be sought in three directions: 1, in certain leading theologians in Great Britain and America; 2, in those who have been influenced by Hegel; 3, in those who have taken the pragmatic path.

It is a singularly significant fact that for the most part, until late in the last quarter of the nineteenth century, one finds little indication that, with few exceptions, English and American theologians had read Kant, or if they had read him, had felt the force of his criticism. The theology of Great Britain was insular, that of the United States provincial, and both were ruled by the Scottish common-sense realism.   Hume, when not denounced as a skeptic, was ignored.   Kant's great work, *The Critique of Pure Reason*, was published in 1781, revised edition in 1787, but Paley, whose *Natural Theology* appeared in 1802, was uninfluenced by Kant; he had not read him and therefore had no suspicion that his own work was to meet an antagonist far mightier than it.   The *Bridgewater Treatises*, which aimed to prove the "power, wisdom, and goodness of God as manifested in the creation," were all cast on Paley's lines.   Even in the first half of the last quarter of the nineteenth century the theologians who still advocated the theistic arguments in their traditional form, present an interesting spectacle.   Some regard all of the traditional arguments as valid, others offer a perfunctory defense of them as perhaps a disagreeable job to be got through with, while still others mix together arguments which are inconsistent with one another.   The elder Hodge, for example, states but does not defend the ontological argument, yet claims the two other arguments as syllogistically sound: the younger Hodge maintains that all are correct and conclusive. A. H. Strong is pro and con through his entire presentation but finally defends the traditional position.   Dr. Shedd, following his Platonic-Augustinian proclivities, argues at great length for the ontological proof. Professor Flint conditions the cosmological argument on the impossibility of an infinite regress of finite causes, maintains the design argument as in full force, but qualifies his assent to the ontological argument. Professor Miley refers to an earlier work of Kant on the "Grounds of Proof for the Existence of God," wherein he finds Kant akin to Samuel Clarke, but appears to be ignorant of the *Critique of Pure Reason;* he adds that he could with propriety omit the ontological argument, but affirms that the theistic conclusion of the cosmological argument in its certainty is little less than demonstration, and that the teleological argument remains unimpaired in its cogency. J. S. Banks classifies all the arguments as *a posteriori,* regards each as sound as far as it goes, not indeed as demonstration but with a high degree of certainty. Professor W. N. Clarke, disinclined to metaphysics, ignores the ontological but accords full force to the other arguments. J. Macpherson fumbles with the cosmological and teleological arguments, but in the end comes out where others had come out before him: with the younger Hodge and Flint and Fisher, he validates the cosmological argument on the ground of the absurdity of the infinite regress; he does, however, throw down the ontological argument. These are samples of influential writers who seem never to have felt the tremendous impact of Kant. They do not all write as if nothing had happened; their dogmatic slumbers are not without disturbing dreams. Professor Samuel Harris was the only American orthodox theologian who grappled with the fundamental question raised by Kant's great work. He maintains that the existence of God must be as necessary as the idea of God. With keen dialectics he endeavors to ground the cosmological argument on causation which conducts to a First Cause. In support of the teleological argument he adduces a five-fold evidence from nature as (1) symbolic, (2) orderly, (3) progressive, (4) telic, (5) harmonious and unified with a spiritual system. This constitutes for him a verification of the theistic hypothesis, that the cosmos is grounded in reason, and that the Absolute Power manifested in it is a Rational Power, the Universal Reason energizing, the personal God. It is an unaccountable fact that men like Professors Park and Henry B. Smith return after prolonged study in German universities as innocent of Kant as if he had never lived. On the other hand, liberal theologians, of whom Professor F. D. Hedge was the most illustrious instance, had found in Kant and especially in his successor Hegel profoundly suggestive material for developing the idea of God.

VII

With reference to those who have been influenced by Hegelian idealism, Kant's solution of the theistic arguments may be regarded as fundamentally sound—pointing out the right approach, and, if not final, as inviting to a deeper analysis by which Kant's ultimate dualism may be resolved into a unity. The latter is the path struck out by the Hegelian idealism. We have then to inquire what this type of idealism tries in general to do. (1) That which is essential in consciousness pushes out in every direction, permitting nothing to stand in the way of its reaching universal validity. Fichte held that reality must be interpreted by what we know to be most real, namely, consciousness or thought. For idealism there is no such object as "thing in itself," unknowable because unrelated to the human mind, nor is there anywhere an opaque and inaccessible somewhat whose bare

existence we can only assert or assume. (2) The ethical
is not to be alienated from the natural, but both are conceived of as essential and complementary aspects of reality, and indeed of personality. Mind and nature, instead
of being independent of each other, are members of an
organic whole. Apart from mind nature has no significance, apart from nature mind has no actuality. Nature
reveals mind and mind finds itself in nature. (3) The
finite consciousness presupposes the infinite consciousness,
and only as it discovers the infinite consciousness within
itself does the finite spirit realize its true being. There
is no complete individual life or separate thought; these
have in themselves as such no absolute worth; only as
they are embraced in the unity of the Absolute Thought
or Life have they meaning or reality. We may distinguish, but we cannot separate the finite from the infinite;
otherwise we make the infinite finite. All distinctions of
the finite from the infinite are only for the sake of affirming their higher unity. (4) Having thus reached the
ultimate unity of thought and being, we are on a vantage-
ground from which the theistic arguments are presented.

Pfleiderer and John Caird, leading representatives of
this general point of view, agree that the value of these
proofs lies in their tracing the steps by which the human
spirit has risen to a consciousness of God, but they are
not at one concerning the rational value of the cosmological and teleological arguments. According to Caird,[1]
the cosmological argument involves a necessary or infinite
Being which is a negation of the finite. This position
becomes a stepping-stone to a higher notion of the infinite,
as that which, instead of annulling, includes and explains
the finite. The logical defects of the teleological argu-

---

[1] *An Introduction to the Philosophy of Religion.*

ment, according to which the infinite is related to the finite world by the bond of an arbitrary will, impel toward a higher and final movement of thought. Pfleiderer [1] discovers in the manifold acting powers of the world not independent substance, but manifestations of a causal unity which is the ground of particular things, the uniform relations of which are the conditions of co-operation and law. [2] The teleological argument means that the cause of the world answers to organic, striving life, and is therefore purposeful, omnipotent reason which we designate as God. Both Caird and Pfleiderer agree in the view that evolution, which is only another name for "essential teleology," presents a form of this proof which is positive and constructive, to which, therefore, Kant's criticism does not apply.

Concerning the ontological argument, Pfleiderer says: "The unity of the laws of thought, which are not drawn from the outer world, and the real laws of being, which are not created by our thought, is a fact of experience of the most uncontrovertible kind." The only possible explanation of this is "the presupposition of a common ground of both, in which thought and being must be one," and this "connection of thought and being . . . points back to the unity of the two in the infinite Spirit." God is "ground and guarantee of the truth of our thinking." [3] Caird held that the meaning of the ontological proof lies in this, "that as spiritual beings our whole conscious life is based on a universal self-consciousness, an Absolute Spiritual Life, which is not a mere subjective notion or conception, but carries with it the proof of its necessary

---

[1] *The Philosophy of Religion.*
[2] Cf. Lotze, *Mikrokosmos,* Vol. II, pp. 596 f, 621 ff. Bowne, *Theism,* p. 60.
[3] *Op. cit.,* Vol. II, pp. 273-274.

existence or reality." [1]   These are impressive statements
of the ontological argument from the idealistic point of
view.   The following words may be added from Edward
Caird: "God is the unity of intelligence, conceived as
necessarily related or manifested in a world of space and
time, yet through that world returning into itself.   In
other words, the ontological argument—the argument
from thought to being—when relieved of its syllogistic
and therefore analytic form, is simply the expression of
that highest unity of thought and being which all knowledge presupposes as its beginning and seeks as its end.' [2]

Reference to other thinkers may complete the idealistic
presentation.   According to Lotze, the cosmological proof
conducts neither to necessity nor to unity of the Unconditioned, but only to the reality of a "Power immanent
in all existence and operative in all change."   The teleological argument is invalid.   The refutation of the ontological argument has been ineffectual.   It would be intol-
erable if what is greatest, most beautiful, and most worthy
is simply an idea, without existence or power, in the world
of reality.   "If what is greatest did not *exist*, then what
is *greatest* would not be; and it is impossible that what is
greatest of all conceivable things should *not* be." [3]   The
positions of the late Professor Bowne are essentially those
suggested by Lotze.   He is, however, satisfied to reach intelligence in the world-ground.   By an inductive process
he infers intelligence from the cosmic order or the structure of the universe, from activity according to rule and
with reference to future ends, and from human intelligence.
By a speculative process he likewise infers intelligence

---

[1] *Op. cit.*, p. 159.
[2] *The Critical Philosophy of Immanuel Kant,* Vol. II, p. 128.
[3] *Microcosmos*, Vol. II, p. 661.

from the constitution of reason, from the nature and implications of knowledge which involves a rational universe, a knowing human mind, identity of thought with principles of being, and such an adjustment of mind to reality that thoughts shall represent objective facts; that is, the intelligible exists only for and through thought.[1]

A recent setting of the ontological argument by W. E. Hocking maintains that we first build up the idea of God pragmatically, by asking what reason we have in the unity of our world, in the presence there of anything changeless and absolute, and in the existence of a personal deity. He shows how God is found in human experience at large and develops in religious experience, and how our knowledge of fellow-men depends on original knowledge of God and not *vice versa*, albeit these are reciprocal in their action. His ontological argument then resolves itself into the statement: "Not I have an idea of God, therefore God exists; but I have an idea of God, therefore I have an experience of God." [2]

VIII

Turning now to those who have been profoundly influenced by the pragmatic aspect of Kant's theory, we come upon two outstanding instances, Mansel and Ritschl. Mansel, who derived the basis of his contention from Sir William Hamilton's "Philosophy of the Conditioned," threw down all rational cosmology and turned to revelation as the sole source of our knowledge of God, the Trinity, and the incarnation. Here the business of reason is not to discover truth, to ascertain what God is, but only what he will have us think of him as conditioned by

[1] *Op. cit.,* p. 132.
[2] *The Meaning of God in Human Experience,* p. 314.

revelation.   Ritschl, influenced by Schleiermacher and
Lotze, yet owing most to Kant, rejected all theoretic
judgments concerning God and placed his entire reliance
on value-judgments.   The argument therefore resolves
itself into a single form, the teleological-moral: according
as the postulate verifies itself in experience, it gathers
validity.   One starts indeed with a great certainty, but
this initial assurance passes into knowledge won through
experience.

Although Herbert Spencer's point of view concerning
the idea of God was in general agnostic, yet he reminds
us of Fichte and Schopenhauer in his assertion that the
Ultimate Reality is of the same nature as that which
wells up in the human consciousness—a new form of the
ontological argument.   This position, if it could be substantiated, would offer a new setting for the presentation
of Anselm and Descartes.   Its pantheistic flavor would,
however, have been exceedingly distasteful to them.

Sabatier bases his conviction of the being of God on
the experience of the pious consciousness and on the necessities of the developing personality.   His affinity with
Kant and Ritschl is disclosed in the fact that he is concerned only with a Being who answers to moral and
religious needs.   His argument does not lead to a Supreme
Being—an Absolute who exists in and for himself apart
from the world—nor does it conduct directly to a Creator
of the universe who controls the forces with which science
has to do.   Piety, however, demands a God who preserves
the soul inviolate against all disturbing forces, whether
within or without.   Following Schleiermacher, the nature
of the Redeemer is deduced from the content of the religious experience.   We are accordingly treated to a twofold
way of approach to the idea of God: he is the postulate
which guarantees the ideal Christian experience, and

he is such a being as may be inferred from that experience.[1]

IX

At the end of this survey we are not surprised that the traditional "proofs" of the being of God are widely discredited. Professor James hardly exaggerates when he says: "That vast literature of proofs of God's existence drawn from the order of nature which a century ago seemed so overwhelmingly convincing, to-day does little more than gather dust in libraries, for the simple reason that our generation has ceased to believe in the kind of God argued for. Whatever sort of a being God may be, we *know* to-day that he is nevermore that mere external inventor of 'contrivances' intended to make manifest his 'glory' in which our great-grandfathers took such satisfaction, though just how we know this we cannot possibly make clear by words, either to others or to ourselves." [2] Reference is here made to such works as Paley's famous *Natural Theology* at the beginning of the nineteenth century, and later the *Bridgewater Treatises*. It is impossible for us now to overestimate the profound and quieting impression made by these works on disturbed and thoughtful minds. Their day has, however, passed; only belated theologians yield them homage and rely upon their outworn principles and methods. To the modern mind these "proofs" when presented in their traditional garb stalk about with the unsubstantiality of ghosts.

"They were mighty, but they vanished;
Names are all they left behind them."

---

[1] Cf. *Outlines of a Philosophy of Religion*, pp. 315 ff.
[2] *Varieties of Religious Experience*, pp. 73-74.

Even if we are no longer convinced by these arguments, we do not therefore conclude that belief in the existence of God is left without support. Men have never believed in God only after they proved his existence; on the contrary, they were certain that they had experienced God before they sought for the rational meaning or ground of that experience. The term "God" here signifies the Power other and greater than themselves which men have always and everywhere depended on. The particular name by which they designated this Power is indifferent, so far as the present reference is concerned. We rejoice if we are able to illumine our faith by the light of reason, but faith stands fast in spite of any and all articulate reasons. With Job plunged into darkness and defeat, the heart cries, "Though he slay me, yet will I trust him!" Belief in God is not innate, but the tendency to such belief is the constant and inexpugnable structure of our consciousness. While, therefore, the theistic arguments, as precisely formulated by earlier generations, may, indeed must, be discarded, and the reasons which were adduced in support of them have lost their meaning, yet the values which they symbolized remain unimpaired.

In the form in which they appeared at the close of the eighteenth century and as they are now commonly elaborated, they are subject to two criticisms. (1) They are *a priori*, leading to an abstract result: God is conceived of as pure being, a necessarily existing being, an all-perfect being, a being than whom a greater cannot be thought, or "thing in itself,"—in a word, a reality irrespective of concrete qualities. Indeed, the question is often raised by the advocates of this way of thinking whether the argument is to prove the being or the nature of God. This is especially true of the cosmological and ontological arguments. The adventure in search of pure being is, however, vain. Hegel has warned us that pure being is pure nothing. Apart from definite properties, the existence of God has no meaning. The only God we can know is not abstract and static, but dynamic and purposeful. A danger similar to that of an earlier day confronts us in the substitution of the Infinite, the Absolute, and the Unconditioned for being, or even if we put consciousness in the place of existence and then treat consciousness as a purely static affair. It would be idle to attempt to prove a divine consciousness as such stripped of essentially dynamic properties. There may or may not be such a consciousness, but either way it could have no concern for us. Only so far as consciousness is revealed in purposeful action can it be of interest or meaning.

(2) A more serious criticism has to do with the way in which the theistic arguments are employed to prove the truth of particular ideas of God or the existence of radically different kinds of God. Since the arguments are *a priori* one would suppose that the first question would have been, What kind of God do I wish to prove the existence of? The term "God" represents a vast variety of notions, some of which are incompatible with others; they are indeed so self-contradictory that if one exists the others cannot. It is a remarkable fact that few of those who deal with the theistic arguments appear to be aware of this dilemma. The God of Aristotle is not the God of the Hebrew prophets. The God of Jesus is not that of the Nicene Fathers. Calvin, Socinus, and Arminius use the word God with no attempt at criticism, but each one attaches a different meaning to it. Spinoza and Leibnitz are worlds apart in the conception of God. Kant in the *Critique of the Pure Reason* and Paley in his *Natural Theology* are at variance in respect to the Supreme Being. There is no common definition of God

back of the manifold conceptions which the theistic arguments seek to validate. Accordingly, in seeking to prove the existence of God it makes all the difference whether it is the God of Plato or of Athanasius or of Jonathan Edwards or of Herbert Spencer. For no reality is ever abstract, nor is there an undifferentiated *substratum* which will be equally necessary and invariably present in every idea of God, be it that of Plotinus, Marcus Aurelius, or Schleiermacher, with which therefore the theistic arguments are concerned. If we reduce the idea of God in Thomas Aquinas and Duns Scotus to its lowest terms, we shall care nothing for the pale residuum. No one would give a second thought to a possibly common element in the conception of Spinoza and Leibnitz. If the nature and properties of God are as Spinoza affirms, then God necessarily exists and acts from the necessity of his nature, the free cause of all things. If, on the other hand, there are, as Leitnitz alleges, finite monads and pre-established harmony is the law of all action, then the assumption of an infinite Monad or God is logically required; or the argument may equally well be turned the other way, in which case the assumption of an infinite Monad of the kind here in question is justified by the character of the finite monads and the relations existing between them. Yet, so far as our idea of God differs from both of these, we shall have to seek other arguments to substantiate the existence of our God. This general judgment is applicable to every idea of God in relation to the theistic arguments. If none of the traditional definitions of God is valid for us, the grounds of belief in such a God become insufficient and others must be sought for our present-day need.

From another point of view the same conclusion is reached. Since every one of theistic arguments has been determined by a particular corresponding world-view, and every one of these world-views has given place to the modern scientific view of the world, these arguments are placed in a critical position. They cannot continue to function in their traditional form and implications. If they are to persist, they must adjust themselves to the new situations, or, if this is impossible, they must be surrendered in favor of other and more defensible positions.

V.   THE IDEA OF GOD AND THE
DOCTRINE OF CAUSE

I

We now enter upon a survey of the idea of God and its relation to the doctrine of cause—the so-called cosmological argument—with the aim of ascertaining its present standing.

The cosmological argument is to-day in a more precarious position than it has been at any time since Kant published his *Critique*. The following considerations which are drawn from a doctrine of the world, the principle of cause, the nature of man, and the idea of God will disclose the invalidity of this argument and the need of carrying over its value from causality to teleology.

II

Two doctrines of the world have been proposed; one, as advocated by Aristotle, that it was without beginning, eternal, yet not static. The church stamped this conception as pagan, contrary to reason and the Scriptures, and subversive of the divine absoluteness and sovereignty, substituting for it the declaration that by a *fiat* God created the world is six days out of nothing. In this doctrine were two implications. (1) The existence of the world was to be referred to a single divine principle, in opposition to dualism or its eternal self-existence. (2) The creation originated not in necessary emanation but in the freely acting will of God. Creation is thus conceived of as an event, having a commencement. Professor Flint, in his oft-quoted and widely approved *Theism* [1] has given a classical statement of this doctrine. He declares that "*the* question in the theistic argument from causality" is "to prove the universe to have been an event—to have had a commencement." The inquiry has therefore to be raised whether or not the universe "bears the marks of being an event." And his conclusion is that instead of matter having existed from eternity "a creation took place . . . and the present system of nature and its laws originated at an approximately assignable date in the past." In support of this view both in Professor Flint's *Theism* and in similar works one is referred to the mutability of matter; the atom as bearing the marks of being a manufactured article; the dissipation of energy which involves at one end a beginning and at the other end a running down of cosmic energy; the impossibility of an infinite regress of finite causes; and the assertion that the notion of cause is satisfied only when one postulates a ground outside of the causal series,—an uncaused cause which is marked by efficiency and sufficient reason. Corresponding to this doctrine of the creation is an idea of God,—a being dwelling apart in eternal self-centered, transcendent isolation, to whom the act of creation is an episode and the world thus brought into existence an incident. Such a doctrine of God as the Absolute perpetuates in religious thought a point of view which is not defensible in philosophy. And it has given rise to a doctrine of irresponsible divine sovereignty, the source of

---

[1] Pp. 101 ff.

the baneful theory of election, limited atonement, and irresistible grace. In this conception no attempt was made to define matter, although the shadow of Democritus darkened the background; and souls were regarded as substances and hence efficiently created even as the world itself.

III

The common doctrine of creation includes two totally different notions of divine action—one by which the material of the world was brought into existence, the other, the shaping of this material into the various inorganic and organic forms. Even if one were inclined to credit the arguments by which changes in the world were referred to the external formative agency of God, he would find these utterly irrelevant to the question of a "creation out of nothing,"—a term to which no intelligible meaning can be assigned. The frequently repeated declaration that we have in human action an analogy of the absolute originative power of God is only another instance of the fatal fallacy of words. Whatever else man has done, he has *created* nothing. As to the material of the world which is the subject of scientific observation, analysis, and interpretation, however the atomic elements are resolved into electrons and these into something yet more simple, we have to assume as an unquestioned postulate that the properties of hydrogen, oxygen, carbon, and the other elements have existed from the earliest conceivable time; they are now as revealed by spectrum analysis changelessly the same throughout the universe, alike on earth and on the most distant perceptible suns, whatever their age or temperature.

"In form's embrace the atoms run
Like planets 'round an unseen sun.
Their world of form they cannot pass;
Their universe in one small mass." [1]

And even if the atoms themselves may be conceived of
as having had a beginning of their present form, the
energy out of which they arose must be affirmed as eternal.

Moreover, it is a violent, irrational, and wholly unwarranted use of the judgment to affirm an absolute beginning of either the existence or the order of the world.
For we have here a total misconception of the meaning
of cause. What we term cause has no other signification
than uniform and concomitant variation among phenomena. All the processes of the physical world are ruled
by mechanical necessity. Contingency which used to be
alleged to account for the changing variation among
phenomena simply does not exist. Mechanical causation
as an antecedent process is universal, but mechanical
causation, as origination of the elements of the world or
their properties, is inconceivable. Any other theory of
cause introduces a perfectly superfluous and futile notion
into our thought of reality.

On the assumption that cause as employed in the traditional sense is a universal principle, we cannot stop
short of the so-called First Cause, but must inquire for
the cause of it. To say that this is a child's question is
itself puerile. To say that God is *causa sui* does not help,
it only arbitrarily shoves the inquiry a step further back,
but leaves it still unsolved. The universe, so far as its
nature and forms are concerned, may, as Hume intimated,
be self-existent, or, as Aristotle held, eternal, yet this

---

[1] Grace T. Davis.

would not be tantamount to denial of the existence of God; it would, however, involve a particular theory of his relation to the world. That the world is intelligible does not prove a cause which lies beyond itself as absolutely originating it, for the same demand would in turn have to be made of the alleged Creator as intelligible. The fact that relations between atoms are susceptible of mechanical and mathematical formulation, that there is uniformity among phenomena, that a rational principle is discovered in the process of the world, does not necessarily thrust us back beyond the universe itself. The world as we know it has a nature and that nature is characterized by order; the question then arises how this order of nature came to be. If, in our consideration of this order, we still feel the need of the notion of cause, we may have to reinterpret it, with the result that efficient or first may give way to final cause. In this way the cosmological will be absorbed into and identified with the teleological argument.

IV

A still more critical situation appears in the relation of consciousness and personality to the idea of creation. Even if one could establish the absolute origination of substance, this would be utterly irrevelant to the genesis of spirits. That persons have always been considered as having a different origin from the inanimate and the animal world is evident in the many theories to account for the beginnings of souls. These may be eternal and therefore uncreated, or, as Origen maintained, created at the beginning of the creative action, or each soul immediately created in connection with the human embryo, or it may be referred to hereditary generation, or to other more scientific explanation. In whatever way, we seek to trace the beginnings of consciousness and personality, one path is barred: we cannot refer its origination to divine *fiat*. "Soul" or "spirit" is not an existence void of content but can be described only in terms of experience as feelings, thoughts, memories, imaginations, purposive actions, character; plainly this is not and cannot be the product of instantaneous creative power. Unless soul, spirit, and personality are defined in terms of substance instead of consciousness, as an instantaneously complete product instead of progressive reaction to its environment,—a definition which neither psychology nor experience will allow,—it has no relation to a First Cause. From this way of conceiving of it, the divine image becomes not the starting-point but the goal and a flying goal at that. And again as in the previous pararaph we no longer look backward but forward, the creative becomes the final cause, and the cosmological gives places to the teleological argument.

V

From the idea of God a similar conclusion is reached. This becomes evident from several considerations. (1) No sufficient reason has ever been adduced for the initiation of creative activity from a condition of the divine consciousness in which such activity was absent. Indeed such a transition is in the highest degree inconceivable. The difficulty is not solved by referring the idea to "revelation," since revelation contains no hint of such a conception. Those through whom the revelation is alleged to have come were wholly unaware of even the existence of a problem of this nature. The question must be answered if at all by the same rational power which raises it, which is that of great thinkers as Plato and Aristotle. (2) It may make little difference in our notion of the world whether it is to be referred to an instantaneous *fiat* or to an eternal process of change or becoming, but the bearing of this alternative on the idea of God is extremely significant. If, for example, we have ground for maintaining that God is forever creating instead of creating once for all, we shall no longer have occasion to picture him as existing in solitary felicity before the creation,—however we solve the riddle of time,—and then as creating and again after an indefinite period as absorbing all things into himself, so that in the end as before the beginning he is all in all. On the contrary, if he is purposive will, he must will something. All speculation concerning God as he would be in himself apart from the world is vain; vain also the assumption that he would be the same apart from the world. The Trinitarian life of God which theologians have alleged to account for the divine activity before the creation; the distinction between foreknowledge and prescience, between omniscience and all-knowingness of God; the doctrine of decrees according to which before the creation God determined in himself what he would have become of every human being,—these and many other related theories of the divine consciousness are without warrant in our thought of God. Accordingly, so far as the cosmological argument involves any of these conceptions of God it is invalid.

(3) The tenability of the common idea of creation is rendered still more precarious by the fact that the farther back we go in time, the less evidence we come upon for the ends of the creative action which we attribute to God or for the God whom our ideals require as their postulate. There are nebulæ, worlds in process of formation and dissolution, molecules in an infinite variety of activity, but

none of the values which give theism its supreme significance—love, justice, personal goodness; indeed, the farther back we penetrate into the past the less need we feel
for a Creator in any compelling sense. Moreover, we can
assign no reason why a Being whose highest quality is
love should bring a world into existence in which for an
immeasurable time appeared no beings capable of conscious response to his goodness. To say, on the one
hand, that man is the end which moved God to create
must be referred to overweening conceit, or, on the other
hand, that the ultimate reason why God created the world
is inscrutable, is to give up argument at the precise point
where argument is most needed.

VI

The assumption that God cannot be the Saviour unless
he is at the same time the absolute originator of the
world is open to serious question. In the entire field of
Hebrew prophetic thought or in that of the early Christian community no such doctrine is to be found. It is
utterly alien from the spirit of Jesus. At a later time
matter was handed over to Satan and evil spirits, and
under the influence of Greek thought became the home of
dark necessity. Salvation meant deliverance from the
visible world and all its destructive forces. In every
Christian land to-day are groups of Christian people who
continue this tradition, looking for the speedy coming of
the Lord to take them out of this "present evil world."
Prose writers as Bunyan, poets as Bernard of Cluny,
F. W. Faber, and Christina Rossetti, and evangelists as
Dwight L. Moody, have voiced their homesickness and
their longing for the celestial country. Such a doctrine

of the world is, however, pessimistic. It is inconsistent with the scientific spirit. It is a repudiation of the very cosmological argument,—that God is the creator of the world,—which those who occupy this general theological point of view maintain. In postponing salvation to another life it robs the present of the meaning which naturally belongs to it. Both the gospel as a principle of individual and social regeneration under a law of evolution and salvation as signifying the conservation of social values are perverted so as simply to present the steps by which one may prepare for a purely fanciful future. According to this conception both this world and the next are unreal,—this one because we do not truly live until after death, the next because it does not grow out of and continue this life. God, if he is anything, is the God of reality; in this view he would be superfluous, and in any case he could not be the creator of the world.

It has been assumed that unless God was the absolute originator of the world,—the God here conceived of is that of the Nicene Creed,—we would have no sufficient ground for the hope of salvation. It is, for example, alleged that unless he had created the material universe he could not control it, and that unless he absolutely controlled it he would be unable to conserve the most precious interests of human life. Several considerations, however, go far toward nullifying the force of this contention. (1) A certain indifference of the universe to moral values. This appears first in the infinite time which elapsed before man emerged on the earth; and we are told by competent scientists that a time is coming again, however distant, when so far as this earth is concerned moral values will have entirely disappeared. Again, on this earth where moral values are in process of creation by man, the embodiments of these are with infinite disregard destroyed

by material forces—volcanoes, earthquakes, floods, tidal
waves, fires, pestilence, incurable diseases, and the slower
but not less surely exterminating erosion and decay.
Furthermore, there is an aspect of unconcern of the order
of nature for moral values which is evident in the fact that
mechanical causation rules from end to end of the universe.   All the exact sciences derive their cogency from
the assumption and verification of this law of action
among all physical phenomena.   Between this causation
and moral values there appears to be no common term
which shall reveal more than a connection in space and
time; at least there is no essential relation.

(2) In spite of universal changeless mechanical causation moral values have appeared. They have been in existence as long as man has been on the earth, and were
foreshadowed before that in the instinctive life of animals.   In human experience they never exist isolated and
detached from connection with the mechanical order.
Neither Plato nor indeed Aristotle in his doctrine of the
Absolute conceived of it in total separateness from the
physical world.   Kant declared that the only perfectly
good thing in the world was a good will, but as he gave this
will no content and no environment—a purely abstract
and formal designation, he was unable to assign to it its
full meaning.   Only that will is good which wills something that is concrete and becomes an embodiment of
value.   It is in connection with willing that all moral
values are created and conserved, even if their form and
continuance depend also upon the structure and function
of the material world.   The history of moral values thus
produced may be traced in the development of the
achievements and institutions of civilization.   If now one
concludes that the world is not to be referred to divine
causality in the way the traditional theology conceived

of it, that the world is more or less neutral in relation to moral values, that at length every visible symbolic embodiment with the living human consciousness in which it was real is utterly to disappear from the earth, even this does not annul the fact that salvation is here and now in process of realization in individual and social regeneration.

(3) If we define "salvation" as the creation and conservation of personal values, together with the customs and institutions in which these are enshrined, we shall not miss the cosmology which has for so long been claimed as essential to it. That we have the power to produce values cannot be disputed and it equally cannot be denied that this is the highest aim which we can set before ourselves. We need have no fear, therefore, lest the hope of salvation will become insecure unless we can refer the absolute origination of the universe to God. If God did not thus create the world and salvation is a fact, then the two positions are not incompatible.

VI. THE IDEA OF GOD AND THE DOCTRINE OF ENDS

I

THE teleological argument proceeds on the basis that the presence of ends in nature is a proof of design, and from design thus indicated is drawn the inference of a designer both intelligent and good; the designer is then identified with God. Although Kant discredited this argument as failing to justify the conclusion derived from it, yet he called it the clearest, oldest, and best suited to the human reason. From Socrates until a recent time it has been received with a well-nigh universal, unquestioning assent. It arose and flourished, however, when there existed a very different conception of the world and of the relation of God to the world from that which now prevails. In the last century and a half it has suffered two attacks, either of which would have been impossible at an earlier day, and each threatened to destroy the last vestige of its validity. Kant's criticism has been referred to already. A still more serious crisis arose with the Darwinian theory of natural selection. Conditions which had been accounted for by special acts of an intelligent Designer had now to receive a different interpretation. Not that adaptations were no longer acknowledged; on the contrary, these, even greater in number and more wonderful in character than were formerly alleged, were freely recognized and attributed not to special design but to the action and reaction of resident forces, mechanical or otherwise. Organizations which have succeeded in establishing suitable responses to their environment have survived, while others in the degree to which they have been unable to effect such responses have either perished or dragged out an impoverished existence. By this process then and according to this law every form of organization without exception has come to be what it is. The earlier claims as to the part played by natural selection in the development of life may have been exaggerated, but after all due allowance has been made, enough is left forever to do away with the teleology of Paley and the *Bridgewater Treatises*. This does not mean that in the operation of Natural Selection all teleology has ceased to figure in our interpretation of the world, for, as we have seen, a greater and more marvelous complexity of adaptation has been brought to light than was ever dreamed of in the earlier thinking. It does, however, mean that teleology must be otherwise conceived. So far as events are themselves concerned, it will make no difference whether they are referred to Natural Selection or divine causality. In either case, as Bishop Butler in another connection remarked, things are what they are, and things will be what they will be. If we have any longer need of God, and if he is to sustain any relation to the facts of life, it must be not as an external control but as an immanent purposive will, inseparable from Natural Selection. By the term "Natural Selection" we may describe the phenomenal aspect of development in the region of scientific causes, and by the term "Teleology" we may refer to the inner principle of divine action operative in the realization of ends.

In addition to the aspects of life in which the law of Natural Selection prevails, there are others from which it is or appears to be absent. These are presupposed but not created by it. They are essentially teleological, although of a different type from the traditional teleology —the persistent law of heredity, the tendency to variation, to self-preservation and to the preservation of the species. These are all purposive principles, immanent in the organism, active with reference to ends.

II

The fact that teleology has persisted through so long a period among men of the highest scientific and philosophical genius indicates that it has a permanent place in the conception of the world. Fundamental to the metaphysics of Aristotle were the two kinds of cause, efficient and final. Efficient cause finds its sole sphere in matter and it operates by necessity; the final cause is the reason which the efficient cause serves. Accordingly we have in our study of nature to "consider the character of the material nature whose necessary results have been made available by rational nature for a final cause." [1] These are the two aspects of the world to which study has to be directed and one is no less real than the other. There is no conflict between them, but each supplements the other and completes the explanation of the whole.

Bacon held that the world presented itself to us in a twofold way—as a mechanism and as teleological. In the scientific interpretation of it, however, mechanism must be separated from teleology. Final causes are indeed there, but in the pursuit of physical science they prejudice and so handicap inquiry. For this reason he refers to them as "vestal virgins," yet not to discredit them as

---

[1] *De Partibus Animalium*, III, 2, 665b, 20.

such, since in their own region they are no less valid than are mechanical causes.[1]

Leibnitz formulates the age-long problems in terms of pre-established harmony. Mechanical causation is universal: every event is rigidly fixed in the order in which it occurs. According to this system bodies act (to suppose the impossible) as if there were no souls at all.[2] No scientist could ask for a more rigid and unbroken connection of events in the physical world. There is final cause also, but this is inserted at the beginning by the thought and purpose of God. Here theology is invoked to find the cause both of the mechanical necessity and of the teleology which gives the world its double character.

Hume, who has often been reproached for his negative attitude in general, has no question that teleology is present in the world. "A . . . design strikes everywhere the most careless, the most stupid thinker; and no man can be so hardened in absurd systems as at all times to reject it."[3] In view of positions suggested by Hume in his further discussion, the term "design" as used by him is ambiguous and may well be the tribute he pays to the usage of his day. Design is unmistakable in the order of nature. He appears to hesitate between two explanations of the existing order. At one time he says, "For ought we know *a priori*, matter may contain the source or spring of order originally, within itself, as well as mind does."[4] In elucidating this conjecture he refers to a tendency toward dynamic equilibrium which had been sug-

---

[1] "Advancement of Learning," *Works*, Vol. I, p. 198, Phila., 1852.
[2] Cf. *Monadology*, pp. 80-81, 209, transl. by Montgomery, Chicago, 1908.
[3] *Dialogues Concerning Natural Religion*, Green and Grose ed., Vol. II, p. 455.
[4] *Op. cit.*, p. 395.

gested by Lucretius.[1]   Referring to the two aspects of nature—perpetual agitation and unvarying constancy—he says: "The continual motion of matter, therefore, in less than infinite transpositions must produce this economy or order; and by its very nature, that order, when once established, supports itself, for many ages, if not to eternity, . . . its situation must of necessity have all the same appearance of art and contrivance, which we observe at present." [2]   Yet he appears not wholly satisfied with this theory, for in another section he refers the present order of nature to a divine source.   Cleanthes remarks: "The order and arrangement of nature, the conscious adjustment of final causes, the plain use and intention of every part and organ; all these bespeak in the clearest language an intelligent cause or author. . . . I have found a Deity; and here I stop my inquiry." [3]   In an impartial inspection of the world, however, he discovered evidences of wisdom and power which are infinite; *"The cause or causes of the universe probably bear some remote analogy to human intelligence;"* [4] but if benevolence and mercy are to be attributed to this Deity they are inscrutable, since there is no resemblance between these and the same qualities in men.   The antithesis of Epicurus remains unresolved: "Is he willing to prevent evil, but not able? Then he is impotent.   Is he able but not willing?   Then he is malevolent.   Is he both able and willing?   Whence then is evil?" [5]   From the order of the world Hume drew the sure inference of intelligence in the cause or causes, but he could reach no conclusion which had any bearing

[1] *On the Nature of Things,* p. 163, transl. by H. A. J. Munro.
[2] *Dial.,* p. 427.
[3] *Op. cit.,* p. 410.
[4] *Op.* cit., p. 467.
[5] *Op. cit.,* p. 440.

whatever upon our human life. The significant thing is
that Hume found final causes in the world,—which the
scientific man is concerned with,—in a universal and unvarying order. Even if there were moral aspects of
human life which baffled his inquiring spirit, he must be
reckoned as one who more than any other in the eighteenth
century established teleology upon an impregnable basis.

In the middle of the nineteenth century Lotze is the
principal representative of mechanism and teleology.
Mechanism is to be affirmed of the entire phenomenal
world. Causation is not so much necessity as contemporary and successive changes—uniform and concomitant variation—among phenomena. All things are part
of a unitary substance, based on substantial unity of being
which underlies and conditions all events: a change in
one part involves a corresponding change in all other
parts. The order of the world is therefore uniform and
unvarying. On the other hand, teleology rests on a foundation as secure, even if not as broad, as that of
mechanism. This arises from the discovery of meaning in
the world. Causation implies law and order; teleology
concerns the ends served by law and order. Yet meaning
is not everywhere discoverable. Some ends appear trivial;
others baffle the moral judgment; still others permit no
definition, save that of malevolence. This mixed impression does not, however, invalidate teleology.

Among contemporary thinkers Professor B. Bosanquet
is the most outstanding representative of this general
point of view. He maintains that "the mechanical
appearance must be granted to be universal and unbroken." [1] Yet he also affirms teleology; "we can freely
suppose the world plan to be immanent in the whole, in-

---

[1] *The Principle of Individuality and Value*, p. 146.

cluding finite mind and also mechanical nature." [1]
Although mechanism is contrasted with teleology, yet
the contrast is "rooted in the very nature of totality,
which is regarded from two complementary points of view,
as an individual whole, and as constituted of interacting
members." This position is still further and with great
learning defended in two discriminating works by Professor F. L. Henderson of Harvard University, *The Fitness of the Environment* and *The Order of Nature*. His
final words in the latter book are: "According to the
theory of probabilities this connection between the properties of matter and the process of evolution cannot be due
to mere contingency. Therefore since the psycho-chemi-
cal relationship is not in question, there must be a functional relationship of another kind, somewhat like that
known to physiology. This functional relationship can
only be described as teleological." [2] In the body of the
work attention is directed to many phenomena which warrant the teleological reference, a few of which may be
cited; the tendency which Hume suggested to dynamic
equilibrium, to order, stability, and the varied conditions
of material objects; systems and gravitation; the conservation and degradation of energy; the living thing,
natural selection, the different cycles—metereological,
organic, harmonious. Not the least significant, indeed,
perhaps the most significant, contribution of Professor
Henderson to the subject of teleology is his discussion of the relation of the properties of hydrogen, carbon,
and oxygen to the order of nature. "There is in truth,
not one chance in countless millions that the many unique
properties of carbon, hydrogen, and oxygen, and espe-

[1] *Op. cit.*, p. 146.
[2] P. 211.

cially of their stable compounds, water and carbonic acid, which chiefly make up the atmosphere of a new planet, should simultaneously occur in the elements other than through the operation of a natural law which somehow connects them together . . . the connection between these properties of the elements almost infinitely improbable as the result of contingency, can only be regarded, is in truth only fully intelligible even if mechanistically explained as a preparation for the evolutionary process. . . . Therefore the properties of the elements must for the present be regarded as possessing a teleological character." [1]

III

We are now to inquire as to the place of teleology in animal and human life. Here the concept of teleology is still further confirmed. Impulse, instinct, and more certainly self-conscious behavior are inexplicable when robbed of their purposive element. The question is not primarily concerning the degree to which the ends involved in action are preconceived. The ends themselves are different from those referred to in the preceding paragraph, more complicated, of many degrees of value, becoming higher the higher we ascend the scale of individual and social activity. Of all ranges of existence known to us, naturally it is the human in which the teleological import is most convincingly evident. Here where the ideal presents itself in consciousness in an endless variety, where values determine the form and the content of action, where alone the supreme values of the world come to expression, is found that aspect of existence where

[1] *Op. cit.*, pp. 187-188, 190, 192.

meaning appears in most condensed and convincing profusion.

1. The meanings which arise in animal and human life are not to be detached from both the mechanism and the teleology which have already been referred to in the inorganic, purely mechanical processes. On the one hand, experience discloses no way in which meaning may exist apart from mechanism. Even the idea of God, however defined, is without content when isolated from the mechanism of the world by which it is conditioned. And, on the other hand, severed from the meanings which have been developed outside of and are contemporary with human life, there would be no meanings in human life itself; in part, these are simple continuations of the lower values and in part a development of these. And we have to add that where the relation of continuity or development has not yet been discovered, it must be presupposed; we have a right to hope that further knowledge and finer analysis will disclose the nature of the connection between the more simple and the more complex collocation of atoms, and between the lower and the higher values.

2. The animal and human organism in which teleology is disclosed is a psycho-physical unity. The ultimate nature of what constitutes organism we do not know. According to experience neither the psychical nor the physical exists in the form of life without its contrasting and complementary "other." Nor do we know the exact relation between the psychical and the physical aspects of the organism. Theories of consciousness as epiphenomenon, or as one element in parallelism, which may be traced to Spinoza and Leibnitz, or as acting and being acted upon by the physical, are under discussion, but no that can at present be said is, that thoughts which are decisive conclusion has been reached. Perhaps the most

non-material and not mechanical appear to modify mechanical and material action. But whatever the truth is, teleology is here the determining principle. In any case meaning is a fact in this correlaton.

3. As to the question, whether some teleology is to be referred to human choice and activity, the whole history of civilization is the answer. If one compares the face of the earth to-day with its appearance at any time since man began to control its forces, he discovers the vast variety of ends which have been already realized. While animals, even the most highly developed, leave only slight and at best very brief changes in the world as result of their action, the changes produced by man are great and enduring, and even so are only the beginning of what is yet to be. By agriculture, architecture, commerce, in the region of chemistry, electricity, and thermo-dynamics, the uses to which the forces of nature are put in the service of human welfare, are incontrovertible evidence of teleology. It is true that if man were suddenly and completely to be swept out of existence, every one of the changes originated by him would begin at once to dissolve and disappear; for while Nature lends herself to his uses and serves his purposes, yet she has undergone no radical transformation, she is at heart *Nature* still, and where man ceases to interpose she reverts at length to her own ways and the bringing to pass of her own ends. We cannot, therefore, maintain that consciousness as we know it is the directing cause of all the ends in nature. In the bodily organism itself none of the fundamental functions are under the direct control of consciousness. They began to be before consciousness in an explicit form appeared. As Kant suggested, the reason has higher uses than to control the physical organism; this is left to reflex action and instinct. Reason cannot teach the heart

to beat, the stomach to digest food, or the legs to walk. Indeed the bodily functions are best performed when the consciousness is wholly oblivious of them.   Instances of organs and functions of the body existing below the threshold of consciousness, serving definite ends, are in great profusion adduced by Paley in his *Natural Theology* —a thesaurus of facts by no means out of date—to be supplemented, if one so wishes, by Schopenhauer, Darwin, and Janet.   In every form of life below the human the purposive action of organisms is infinitely more subtle, sure, and wonderful than is to be found in human self-conscious purpose; on this one has only to consult von Hartmann in his *Philosophy of the Unconscious* and Fabre in his fascinating stories of insect life.

4. A further question rises, whether the finite consciousness and its purpose are themselves an integral part of the universal teleology.   If there is a world-plan,—and our conception of the world as a universe, of the two laws of thermodynamics, and of evolution is meaningless without it,—it would seem that there must be included in it not merely mechanism, but also consciousness, together with all the products of its action.   From a theological point of view, a doctrine corresponding to this has been fundamental to Calvinism (cf. *The Westminster Confession*, Chap. III).   How to reconcile such a postulate with our conviction of freedom, slight as that freedom may be, is at present beyond our reach; this, however, instead of discrediting, only adds another to the many unsolved problems, one may even say antinomies, in our world-view. That the purpose of the individual grows out of the universal, that it is taken up into and becomes a part of a wider social purpose and even of the mechanical process of nature, is a commonplace of experience and a recognized fact of history and science.

IV

A final question remains, as to what conclusion may be drawn from the facts before us in their bearing on the idea of God. We are indeed enjoined against trying to proceed further: "Science must put aside the problems which thus arise; and philosophy must deny to all men the right to found a system of natural theology upon the fact.[1] Yet in spite of this injunction, we must press forward to several well-grounded positions, and we must be modest in our inferences and conclusions.

1. A universal teleology justifies the assertion of a universal, immanent, purposive principle to which the adaptation and ends are to be referred. There is no indication of an external force, contriving, adjusting, bringing to pass results for which the elements of the world have no inherent fitness. The activity is purposive and always purposive. The ends are not all of equal value, nor indeed could they be, since they are of infinite variety. Nor may they all be judged by human uses and standards. They are, however, all equally necessary as indispensable parts of the whole. Some ends are realized which lie outside of any actual human experience.

> "Full many a gem of purest ray serene
>   The dark unfathomed caves of ocean bear;
> Full many a flower is born to blush unseen,
>   And waste its sweetness on the desert air." [2]

But the hidden gem which human eye will never see and the flower whose fragrance no human sense will ever per-

---

[1] Henderson, *The Order of Nature,* p. 118.
[2] Gray, *Elegy in a Country Churchyard.*

ceive are elements in the universal order. Moreover, some embodiments of ends stretch out beyond possible human experience, as suns which are so far distant from our planet that their light will never be brought within the vision of man. Still further, there are ends so remote from the interests of men, so utterly indifferent or even hostile to him that they are beyond comprehension or reconciliation with his existence, and yet are integral parts of the vast unity of ends of the universe. And although these ends are innumerable, complicated, confusing, sometimes at cross-purposes, perhaps inscrutable, yet they are no less truly ends and must be included in the all-embracing Reality. The prophet gave expression to a feeling something like this when, speaking for God, he exclaimed, "as the heavens are higher than the earth, so are my ways higher than your ways, and my thoughts than your thoughts."

2. It is not necessary, indeed it is not possible, to refer all teleology to self-conscious, selective intelligence as external. Teleology may have two meanings: first, conscious design due to preformed divine purpose. This is the common theological notion of it. Secondly, ends in nature are referred to an inherent principle or tendency to organization and harmony of the elements of the world. With respect to conscious purpose as involved in the argument of design, whether it be to or from design, the criticism remains in force. The argument to be valid would have to substantiate (1) a universal order which can spring only from design; (2) which is not inherent but foreign to the nature of things and accidentally attached to them; (3) of which the only assignable cause is a free intelligent agent; (4) from the necessity of the facts of the world thus accounted for, the unity of the cause is to be inferred, with certainty within, with prob-

ability beyond, the region of observation.[1] The argument,
however, conducts only to an Architect, not a Creator,
to very great but not infinite Power. Since Kant's criticism other objections have been added and to-day the
argument in its traditional form is set aside. Moreover,
with this form of the argument the facts of dysteleology
have never been reconciled. Hume called attention to
"the curious contrivances of nature, in order to embitter
the life of every human being." [2] Since biology took the
field, just as the adaptation, so the "contrivances"—war-
ring and destructive organisms—have become known in
immeasurably increased and perplexing variety. If one
attributes these to the purposive activity of an all-wise,
all-powerful, and all-loving God, and then with St. Paul
exclaims, "How unsearchable are his judgments, and his
ways past finding out!" he simply abandons the argument
in its most critical point and takes refuge in the inscruta-
bility of the world.

We turn therefore to the other definition of teleology
which seeks the explanation of it in the nature of Reality.
Spinoza broke ground here, although he was not in position to work his lead without the aid of modern scientific
tools. From the point of view of the active elements of
which the universe is compounded, there is an abstract
possibility of an immeasurable number of universes,
included in which is naturally the present order. The
present material order is, however, conditioned, if not
determined, by the properties of the atoms and their
psychical concomitants. There is everywhere complete
absence of any external force, originating or shaping
conditions and results in an arbitrary manner. Within

---

[1] Cf. Kant, *Critique of the Pure Reason*, pp. 536-537, Mueller's
transl.

[2] *Dial.,* etc., Vol. II, p. 436.

limits there are degrees of freedom, in the scientific sense, according to which the ultimate particles of the universe produce all results. The results produced, of whatever kind, have a teleological character and they have arisen in a fitness of the environment without which they would never have become what they are. In the action of the ultimate particles and their psychical concomitants, together with their relations with one another, there is an essential and changeless tendency toward co-ordinating activity, combinations, systems, adjustments, and ranges of development which involve meaning. To us the meaning appears to be more complex and richer in value in the animal, and especially in the human realm—the sphere of individual and social ideals.

V

We have now to inquire whether the source of this universal purposive activity is self-conscious or may be described as consciousness. According to the traditional view which arose when God was conceived of as independent of the world and essentially separate from it, he was the absolute, self-conscious, originating cause of all. The belief found expression in the doctrine of decrees: before the creation of the universe God determined within himself what he would have come to pass with every single thing. Naturally there was no proof of such a doctrine; although the authors of it claimed to draw it from the Scriptures, yet the biblical writers had no means of discovering or by revelation becoming aware of it. Prophecy as predictive which was formerly urged in support of divine foreknowledge is itself hopelessly in need of corroboration. Ethically the doctrine, whether that of Calvin or that of the *Westminster Confession*, breaks down. No more acceptable is Leibnitz's theory of pre-established harmony, originating in an optimistic choice by an omniscient will. The doctrine of omniscience may be so defined as to assert that all the changes and events of the universe, past, present, and to come, are eternally in the divine mind, but the definition is purely *a priori* and can never be substantiated in experience. There is, however, in this conception the presentiment of a deep truth: reality as a whole being infinite, of which the visible universe is a part, is marked by intelligence or order, and the form of the present order or intelligence not only is what it is by reason of all the past, that is, it *contains* the past in its entirety, but also bears within it the promise and potency of all that is to be. In one sense time is "the moving finger of eternity"; in another and most real sense, it is the process of eternity, of the All-Real in changeless transition. But whether the All-Real is "conscious" or not, will depend upon the meaning which we assign to consciousness. If we identify it with the principle of order or intelligence, the answer is plain; yet in doing so we give consciousness a significance which is only partially warranted by our experience; the word order or intelligence is preferable to consciousness. If, on the other hand, we take the human consciousness as a standard, we cannot exhaustively describe God as self-conscious or even as conscious.

Self-consciousness is a late comer in the evolution of reality, at least in one of the most insignificant of all the bodies which float in space. There was an inconceivably long period before it appeared in our world, and we are told by competent authorities that there will be an immeasurable period after it has ceased to exist in its human limitation—itself but a moment in the Eternal Silence. Self-consciousness as we know it is made up of sensations, perceptions, feelings, intuitions and discursive thought, recallings and forgetting, imaginings and dreamings, purposes, passions, acquiescence, hopes and fears, faith, love, pains, sorrows, disappointments, social action and reaction. A reality of which these were not characteristic experiences, whatever else it might be, would not be conscious in any sense of the word true to human experience. The human self-consciousness is further marked by several aspects or stages: an initial impulse from a previous condition of inertia in that direction; interest determining a longer or shorter attention; goodness as a result of effort becoming habit in which the feeling of effort ceases. The condition of attention is that we cease to attend; of knowledge that we ignore; of recalling that we forget; and of all conscious processes that they pass into the sub-conscious, until at the end of life we lose ourselves in the Great Unconsciousness. On the other hand, to speak of consciousness as infinite or perfect is to exclude the very condition of its existence. According to Aristotle the consciousness of God is pure and perfect intelligence; it is that eternally which man, that is, the philosopher, strives to become. But this is to raise to the nth power a single aspect of man's life and to imagine that he could realize this in total abandonment of all that gives to experience its meaning or value. Plato's supreme Idea was that of an absolute Good, a formless, colorless, changeless Reality, detached from the material world, essentially alien from it, perfect in itself. The church doctrine of the being of God not only denied to him "body, parts, and passions," but defined him as complete within himself, in total isolation from the world. It follows, therefore, that

God would not think as we do,—the infinite content of his consciousness would be present as an eternal intuition; his purposes would be unlike ours,—he would changelessly and from eternity will whatsoever comes to pass. The traditional contrast between the human and divine consciousness is perfectly presented in the well-known stanza:

> "Our lives through various scenes are drawn,
>   And vexed with trifling cares;
>   While thine eternal thought moves on
>   Thine undisturbed affairs."

We may sing such words,—they were written when theology was ruled by Plato, Aristotle, and the Schoolmen, and not by Darwin and the modern scientific spirit, —but like many of our hymns the words are unreal to us. If God were such a being we could never know him, and even if it were possible to know him, he might be an object of intellectual interest, but he could awaken in us no devotion. This is not consciousness, however the aim is to exalt the life of God to the highest degree, but a theological construction.

There are many forms of cosmic activity to which the term "conscious" seems not to apply. There are, for example, the organization of systems, gravitation, cohesion, the conservation and degradation of energy, radio-activity, and growth of living beings. The question now is not whether back of these phenomena there is consciousness, but whether we can frame any description of consciousness which shall embrace these activities as constituent elements of it. To this question a negative reply must be returned. We must accordingly seeks some other word than consciousness, but we know of no single one which is capable of wholly expressing it. It must be understood that we do not degrade but rather exalt the meaning of this reality when we disallow consciousness as the alone characteristic of it; there is, on the contrary, infinitely more in this cosmic force than is contained in consciousness as we experience it.

If now from our knowledge of the universe we inquire whether in the teleological activity which we have affirmed we can discover forethought or preconceived plan, our reply would depend in part on definition. If we insist on forethought as an element in plan, it might be difficult to establish such a position. On the other hand, if one were allowed to select his facts, ignoring all others which were in conflict with them, although not less significant, one could make out a plausible case for purpose determined by forethought and choice. No doubt, too, one can so define omniscience as to include knowledge of all future events, possible and actual; but since this is only a definition of an *a priori* notion and is neither based on an induction of facts nor capable of verification, it is not authoritative for us in the study of the problem at hand. In the older works on the evidences of Christianity and in those to-day which follow the traditional method, the argument from prophecy is so treated as to prove the fact of divine prescience, particularly in the field of human action. This was based on the conviction that an essential function of prophecy was prediction. It was further based on the assumption of a miraculous inspiration by which the sacred writers became the amanuenses or mediators in communicating the purpose of God with reference to future events. The prophets did not need to be aware of what they wrote; this might be wholly enigmatical to them. Their writing was in no sense determined by their insight into the tendencies and hopes of the national consciousness; it was enough that they set down with accuracy the divine message. Several considerations, however, rob this argument of all its force.

Prediction is no longer regarded as essential to prophecy. Not that the prophet did not often gaze intently into the future, and there on its ominous or inviting background behold reflected the meaning of the aims and struggles of his people. The theory of inspiration which was essential to this view of prophecy as predictive is supported by an appeal neither to the documents nor to the psychology of the writers. These men were religious teachers, poets, statesmen, searchers after spiritual reality, trusted counselors or courageous rebukers of kings; and the least truthful thing one could say of them would be that they were tools, passive tools of divine revelation, and did not know what they wrote. We might further ask, how one could know that the word of the prophet was an immediate and infallible message of God, and not the product of his own contemplative and purposeful spirit. Of many predictions uttered with solemn assurances of their certainty, some were reversed within a generation of their utterance, others by reason of changing conditions were unfulfilled, and still others in the very nature of the case were never possible of fulfillment. From prophecy, therefore, we cannot establish the fact of infallibly precise and complete divine foreknowledge of events to come.

VI

In the order of nature there is a "hit or miss" method which seems difficult to reconcile with definite foreknowledge. From this point of view two aspects of the world are equally evident; one is an element of certainty in events, the other is an element of chance. Tables of mortality figure an average number of deaths among the assured, but there is a margin of variation above and below this number, and no insurance company will venture to point out the individual beneficiaries who will die in a given year. In the meteorological cycle the amount of rainfall of each year in a century is fairly uniform, but the months and days in which a certain amount will be precipitated cannot be foretold. Seeds that are sown by the wind are provided with springs and hooks and wings and parachutes and, as in the case of the water cat-tail, a thousand seeds will be blown in all directions and perhaps nine hundred and ninety-nine of them perish, but a chance wind will carry one to a congenial soil. And nature is not balked.

> "So careful of the type she seems,
> So careless of the single life."

Thus the evidence of plan is overwhelmingly manifest —order, stability, purposiveness, adaptation, realization of ends; in some aspects of the world too more than in others—the astronomical cycle, the behavior of atoms in compounds and systems; while in the region of organic existences the accidental, the non-significant, the maladjustment is often in evidence. In order to meet the problem thus arising in natural theology it has been affirmed that God governs the universe by general laws and second causes. In any system originated by divine wisdom a certain amount of imperfection and failure is inevitable; this is to be referred to the nature of the system which is on the whole, with all the infelicities incidental to it, the best possible. The merit of this theory lies in its recognition of patent facts, but in its assumption of divine foreknowledge it begs the very thing which is most in need of proof.

Another method which appears to characterize the order of nature is that of "trial and error." The creative activity, instead of proceeding in direct and unending lines, at times moves forward till arrested by blind alleys or turns backward on its track. It produces gigantic, unwieldly forms of organic life, and as if disappointed at their impossible bigness puts an end to them but preserves them in fossil form, as if to remind itself not to repeat the futile endeavor. The remains of extinct species on land and sea testify not only to the fecundity of nature but also to a certain groping and unforeseeing aspect of her action. It may of course be objected that if we knew perfectly the nature of the power operating in the world and the principles of its action, we might see that it moves in straight lines and inerrantly to its goal. But this hides an *a priori* premise, is an appeal to our ignorance, and is without validity in view of the fact that of the countless secular trails struck out by nature many have been deviated from or abandoned. The method of trial and error is possible by reason of the large degree of freedom in the world,—a freedom which allows of development in the way of variation as well as of heredity, of struggle as well as of natural selection, of many successes as well as of many failures. Freedom is, however, not merely caprice but active in accordance with general laws and a special environment. However far it may proceed, it is always ultimately checked by the fitness of the environment; having pushed to the limit, it may defeat itself by the very egregiousness of its achievement. The wind-swept wave lifts itself to a dizzy and unstable height only to fall back once more to the sea level, and the megatherium developing bigness to the furthest degree exhausts the impulse and capacity of animal structure and function and so knells its own doom.

This method of trial and error appears also in the social organism. No form of human social life is stable. Society is a continuous experiment. One type of organization is no sooner established and its value proved than its defects also emerge—an inevitable shadow cast by the ideal—and force an endeavor after a better adjustment of the social order. The shores of history are strewn with the wrecks and discards of past trials, tribal organization, theocracies, despotisms, oligarchies, kingdoms and empires, representative governments, democracies; and always something more workable and attractive beckons the race onward. In an enthusiastic passion for democracy, the poet sings:

> "God said, I am tired of kings,
> I suffer them no more." [1]

But kings were created by the same power which throws them down. At a stage of human experience when they were the only recourse, God set them up. They seemed ideal, and indeed were the only possible ideal, for the time being; with them a new millennium dawned. Yet afterward, for the further uses of humanity, they are outgrown and have to be cast aside. What will be the final form of social organization no one can predict, for in the first

---

[1] Emerson, *Boston Hymn.*

place there is to be no final form, and secondly, the experiment must go on as long as human life endures. Something of value will be retained; the old is transformed into the new. What is unworkable and a hindrance in the social experiment is rejected. The different experiments are going on side by side contemporaneously, and side by side kingdoms and empires and republics and democracies, no one of which is more than a brief stopping-place in human progress.

In explanation of this experience, the law of evolution is appealed to. It is alleged that in the process, a certain amount of waste and reversion to type is unavoidable. Moreover, what is fitted for one stage of development is by that very fact unsuited for another. This does not, however, prove that the Power operating through evolution has chosen this in preference to any other method of realizing ends. For creative evolution is eternal. There was no "before" when a choice could be made. And we have not the slightest reason for supposing that any other than the present order of human events is or has ever been possible on the earth.

The use of the terms "hit or miss" and "trial and error" should not lead us to the judgment that the method thus characterized is imperfect. It is not a question of perfect or imperfect. Such words and the notion they suggest are out of place here. If the term "perfect" has any meaning, it must be in reference to the possible. If no other order than the existing one has any place in our thought, then to all intents and purposes the present order is perfect and the error is as truly a part of the perfection as is the attainment.

Moreover, in spite of the handicaps referred to—the "misses" and the "errors"—whatever is true in the rest of the universe, here on this earth and in the circle of our experience, with all their apparent failures, nature and human life do not fail. Fire and flood may devastate here, but there tall forests grow in secure luxuriance and yellow harvests yield abundant grain; pestilence and war may decimate one nation, but in another, peace and health are plentiful and the death-rate normal. In the meteorological cycle, the average of heat and cold, rain, sun and shine, light and darkness varies but little from century to century; within this range human life flourishes, indeed it could exist in no other.

VII

The force of these considerations does not, however, in any way militate against the certainty that the universe is pervaded by "plan." The structure and constitution of the world, the co-ordination and behavior of its parts, the unity and adaptation throughout the entire range of experienced reality, the fact that we employ such terms as nature, organization, system, and evolution, the very term universe in which these are embraced, betrays the common conviction that plan is everywhere. That we are not yet able fully to define nature, and that the principle of organization remains in great part hidden from us does not detract from the judgment referred to. The instruments of scientific investigation and discovery and the sciences themselves—astronomy, geology, biology, chemistry, and chemical analysis—all imply the existence of an order which is as wide as the reach of human intelligence, and is moreover presupposed for all regions inaccessible to man's utmost reach.

When we use the term "plan," the question presents itself whether this involves what we usually associate with it—a purpose fully formed before its execution is entered upon. This, which seems to be the ideal, is rarely if ever the method and fact of experience. However wisely and with long forethought we determine the form of future action, we are confronted by contingencies which require revision, correction, enlargement, abandonment, or the substitution of another scheme more promising. Great works of art are never like Minerva in an instant thrown out perfect in conception; on the contrary, they unfold from the germinal idea, developing according to their peculiar genius steadily from within, growing as a tree grows, its form implicit in the seed, expanding true to its type according to an immanent impulse. If the work is a tragedy, each event grows out of what preceded, and it determines that which follows, ever moving steadily forward to the catastrophe; its coherent and developing detail, however, instead of being present all at once in the initial concept of the drama, emerges gradually with its inner necessary connection in the progress of the author's thought. The magnificent system of the Roman Catholic church, together with its impressive dogmas, was indeed implicit in the apostolic age and has gradually developed as an organism according to a perfectly intelligible type; but the present consciousness of the church, its dogmas, and the forms of worship and administration were at the outset only potencies among many other potencies of ecclesiastical development. There is also a plan of human life; Dr. Bushnell states it, "Every man's life a plan of God." Among many people there is a belief that a guardian genius presides over the birth of each child, to guide him into the realization of the plan of his life. Others, as Plato, regard this life as only reminiscence and recovery of a former state of perfection in which alone lies life's true plan. Theologians have affirmed that every event in man's earthly existence was foreknown and predetermined in the thought of God; the life of each man therefore simply repeats in earthly form what was eternally present as a purpose in the mind of God. Of such a plan, however, in the mind of God, in the sense outlined, we have and can have no knowledge. What we know is that in the successive generations of living men, there is something which for the want of a better word we call "plan," according to which personality and character develop. This it is which determines the structure and function of the human body and the human consciousness. It is implicit in the nature of man; it is presupposed in all his acts; out of it arises his authoritative and convincing ideal. We see, therefore, that "plan" is not necessarily dependent on forethought, whether perfect or partial. It requires only development on structural lines by which functional activity is in part determined, be the activity that of the inorganic, the organic, or consciousness. The question of its absolute origination is irrelevant—there is no such origination; such origination as there is is progressive and may be traced in the stages of its development. Accordingly, the originative activity is immanent, gradual, continuous, ever changing, yet ever the same, without beginning and without end.

In our experience we find nowhere complete, perfect, and permanent expression, but only approximations, with many failures, in the products of this ideal-forming tendency. Here, neither unrelieved pessimism, nor unqualified optimism, but only meliorism, and that in modest measure, is warranted. Aristotle's dictum that the perfect must already exist, else all striving after the perfect would be without rational ground, rests upon an assumption which is not justified by experience. Impulse and effort are not for the perfect, save as the perfect is conceived in a purely abstract fashion; men strive for what appears to be concretely better than existing conditions. No truer statement of the point in question has ever been made than in the following by Professor Dewey:

"The ultimate ideal (standard) seems to me to be chiefly what keeps all moral discussion from getting on. . . . We can talk intelligently about the beginning of a specific concern and so we can talk about *its* end, actual or desirable, but when we go beyond some specific matter, I think we talk nonsense. I am more and more convinced that all reflection is an analysis of some specific situation, and that moral theory can only give the general tools for such analysis. As a sort of limit of comprehensiveness, or adequacy, of such analysis, the term ultimate or absolute ideal may have a meaning, but in no other sense."

Every one who stops to consider is aware that individual, in the sense of absolute, perfection is beyond finite reach. Such perfection, if it is to be held as valid, is possible only to the total Reality of which each individual is an integral part. And such "perfection" would have to include evil as well as good, limitation no less than completion, infinite diversity and not simply undifferentiated sameness. Nor is it something that is wholly in the future; it already is; it has always existed; it will never end. But this concerns us only in an abstract way. Even so, it does not conduct us beyond an immanent teleology.

VIII

The results thus indicated—the unity of the world, and indeed the whole process of evolution—can be referred to one principle only, that is, to an inner tendency to unity and co-ordination and development. This tendency is present throughout the entire inorganic world. Instead of an aimless and unending play of forces, moving to and fro, whirling in fixed and separate orbits, like the tide ever returning to the same line—an eternal recurrence to the original starting-point—there is a process in which ends are realized, a necessary condition for the appearance of life. This tendency is in every atom, but it is super-atomic; it is in every inorganic combination, but it is super-inorganic; it is in every organic existence, but it is super-organic; it is in the ethical endeavor of every individual, but it is super-individual; it is the secret force in all social progress, but it is super-social. That is to say, the tendency in which lies the controlling direction of all things is forever active and forever unexhausted by any and all ever-changing finite forms. It is not merely that the possible permutations and combinations are infinite; if this were all, the result might be a mere kaleidoscopic shuffle of unstable and meaningless combinations. It is not simply action or movement, but tendency. It may for long periods be inevident; it is never wholly quiescent. It waits only for the fit environment, which other contemporaneous activities produce, in order to invoke the inherent capacity to further fulfillment. The tendency to development through variation is the secret of the entire creative process. An instance of this law is that of the little four-toed eohippus of millions of years since, as his fossil remains reveal the several stages of his evolution—four toes, three toes, two toes, to the one-toed magnificent creature, the horse of to-day. This tendency which is seen actually at work in the creation of the horse is everywhere active in all organic forms of existence.

We have to observe that this tendency, instead of operating on independent, isolated lines, irrespective of all others, co-ordinates its activity so as to constitute environment. Particular forms of life can exist only if other forms also exist. And all are dependent on certain degrees of heat and cold, light and darkness, humidity and dryness, gravity and countless other conditions, many of which are unknown to us. Hume called attention to the connection here referred to: "It is in vain to insist upon the uses of the parts in animals or vegetables and their curious adjustments to each other. I would fain know how an animal could subsist, unless its parts were so adjusted." [1] A previous question arises, as to the simultaneous, co-ordinating, teleological activity by which the adjustment is produced. The conviction is irresistible that we have here to do with a unitary force whose activity is twofold—toward individuation by which the organism comes into and is maintained in existence, and toward totality in which the individual becomes an integral part of a harmonious whole. For this we invoke no external power, arbitrarily manipulating the ultimate particles of the universe; instead, we discover that we are here in the presence of a fundamental characteristic of Reality, namely, a creative tendency toward ends of whatever kind. We may define this tendency by various terms, as Nature, Cosmic Force, the Will to Live, Creative Impulse, Infinite

---

[1] *Op. cit.*, p. 105.

and Eternal Energy, or, taking into consideration the
ethical values which have emerged in evolution, we may
say the Power, not ourselves, that makes for righteousness, or, having regard to the experience and custom of
the Anglo-Saxon people, we may call it God.

The tendency here referred to is toward infinite vari-
ability and infinite development. The atoms are of such
a constitution and their mutual relations are such as to
permit an inconceivably vast number of combinations,
components, phases, systems, and organisms. It is precisely here that the suggestion of Lucretius has its truth.
"For verily not by design did the first beginnings of things
station themselves each in its right place by keen-sighted
intelligence, nor did they bargain, sooth to say, what
motions each should assume, but because the first beginnings of things, many in number and in many ways
impelled by their own weights, have been wont to be carried
along and to unite in all manner of ways and thoroughly
to test every kind of production possible to their mutual
combinations, therefore it is that spread abroad through
great time, after trying unions and motions of every kind,
they at length meet together in those masses which suddenly brought together become often the rudiments of
great things of earth, sea, and heaven, and the race of
living things." [1]   Spinoza has been reproached for his
proposition that since thought and extension are infinite,
they must of necessity express themselves in all possible
forms, not, however, all at once, or at every instant, but
eventually, in the limitless range and duration of phenomenal existence. [2]   The entire activity of the world is determined along certain structural lines, and it is within

---

[1] *On the Nature of Things,* p. 163, tr. by Monro.
[2] *Ethics,* Part I, Prop. XXXV.

these that the variations occur. This must be regarded not as a limitation, but rather as a perfection. It is what Aristotle referred to when he spoke of "the material nature whose necessary results have been made available by rational nature for a final cause." If we interpret "rational nature" by the present-day term "laws of nature," we can perceive the bearing of his most suggestive statement. All the variations are rightly assumed to be according to law, that is, they are intelligible, even if their principle has not yet been fully ascertained. Every one of these variations is at the same time a revelation of universal and continuous activity of the unifying power at the heart of things. In this unifying activity we may find a part of our definition of God. And we need have no fear lest we belittle God if we think of his working as completely absorbed in the universe. A universe infinite in space and time, with an infinite possibility of combination and system, is a field broad enough for infinite power, wisdom, and goodness. Moreover, if any energy were to be alleged in addition to what is here involved, it would be purely supposititious; it could never come within the scope of human experience or apprehension. Such supposititious energy is therefore wholly negligible; not only so, but it becomes a serious handicap to a constructive idea of God.

Reference has been made to the psychical aspect which accompanies physical phenomena in the sphere of life. Greek philosophers thought of all the heavenly bodies as living beings. The Stoics conceived of the universe as pervaded and determined by a dynamic rational principle. At present, within the sphere of personal life, where the problem of action is most complex and difficult, many thinkers propose a "vitalistic" explanation. Without at-

tempting to adjudicate concerning this theory, attention
is directed to the psychical factor concomitant with every
physical form of life, whether beast, bird, or fish, or even
vegetative existence. The physical and the psychical are
in the most thorough-going correspondence. If we use
the term "conscious," we should say of the spider, the
wasp, the rattlesnake, the shark, the tiger, the eagle, and
indeed of every animal life, that in each is a conscious
principle which answers perfectly to its physical organism,
in each different as the physical organism is different.
These psychical accompaniments appear to rise out of a
common background of reality, so that, however differen-
tiated, they are never wholly separate from their source.
Here is an infinitely subtle and varied activity producing
infinitely varied and subtle aspects of life. And this constitutes a further revelation of the Reality which is cre-
atively active in the world.

The tendency to develop the psychical in connection with
the physical appears in a supreme degree in the human
experience. This may be traced along two main lines—
the individual and the social aspect of personal life. While
they never exist apart from each other, yet for purposes
of study, each may be isolated from the other. The richness of the individual aspect is discovered in the revela-
tions of psychology, in the manifold forms of consciousness, and even more in the mysterious and exhaustless
treasures of the sub-conscious self. The content of consciousness is still further disclosed in the products of the
human spirit, in literature, art, music, science, philosophy,
invention, finance, commerce, exploration, and yet more
in the inexhaustible impulse of which these are the progressive but always imperfect expression. If the self is
a "force which can draw from itself more than it contains,

yield more than it receives, give more than it has," [1]
then here is a point at which the tendency active in
the world is realizing the ends of individual personal life.

Side by side with this is the tendency to social evolution, disclosed in the language, customs, laws, and institutions which have come into existence in the developing
life of man. How diverse and significant these are only
the student of history knows. No dreamer can imagine,
nor can any prophet comprehend "the vision of the world
and the wonder that would be." Splendid as are the
already achieved moral results when referred to purely
human intention and agency, they are not explained from
human agency and intention alone; they involve a psychical activity of far wider scope co-ordinating and completing individual activity. Human purposes are merged
into and become part of a larger plan which seems to be
in process of realization,—a plan which cannot indeed
be effected without man's agency, yet for which man's
consciously directed agency does not suffice. Instances
of what is here meant are not far to seek. Joseph said
to his brethren, "Ye meant evil against me, but God
meant it for good to bring to pass as it is this day, to
save much people alive." [2] In his address at Pentecost,
Peter employed the same principle, but with a more rigid
reference to a divine purposeful activity, which took up
into its plan the perverse and short-sighted aims of the
Jewish rulers: "Jesus of Nazareth . . . being delivered
up by the determinate counsel and foreknowledge of God,
ye by the hands of lawless men did crucify and slay;
whom God raised up," and "hath made him both Lord

---

[1] Bergson, *Mind-Energy,* p. 39, transl. by H. Wildon Carr.
[2] Gen. 1:20.

and Christ, this Jesus whom ye crucified." [1] An unknown writer of the Exile gave unwitting expression to this principle in his reference to the Persian king, Cyrus, who was consciously absorbed in pressing forward the conquests of his kingdom, and yet was at the same time a chosen servant of Jahweh, fulfilling the will of God for his people.[2] Alexander meant only to subdue the nations of the East, but he knew nothing of the roads he was preparing for the Greek language and the Greek ideals to invade the civilization of those lands, and later for the Roman rule to extend its powerful sway over the same peoples. Both Luther and Wesley set out to correct abuses of their respective churches, and the great Lutheran and Methodist communions are only the more immediate and obvious fruits of their endeavor. Columbus sought only a new route to India and the Pilgrims a free church in a free land, but a new Continent and a new Republic crowned their simple but sublime endeavor. In his Second Inaugural, Lincoln, referring to the conflict between the North and the South, wrote that "Each looked for an easier triumph and a result less fundamental and astounding." In the recent War certain definite ends were present to those who precipitated the struggle, yet not a single one of these has been realized; others unforeseen and infinitely more significant are now taking their place on the field of history. In our survey of the past we cannot escape the conviction that a continuously active ideal tendency is realizing ends richer and more enduring than the transient, fragmentary, conscious purposes of our human world.

---

[1] Acts ii, 22-24, 36.
[2] Isa. xliv, 28—xlv, 6.

"There's a divinity that shapes our ends,
Rough hew them how we will."

We must not, however, present this to ourselves as
something external, arbitrary, and coercive, but as an
immanent impulsion toward a more inclusive unity, better
balanced, more harmonious, and greater ends. Here again
is a further disclosure of the essential nature of Reality.

It is in the nature rather than in the fact of ends that
the character of the tendency referred to is revealed.
Plato in the farthest reach of his speculative gaze beheld
the Good as the eternal, transcendent summit of being,
the end toward which all existence strives. And a poet
in our own time has written,

"O yet we trust that somehow good
Will be the final goal of ill." [1]

Experience has not, however, left this word "good" to
dwell in an inaccessible height or to remain an indeterminate something which haunts the imagination, but forever eludes definition in human life; experience has instead
brought it down to earth to make its home with men.
The good is not a glittering abstraction, but a concrete
reality with many facets, presented variously, now this,
now that—truth, justice, beauty, goodness, sacrifice,
social welfare. The one end—the good—is thus divided
into many ends, and these again instead of remaining
abstract become particular and concrete, incorporated in
words and deeds and a spirit of life. Wherever men and
women exist, they are urged onward by an inner, indefeas-

---

[1] Tennyson, *In Memoriam*, Canto liv.

ible impulse to be truthful, just, loving, to live for others, and to create social well-being. This impulse is back of all choice, back of all thought, back of all desire, having its source in the value-creating principle of the world. To this principle are to be referred the great loyalties, heroisms, sacrifices, sympathy, and co-operation of the social consciousness. In every phase of social activity the ethical ideal is in process of enlargement and revision, in respect of definition, functional efficiency, and emancipation from the stupefying power of tradition, with more or less of groping and experimentation, yet withal becoming at every point—industrial, economic, political, educational, community-wise, religious—more truly human and therefore more divine.

This inherent tendency of Reality to realize the highest individual and social values, instead of being exhausted by any and all existing conditions, contains the promise and potency of an immeasurable advance. This is evident from two considerations: (1) The capacity of the psychical aspect of being for an infinite content. (2) The fitness of the world for embodying an infinite variety of ends. If one asks concerning the relation of the psychical, ideal-forming, and efficient tendency of Reality to the ends in process of becoming, he is met by two answers: one, which has held the field from an early time, that the ends are partial and progressixe disclosures of an infinite, transcendent content; the other, of more recent origin, that the psychical aspect of reality, which at every instant completely expresses itself in the ends realized, changes as these change and is as these are: hence, if at any moment we could comprehend all the ends which are then existent, we would at the same time comprehend the entire content of the psychical Reality. In case we find neither the static nor this particular dynamic theory satisfactory, we may turn to another conception, that while Reality is as it manifests itself at every instant throughout the universe, yet its immanent causality contains the possibility of an infinite variety of not-yet-realized values. It is, however, necessary to suppose neither that in the Ultimate Reality all that is yet to be is present in the form of consciousness, nor indeed that all that is past exists in the form of explicit, conscious memory. It is another question whether Truth, Justice, Beauty, and Goodness, as absolute entities, subsist "in a heaven by themselves," independent of the world of space and time, in some way the secret source and explanation of the finite forms of truth, justice, beauty, and goodness.

VII. THE IDEA OF GOD IN RELATION TO EVIL

I

WE ARE now to consider the relation of evil to the ends in process of realization by the creative action of Reality. "Evil" and "ends" seem to be mutually contradictory: if ends are to be referred to a Creative Good Will, then evil appears to require a totally different cause. The two have always existed contemporaneously in the same world of human experience, both equally real, neither one able to overcome or abolish the other. Naturally all the early theories concerning evil took their rise in the world-view of different peoples. For Greek thinkers there was a deeper element of life than free-will and responsibility— primordial, dark, non-rational—a background of fate and necessity and Nemesis, over which gods and men had no control; before it they were powerless, and their only right attitude was one of submission. For the Persian Zoroaster the contrast of good and evil was absolute, symbolized by light and darkness, presided over by Ahura Mazda and Ahriman. While these co-existed in the same world and in the same human breast, their mutual antagonism was absolute, reconciliation was impossible, and neither could triumph save as the other was destroyed. The book of Job brings to the solution of this problem all the resources available to the moral and religious consciousness of the group in which it originated, but the author of it sought in vain for an explanation of the dilemma in the nature of the world or in man's relation to it, in man's moral condition or in the known principles of the divine action. The problem had therefore to be given up as insoluble, or rather the problem was merged into the far larger problem of the divine providence to which one resigns himself in uncomplaining and confident trust. Augustine as a philosopher, following his great Master Plato, thought of evil as defect of being, privation of good, and therefore as that in the world from which the divine was more or less absent; between good and evil there was, however, no absolute opposition; evil was relative and might gradually give place to good. To Augustine as a theologian, concerned with the vindication of the divine sovereignty, evil found its explanation in the divine will; here good and evil were sublimated to a shadowy distinction. Since Spinoza identified reality and perfection and held that from the essential nature of God everything arises by an eternal necessity, he had no place for evil except in our mistaken notions of perfection and imperfection: *sub specie aeternitatis*, everything is good; only from the finite point of view may one speak of evil. According to Leibnitz, evil involves three aspects—metaphysical, physical, and moral. As metaphysical, it is to be referred to the imperfection inherent and essential in finiteness. As moral, it is inevitable in a finite moral order, even in the best of all possible worlds. As physical, it is a necessary result of the metaphysical or moral limitation of finite existences. Accordingly, the relation of God to it is either causative as its source, or at least permissive, since he beholds it as a means to the greatest good. For Kant, evil, which is moral evil, has its source in a deed of intelligible freedom, not indeed temporal, but non- or extra-temporal; this evil is a "radical badness" whence all other evils spring; there are no shadings by which it may approach and gradually melt into good. A doctrine in some respects cognate with this has been advocated by Mueller and others: moral evil is referred to a prenatal free act, resulting in the fall of all souls previous to their entrance into this world. In this way universal sinfulness as selfishness is explained.

Other theories having a metaphysical reference have appeared. No one of them is, however, new. (1) In the common doctrine of the church it is assumed that by reason of the ignorance and frailty of men evil is inevitable; it is in a sense permitted and certainly overruled in the interest of a higher good. When, therefore, one passes in retrospect the long way over which one has come, recalling his sicknesses and losses, his pains and griefs, and even his sins, he yet thanks God for it all. (2) Evil is explained as an error of mortal mind, a false belief, an illusion: it has no reality. All that is real is "infinite Mind and its infinite manifestations." Since man as real is from the essence of God he is "incapable of sin, sickness, and death." Accordingly, sin, suffering, sorrow, disease, and all mortal woes are delusive phenomena, to be denied by a spiritual understanding of divine reality as not only without objective existence, but even any right in the human mind. (3) According to Professor Royce, evil in general is constituted by all finite facts as such, that is, regarded as individual and separate, and therefore incomplete, in relation to true Being. Since we are destined to find our satisfaction only in the perfect Idea and the absolute Will, all that falls short of this is occasion of unrest, longing, and disappointment. Yet *sub specie aeternitatis*, evil is never total;

the fact in which it appears is undefined save by reference to all other finite facts and to the absolute Idea and Will. Moral evil is to be traced to the will of a free agent, but even so it does not become an isolated, disconnected deed; somewhere and at some time it must be atoned for either by the evil-doer or by another; in some way the evil will must be thwarted and overruled and supplemented by his own or another's will, even the absolute Will.

II

Leaving the *a priori* path of metaphysics, modern thinkers have sought in experience a solution of the problem of evil in relation to God. Hume, who blazed the way for so many inquiries in various directions, is fruitful in suggestions here. He calls attention to four circumstances in which evil arises. (1) The function of pain as incitement to the activity and preservation of animal life. (2) Evil as incidental to a world conducted by general laws. (3) The frugal conditions in which all the powers and faculties of living beings exist. (4) The imperfect workmanship of the great machine of nature. So far as these considerations find a place for evil and assign a meaning to it, they relate it to ends which are in process of realization in the order of the world. Other solutions have been more recently proposed. One, the pragmatic, holds that both good and evil are relative to each other and to the time; there is therefore no absolute evil; what is evil to-day may be good to-morrow. If, through better adjustment, that which was evil ceases to be ineffective and "works," to that degree it ceases to be evil and becomes good.

The evolutionary view recognizes two aspects of evil—physical, in the animal world and in relation to men, and moral, as related to man alone. In the struggle for existence animals have been confronted by conditions which are from one point of view hostile and destructive, but from another advantageous and promotive of fuller life. Every function, and indeed every organ of animal life, has been created by the united action of two forces: one, an inner tendency to development, to which reference has already been made; the other, reaction to an environment which is at the same time both unfavorable and favorable, which calls out the resisting and adaptive capacity of the organism. The structure and color and quality of every living thing record the kind of enemies it has been confronted with and the degrees to which it has met the challenge. Many species, unable to turn their changed environment to account, have disappeared. Millions of individuals have been destroyed by enemies always on the watch for prey, yet in the long struggle for existence the fittest have survived. Swiftness, strength, cunning, alertness, endurance, beauty, witness to obstacles encountered, often fatal, yet finally in great part overcome. Evil has been omnipresent—fear, hunger, accident, violent death, and a host of disturbing conditions. Constituted as our world is, these are indispensable to fullness of life. That which robbed has enriched, and that which killed has made alive. By the alchemy of the Creative Good Will a part at least of the evil has been transmuted into good. And what is true of physical evil in relation to animals is even more true in relation to man.

The same law holds good in the moral evolution of humanity. Here evil has been described as the misuse or survival of tendencies and habits in a higher stage of development, where they are no longer sanctioned. It is further claimed that both individual and social development is from innocence through conflict to virtue; but since the path is devious and unfamiliar, and solicitations crouch by the way, inexperience betrays the unwary, and mistake and failure are inevitable. The conflict of the spiritual with the animal impulses, of the individual with the social, has issued in such defeat and degradation and selfism that to some it seems as if the way out of the dilemma would be either to suppress or else to exterminate the animal for the sake of the spiritual and the individual in the interest of the social; whereas the ideal is satisfied only by the mutual and harmonious action and reaction of the two conflicting yet complementary elements of experience. Good and evil have a common root. To the same impulse, the same appetite, the same desire, the same social relation may be traced the most splendid virtue and the most hideous vice. The natural impulses and appetites are, however, as such, neither good nor evil; they are simply the raw material out of which are fashioned the glory and shame of personal life. In themselves they are non-moral; man's most difficult and splendid task is to moralize them. For uncounted ages before the advent of the human race animals had been developing the impulses and appetites which were the springs of their existence. They were not, however, without foreshadowings of the higher personal qualities of man who was to crown their history, for they had already developed spontaneous and unreflecting love, sympathy, tenderness, loyalty, heroism, and sacrifice. And to-day, before the moral consciousness awakens in the child, the animal impulses and appetites have already taken possession of the infant self,—they are indeed the self; and they behave as if there were never to be anything else in the unfolding human life. When the higher self begins to awaken and assert its right of control, it is met by a lower nature already vastly more powerful, before which it goes down again and again in defeat. One may feel that if the sensuous nature were not there to oppose and overthrow the higher self, the higher self would develop in unhindered, ideal strength. "The light dove, dividing the air in her flight and feeling its resistance, might perhaps imagine that she could succeed much better in a vacuum." Without the sensuous nature and its opposition, however, the higher self could not develop at all. Thus the evil is good in disguise.

> "Let us not always say,
>   'Spite of the flesh to-day
> I strove, made head, gained ground upon the whole!'
>   As the bird wings and sings,
>   Let us cry, 'All good things
> Are ours, nor soul helps flesh more, now, than flesh helps
>   soul!' " [1]

This becomes only another instance of the universal law, that "our antagonist is our helper."

In addition to the conflict set up in the individual experience between the lower and the higher self, there is a not less precarious condition which owes its existence to two social relations. (1) No sooner does one begin to assert his simple individual impulses than he is met by checks which originate in the customs, prescriptions, and ideals of his social environment. How momentous, indeed

---

[1] Browning, *Rabbi Ben Ezra.*

how ominous this experience is for the moral consciousness is suggested by St. Paul in a revealing word: "When
the law came, sin revived, and I—died!" To him it
seemed as if the fierce resistance which blazed up under
the touch of social restraint already existed within him as
a latent power, a spark of evil which awaited only this
occasion to burst into flame. He interpreted the experience as if the entire meaning was embraced in the opposition and struggle of the lower and the higher nature. He
had, however, only to include in the "higher nature" the
social group into which he was born, with its institutions
and ideals, and hence its claim upon him, to understand
that personality is undeveloped save in harmonious and
happy adjustment of individual and social interests, and
that in this adjustment conflict is unavoidable. Instead
of the consciousness of the initial antagonism between
the two being an evil, and the conflict and even momentary defeat of the "mind" by the "flesh," of the social by
the individual an "evil," it is an indispensable condition
of self-realization.

(2) The other condition referred to is birth into a
social heredity by which one is plunged into an environment already saturated with ancient and still powerful
wrong-doing of the race. Yet this condition is not wholly
evil; that it does not preclude virtue is evinced by the fact
that in the darkest periods of history and the most cor-
rupt civic centers there have appeared men and women
and even children of majestic personal worth. And not
only is this true, but even knowledge of good is possible
only on a background of knowledge of evil. A German
poet has written: I learned truth from liars, hypocrites,
and scandal-mongers, the nature of charitableness from
fault-finders and scoffers, love from haters, egotists, and

envious persons, to be silent from tattlers, truth from flatterers, loyalty from the fickle, and steadfastness from weather-vanes. Moreover, goodness reaches its goal only in conditions which subject it to severest trial and threaten its very existence. The more desperate the straits into which it is thrust the more glorious the triumph. "These which are arrayed in the white robes . . . are they which come out of the great tribulation, and they washed their robes and made them white." .

> "Then welcome each rebuff
> That turns earth's smoothness rough,
> Each sting that bids nor sit nor stand but go.
> Be our joys three-parts pain!
> Strive and hold cheap the strain;
> Learn nor account the pang; dare, never grudge
> the throe." [1]

III

There are to-day two aspects of the moral and spiritual ideal which were subordinate and little thought of in the ancient Greek and Hebrew world, the impulse to which may be traced directly to evil. These are in addition to the highest virtues known to them: for Plato, love of the true, the good, and the beautiful; for Aristotle, high-mindedness which lifted itself above all common and ignoble things or found its satisfaction in divine contemplation; for the Stoic, an undisturbed self-mastery; for the Epicurean, happiness resulting from rationally moderated desires,—all in high degree individual and self-centered.

---

[1] Browning, *op. cit.*

Among the Hebrews the ideal was both religious and social: as religious it was defined as a severe, uncontaminated holiness; as social it prescribed justice between those who were of the same family or nation. "What doth Jahweh require of thee, but to do justly, to love kindness, and to walk humbly with thy God?"

Splendid and indispensable as all these virtues are, they have been crowned with two others not less shining, both of which owe their rise and development to evil. The first has for its aim the alleviation and, as far as possible, the removal of particular, temporary privation and suffering. In the ancient world few agencies existed for the relief of physical ills and fewer still were fostered by charity. Owing to various theories as to the cause and meaning of suffering there was an indifference to it which was antipodal to the mind of to-day. The modern attitude was prefigured by Jesus in a parable of judgment; in the order which he came to establish he introduced a new type of virtue which found its sole opportunity in various forms of suffering and need. It was to be a prime excellence to feed the hungry, to clothe the naked, to minister to the sick and to those who were in prison. This spirit received a powerful impulse from him in his compassionate healing of the sick. Dating from that hour with varying fortunes, the story of charities in Christendom is a remarkable witness to the growing sensitivity to pain and want, to disease and every kind of physical defect. In the Great War this spirit burst into glorious bloom; in our own country outstanding instances were the Jewish Relief Society, the Knights of Columbus, the Y. M. C. A. and the Y. W. C. A., Christian churches, singly and in combination, units of physicians and nurses, and the Society with widest appeal and most efficient service, the Red Cross, the most

comprehensive embodiment and expression of good will
wherever calamity, famine, war, pestilence, or any other
form of physical evil has laid its devastating hand upon
the welfare of men.   In addition to these agencies are
innumerable others, often little known, for the relief of
human suffering, for prisoners, for the sick, the blind, the
insane, for the deformed, the unfortunate, the dependent,
and even for the protection of birds and kindness to
animals.

The second aspect of the Christian ideal is called into
play in relation to conditions which either beget sin or
are directly begotten by sin, whether the sin is from ignorance or weakness or perversity of will, or from unworthy
and contaminating environment. The aim and motive thus
awakened were defined by Jesus, both negatively and positively. "I came to seek and to save the lost." "I am
come that they may have life, and may have it abun-
dantly."   All permanent rescue from evil is with a view
to fullness of life; neither can be realized apart from the
other; and evil is not the last word. The greater the evil
the greater the energy of good to bring it to naught.
"Where sin abounded, grace abounded more exceedingly."
In no way is the excellence of the good so truly revealed
as in its bearing toward evil—patient, sympathetic, undis-
couraged, resorting, if need be, to temporary expedient,
but never satisfied with anything short of its radical elimination or transmutation. Here is the sphere and function of the community founded by Jesus and of all others
kindred with it. The vast missionary activity of our
time, whether home or foreign, and all the agencies which
have sprung from the same spirit—educational, medical,
sanitary, industrial, economic, charitable—find their
meaning in individual and social regeneration. Outside of

the circle of the church there are innumerable agencies which aim at the eradication of evils: Women's Clubs, Societies for Civic Betterment, Societies for Advancement of Science, Medical Societies. Animated by the same spirit are peaceful political changes brought about by the ballot, together with upheavals and overthrow of government by violent means. All of these and many others are integral parts of a great movement, to gain control of nature's forces by discovering the secret of their action, and control of social forces by discovering the laws of their harmonious and beneficent working, with the single aim of deliverance from evil into fullness of life.

If we seek for the element common to all the individual and social endeavors to relieve suffering, to remove sin, and eradicate every kind of evil, we shall find its full explanation neither in one person nor in particular groups of persons, but in "an inward perfecting principle," of which the activity of persons and the persons themselves are a product. A tacit acknowledgment of this is involved in the terms with which recent movements, accelerated by the World War, have been characterized: "A wave of idealism has swept over our world"; "A new democracy has been born"; "A spirit of freedom has taken possession of the human consciousness"; "A new feeling of justice has been awakened in humanity"; "A new sense of the community of human interests has drawn the nations together and created higher ideals of national and international responsibility." One may allege that this is just a figurative way of speaking, and that therefore one has no need of recourse to aught save human agency. Accordingly, the explanation of this altruistic atmosphere and achievement is sought in the capacity of the human spirit for development and in the psychology of the crowd.

These are indeed real and have to be reckoned with; but after we have assessed their highest efficiency at its full value, we are aware of a remainder, a something more, a power, an activity which comprehends and gives fuller meaning both to the developing human spirit and to the common social consciousness. This is no other than the purposive principle already so often adduced, which impels, controls, and carries forward all human endeavor. The nature of this principle, as it embodies itself in the social consciousness in relation to evil, is disclosed in sympathy, justice, patience, resourcefulness, hope, courage, wisdom, scientific method, self-sacrifice. These are particular aspects, *shinings through* of the Reality in whom "we live and move and have our being."

IV

It might be supposed that in a world pervaded by an ideal-forming tendency of the kind here suggested, there would be no evil. This, however, loses sight of several considerations. (1) We have to take the world as it is. There is evil in it, as there has always been ever since life appeared, and as there will continue to be while human life endures. This is conditioned in part on the nature of things, and in part on the indeterminate freedom which emerges in the process of life. (2) While by the action of this ideal-creating principle form arises from the unformed, beauty from what was not beautiful, virtue from the non-moral, and social consciousness and activity are blended from many individual wills, yet form, beauty, virtue, and social consciousness are never perfect. If evil is to be identified with the imperfect, then evil must forever be. In any case, the "World-creating God" works only with imperfect materials and produces and can produce only imperfect results, whether these results are things or persons. At best they are approximations; there is always a "more" either of quantity or quality. The ideal ever beckons, yet is never fully realized.

(3) The common judgment of mankind is and has always been that this is, on the whole, a good world. If, with the hedonist, good is defined in terms of happiness, there is, whether among animals or men, more good than evil, more pleasure than pain, more joy than misery. Moreover, no one who looks back on his own past or the past of the human race wishes that there had been no pain or supposes that happiness would have been greater without the shadow of evil. If good and evil are defined in terms of ethics, there is and has been from the first more truth than falsehood (even in the Garden of Eden!), more virtue than vice, more justice than injustice, more sympathy than disregard of others' welfare. In addition, some forms of evil have either disappeared or become greatly mitigated; many new forms of good have arisen, the very coming forth of which was conditioned by evil. Some new evils have sprung up which could have originated only in the historical conditions which gave them birth, but even these are met by a corresponding, mightier good. It was no mere hallucination of an idle dreamer when Jesus, the very incarnation of Good Will, beheld Satan as lightning fallen from his seat of power. Moral evil in a social form exists only by sufferance of the good. The good will never consents to moral evil or acquiesces in it when it is recognized as such. That evil will gradually diminish there is every reason to believe; that it will at length wholly disappear, there is little ground to expect.

(4) In the long run, the nature of things favors righteousness and is against evil. One could not define righteousness better than to call it an attitude or action which is in accord with the nature of things, and evil as an attitude or action which ignores or opposes the nature of things. To say that the nature of things is wholly indifferent to good and evil would be to deny the uniform testimony of experience. Individual evils survive from generation to generation, but the proverbs of every people, which are the distillation of experience, bear witness to their ineffectiveness and impermanence. Yet in spite of the great moral teachers and the total experience of the race, it is one of the most difficult lessons that humanity has to learn, that particular moral evils are evanescent. This was the haunting problem which agitated the spirit of the Psalmist as he contemplated the wicked—their prosperity, their immunity from trouble, their arrogance, their satiety, their unbridled boasting, their covering the righteous with confusion. He was stunned and dumb at the contrast between them and the quiet, humane, and devout servants of Jahweh. His envy at their lot and his rebellious, atheistic doubt gave place to peace only when he "went into the sanctuary of God and considered their latter end." For him the house of God symbolized the moral order of the world which, notwithstanding all appearance to the contrary, was inviolate and would react with infallible retribution against all who set it at naught.

(5) The world is not organized on the pacifist plan. The glacier plows its path deep into the iron heart of the hills, thunderstorms plunge headlong over the mountains, and cyclones spread havoc over cultivated fields and populous cities. The "Power, not ourselves," is no milk and water energy, no subject done up in cotton-and-wool,

no gentleman in a dress suit, a drawing-room *dilettante*, unwilling to roughen his hands or soil his garments in the necessarily coarse work of the world; on the contrary, this "Power" is mighty, swift and direct-moving, not always tender, sometimes violent, and always resistless. Forms of this Energy are indeed the dove and the lamb, but nature has not in vain developed talons and beaks, teeth and nails, stings and poisons, strong paws and powerful tails, animals fierce and devouring,—all integral and necessary in a world which is tending toward fullness of life. Men and women are not ghosts, but flesh and blood, with appetites and passions and prejudices and determined wills. Institutions and aims which have become consolidated by generations of thought and struggle and habit are not suddenly dissipated by the waving of a magician's wand. In some instances by a silent and gradual evolution of the higher forces immanent in the condition itself they are transformed; in others they have to be overcome and reduced to naught by crushing power. To find God in one process and refuse to find him in the other is arbitrary and unwarranted. Neither a philosophy of nature, nor a philosophy of history, nor a philosophy of redemption justifies the word of the prophet, that the Lord was not in the mighty wind, nor in the earthquake, nor the fire, but only in "the sound of gentle stillness." One may wish that it were so, and that the particular idyllic dream of other prophets was already or could ever be realized.[1] Such visions are, however, the Eldorados of our hope, the Utopias of our imagination. They may haunt and console the troubled spirits of men, but they are not real, and in the nature of the case cannot be. We live in no such world and God lives in no such

---

[1] Cf. Isa. xxxv; Rev. xxi-xxii, 15.

world, for no such world either exists or subsists. In the only world of which humanity has experience, the higher good has been realized in part by the overcoming of one evil by another; and this is also one of God's ways.

V

These considerations have a profound bearing on our idea of God. They show, among other things, that the most significant fact about our human world is not man and his deeds—glorious as these are—but a "Power, not ourselves, that makes for righteousness." The Cosmic Reality is all that science affirms and more; but for us its supreme quality is ethical. In defining this Reality as ethical we may use the religious word "God," or, appealing to experience, call it "Nature," or we may employ abstract terms as "Justice" and "Goodness," yet in all alike we mean the same thing. We do not know, although we may believe that beyond the planet on which we live there are moral values in process of evolution: nor need we inquire how far such values exist in the animal world. It is enough for us that these values are real, and that they constitute the highest elements in our definition of Nature or God. They have not come up in a straight line or without hindrance. Their course has been zigzag, interrupted at one point, resumed at another, on the whole gaining in purposive content; yet not without fighting against and sloughing off evil. Besides the ethical and the spiritual there have been other rich acquisitions, scientific and esthetic, but the most precious gains are here. They have made themselves at home in human life and are preserved both in the consciousness of man and in his language, customs, institutions, and ideals. Nevertheless, not to man alone is to be attributed their creation and conservation; a Power within him and beyond him has energized for this result. There is a conspiracy throughout the entire world with this as the aim of its action. It was a feeling of this sort which inspired the prophet to write: "And it shall come to pass in that day, I will answer, saith Jahweh, I will answer the heavens, and they shall answer the earth, and the earth shall answer the grain and the new wine and the oil, and they shall answer Jezreel." [1] But the opposite is also true. Another prophet voiced the deep conviction that the overthrow of moral evil is to be referred not to man alone, but to a power mightier than man which reinforces and crowns his utmost endeavor. "From heaven fought the stars, from their courses they fought against Sisera." [2]

If we inquire as to the way in which the "Power, not ourselves," is overcoming both physical and moral evil, we shall discover that it is not by one but by many ways. The aim of this inquiry is to ascertain what light is thus thrown upon the nature of God; in no way is that nature more clearly revealed than in the history of evil. And yet so many baffling mysteries have been associated with the problem of evil and God's relation to it, that the pious heart has ever been ready to confess that "His ways are not our ways, nor are his thoughts our thoughts." [3] St. Paul, after an effort to adjust his thought of God to evil, exclaims, "How unsearchable are his judgments, and his ways past tracing out." [4] Involved in this attitude is a

---

[1] Hos. ii, 21.
[2] Judg. v, 20.
[3] Is. lv, 8.
[4] Rom. xi, 8.

suggestion that, since God is so different from man, he may act on other principles than those by which man's action is determined. This has carried with it two other implications concerning these principles and methods. First, that these are hidden from man, and secondly, that although man could not discover them, they have been in part at least supernaturally revealed to the human understanding. The first attitude is that of the agnostic; the second that of the traditional theologian. If, however, the position of the agnostic is valid, it would be all the same whether God had any relation to evil or not, or indeed whether there is a God at all. The second attitude is exceedingly unsatisfactory: it involves many notions of revelation, various and contradictory contents of the alleged revelation, and interpretations as different as the presuppositions of the different schools of theology. We are therefore thrown back upon a study of human experience, that is, we are forced to adopt the inductive method of inquiry.

We turn our attention first to physical evils. Outside of earthquakes, floods, tornadoes, and other cataclysms, no form of evil is remediless. Scientific men, working in different fields of research, are confident that all accidents and diseases, and, by wiser economic and sanitary administration, all famines and pestilences will be replaced by healthy, wholesome human life. Whatever Kant may say, Nature is not a niggardly step-mother. We are her children and in the wealth of her resources is provision for every physical good. She gives with no grudging hand; yet she is not inconsiderate and prodigal. Of him who would receive of her bounty, she requires only an open mind, docility, patience, insight, application of means to ends. Once the right key of knowledge has been found, there is no secret chamber of medical, surgical, sanitary, or economic riches but is at the disposal of him who seeks. Meanwhile, for such evils as we still have to bear, there are physical and mental alleviations, and there are remedies which heal or palliate if they do not cure—sympathy, fortitude, prayer, and co-operative charity. From the religious point of view, "To those who love God, all things work together for good"; in the field of science and physical welfare, to those who know Nature—the dynamic form of God—all things work together for good.

VI

With reference to moral evil there are two ways, in addition to those already mentioned, in which the Cosmic Energy is active. According to the first, evil is self-destructive or is brought to naught by means of evil. The world is so organized that many evils as lying, avarice, theft, hypocrisy, and slander correct themselves or carry about with them the seeds of their own dissolution. Moreover, there are evils which appear to go unchecked until they reach their climax and their doom. Their natural history has been described by an observant moralist: "Lust when it hath conceived beareth sin; and sin when it is full grown bringeth forth death." [1] In like manner cities and nations have perished through their vices—covetousness, luxury, licentiousness, cruelty, improvidence and economic waste. The nature of Reality is such that it will not tolerate attempts to set up within its domain kinds of life which are radically hostile to its energetic

---

[1] Jas. i, 15.

and all-powerful ends. Evil is also brought to naught by
means of evil—by the same or by a different kind of evil.
An instance of this is war. Jesus said, "They that take
the sword shall perish with the sword." We are told that
war can be vanquished only by the pacifist way. Without
stopping to argue whether there is only one path by which
war can be made to cease, it is enough to say that a particular warlike attack may be utterly defeated by a
stronger opposing attack. But this way of overcoming
one evil by another is condemned as unethical. And God's
skirts are cleared of all complicity in such conflicts by
the assertion that such conflicts are in direct contradiction to the principle of the divine nature. The Ancient
Hebrews, however, took a very different view of their
God. He who had been a storm- and later a war-God
entered the lists with them to beat down people and gods
hostile to them. A writer in the Old Testament does not
hesitate to use the most daring hyperbole: "Jahweh is a
man of war"; and as if one might shrink from identifying
Jahweh as a man of war, he quickly adds: "Jahweh is his
name." [1] Nor may we overlook the splendid passage in
Isaiah: the single-handed, vengeful, victorious warrior,
striding along on his return from the battle-field and the
slaughter of his enemies, his bright red garments dyed in
blood,—a picture which kindled the imagination and inspired the terrible vision of the seer of Patmos: the celestial warrior, his garments sprinkled with blood, smiting
the nations, ruling with a rod of iron, treading the wine-
press of the fierceness of the wrath of God.[2] This may
seem to us harsh, cruel, ungodlike, far removed from the

---

[1] Ex. xv, 3.
[2] Isa. lxix, 15-18; lxiii, 1-6; Rev. xix, 13-15.

spirit of the Suffering Servant and of Jesus. Yet in the last century, in a great national crisis, one who was imbued with the spirit of love wrote:

> "Mine eyes have seen the glory of the coming of
>   the Lord;
> He is trampling out the vintage where the grapes
>   of wrath are stored;
> He has loosed the fateful lightnings of his terri-
>   ble, swift sword;
>
> .   .   .   .
>
> Our God is marching on!" [1]

It seems but yesterday when a staggering blow was aimed at the peace and welfare of the world. A huge evil, prepared to destroy the civilization of a thousand years, arming itself with weapons which seemed irresistible, set forth on its arrogant career of conquest, but just as its hand was fast closing upon the prize, was paralyzed by a yet more powerful force. When diplomacy had failed and the mighty struggle was precipitated, only one course presented itself—to bring to the conflict all the resources of government, all the engines of destruction, the inexhaustible enthusiasms of youth, all the sacrificial offerings of religion and humanity, in a word, all the energies of mighty nations for the sake of ends dearer to men than life itself. To suppose that God was not in the roar and carnage of battle, in sinking ships and flying airplanes with their heroic daring and sacrifice of human lives, but only afterward in the conference of the Powers to settle terms of peace and discuss resumption of diplomatic, territorial, and economic relations, would be tantamount

---

[1] Julia Ward Howe, *The Battle Hymn of the Republic.*

to excluding him altogether from any part in the great
struggle.   No, our God is a "Man of war" as well as of
peace.   There is in him a terrible as well as a tender side.
It was the same Jesus who drove the money-changers from
the temple court, who also wept over the doomed city,
who shuddered with anger at men's unbelief, who also
spoke the word of forgiveness to the penitent sinner.   War
is not for the sake of war, nor peace for the sake of
peace, but both war and peace are with reference to
ends without which neither would have meaning or justification.

When we say that particular moral evils are overcome
by other evils, as by a superior force in war, what we
mean is, that the evils so overcome are for the time being
depotentiated, rendered impotent to continue their effective working.   The disposition of which the evil is an
expression is not necessarily changed, and conditions being
favorable, it may break out again in wrong-doing.   Trees
are felled, rocks blasted, swamps drained, large tracts
burned over—all so far negative—only that on this
ground there may spring up happy homes, fruitful harvests, schools, churches, business, and a commonwealth of
human good.   The old things are passed away; whether
they will become new depends on something other than the
destructive process.   The only radical and permanent
cure of evil is replacement of it by truth, justice, loyalty,
love.

In Greek thought the question of overcoming moral evil
had risen scarcely above the horizon.   Sophocles conceived
that to one who was threatened by unjust and fright-
ful torture and even death, but a single course was
open—obedience to a higher than a human authority,
namely,

"Unwritten laws, eternal in the heavens;
Not of to-day or yesterday are these,
But live for everlasting, and from whence
They sprang none knoweth." [1]

Socrates knew only that it was better to suffer evil
than to do it; the suffering was borne with reference to
the laws of the state and in obedience to an inner divine
behest. Aristotle would have his magnanimous man ignore
minor evils, while for such as were of sufficient gravity he
would strike back with scornful and unsparing hand. The
Stoic would receive with undisturbed spirit such evils as
men thrust upon him, and he would teach others to bear
these with equanimity. The message of the Hebrew
prophets was concentrated primarily on the national and
later on the racial religious interests; the people were to
cultivate holiness in social and personal life. Moral evil
was to be put away by amendment of life and by sacrifice,
but the aim was limited to the evil of the community.
Little or no consideration was given to the wiping out
of sin among those who were outside of the Jews. The
ideal is well symbolized in the New Jerusalem of the Revelation. The walled city lay four square; within it dwelt
only the redeemed who had been delivered from every
earthly ill, now crowned with unalloyed and perpetual bliss.
None from within ever passed outward through the gates
to share their blessed life with the "nations," but from
without the nations bring their glory and honor to enrich
the fullness of joy of those within. With Jesus, however,
a new day dawned. It was not enough for him to offer
blessings to the needy among his immediate neighbors; he
must "go to the next towns" also. It was not enough that

---

[1] *Antigone,* transl. by J. H. Mahaffy.

his disciples "be with him," and enjoy his high companionship; he must "send them forth" through Galilee with
the supreme good; after his death the same impulse carried them into Judaea and into the uttermost parts of
the earth. No one was to seek to overcome evil with evil
and no one was to be overcome by evil.

Evil was to be met in two ways. One was suggested
by the precept, "Resist not him that is evil; but whoso-
ever smiteth thee on thy right cheek, turn to him the other
also" (Matt. v. 39) ; that is, retaliation tends to increase
anger and malice in the wrong-doer. On the other hand,
suppression of revenge, instead of adding fuel to the flame
of the offender's wrath, leaves the fire to burn itself out
for the lack of further provocation. The other way is
still more positive and effectual: "Love your enemies; do
good to those that hate you." "Be not overcome of evil,
but overcome evil with good." [1] This path had already
been trodden by a Jewish king under a prophet's direction,[2] and the principle of it was found so true that it
had passed into a proverb.[3] But it had never taken its
place as a general law of life in the overthrow of moral
evil until Jesus announced it his teaching and made it
real in his conduct. Significant as have been other discoveries concerning an ideal order of human life, none
surpasses this in the interpretation of moral experience
in relation to overcoming evil, and indeed in the light
which it throws upon the meaning of God. In the attitude
of those who love their enemies, pray for such as treat
them with cruel scorn, who thus seek to overcome evil with
good, one beholds the children of "the Father which is

---

[1] Luke vi, 27; Rom. xii, 21.
[2] II Kings vi, 21-23.
[3] Prov. xxv, 21-22.

in heaven." Here then is disclosed in the highest degree the nature of the "Power, not ourselves, that makes for righteousness," and the divine alchemy by which the spirit of the evil-doer is transmuted into good. This is no arbitrary requirement. This is no obligation which an absentee God has enjoined upon men, by which he is himself not bound. Here we penetrate to the very nature of things and the heart of reality. Only good can call out good from the soul of the evil; only love can waken love. Where love is there is God, for God is love. Where goodness is, there, too, is God.

VIII. MORAL VALUES AND THE IDEA OF GOD

I

A NEW approach to a "proof" of the idea of God has been opened in a comparatively recent time. For several centuries now the ontological argument—from thought to being, from the idea to the existence of God—has been regarded by many as resting on an impregnable foundation, and it still wins recognition from serious and responsible thinkers. On the other hand, an even greater number of philosophers and theologians deny validity to its traditional form. Attempts are, however, made to rehabilitate it so as to bring it into accord with the requirements of modern intelligence and world-view. Two of these are here adduced. According to the first, the argument is based upon a profound confidence of reason in itself: the necessary implications of thought and of reality are not unlike. Thus the conviction is irresistible that "the best we think or can think, must *be*"; or, as another writer puts it, "Existence must correspond with our ideas." In the second view the ontological argument rises out of two motives: that our highest ideal, which represents the highest conceivable being, shall not be severed from reality; that an intellectual desire is satisfied only with completeness in our conceptions.[1]

---

[1] Cf. Pringle-Pattison, *The Idea of God*, pp. 240-241, 315.

These are cited not because one yields assent to them—
they are indeed subject to serious criticism—but to indicate the values which idealistic thinkers still find in the
a priori approach to the existence and nature of God.
In any case, the argument, in its more common form, presupposes a gulf between thought and being; if God exists
he must be transcendental.

II

The approach to the idea of God to which attention is
now to be directed belongs in part to the teleological and
in part to the ontological argument. It concentrates
interest upon the interpretation of values. So far as
these are related to ends, they may be classified as teleological; so far as they have a bearing on reality, they
belong in the region of ontology. If we would define God
in terms of value—and no other point of view offers so
attractive promise as this—we must first inquire what we
mean by "value." When we speak of values we think of
ends which are desired and striven for, together with the
means by which the ends are to be attained. They involve
ideal aims and corresponding activities. Values are of
many kinds—physical, esthetic, moral, scientific, philosophical, economic, religious. Aspects of these are happiness, welfare, truth, beauty, goodness, more particularly
justice, art, friendship, love, loyalty, sacrifice. There are
also degrees of value, permanent and changing, higher and
lower, ends and means.

Before we proceed further we must dispose of one or
two preliminary questions. The first is whether we are
to conceive of values as existing "in a region above the
heavens," irrespective of the human consciousness. Some-

thing like this appeared to be the view of Plato [1] in his
myth describing the life of the gods; they maintain their
existence in blissful contemplation of the divine, supersensuous, utterly transcendent ideals.   In "the heaven
which is above the heavens" is the colorless and formless
and intangible reality—justice, temperance, knowledge,
and other realities in their absolute, eternal essence.   This
picture is indeed one of surpassing splendor, and in its
pure sublimity has never been equaled by the human imagination: in moments of detached and rapt contemplation
it exerts a powerful fascination over the spirit.   Countless
souls have been inspired and strengthened by the assurance
that there is a world in which justice, which here below
is imperfect, subsists in perfect degree; where knowledge,
which here is incomplete, is absolute; where, undisturbed
by human striving and anguish, is eternal and changeless
calm.   Not that man may ever hope to win such height.
It is enough to be aware that such a world *is*, that beyond
these shadows there is Light, that Truth, and Beauty, and
Goodness *are*.   Such is also the doctrine of the New Realism.   The ideal is the only real.   Above time and space,
in no sense entering into or determined by these, neither
enduring in time nor extended in space, subject neither
to development nor to any kind of change, the Perfect subsists "in a heaven by itself."   It is independent of the
world as we know it; it is not conditioned by man's intelligence or ends.   It subsisted before any finite creatures
began to be, and it would be the same if all finite existences
were swept into nothingness.   This does not, however,
mean that if space and time, "the choir of heaven and fur-
niture of earth," were forever dissolved, all values would
come to an end.

---

[1] *Phaedrus,* 247.

"Though earth and man were gone,
    And suns and systems cease to be,
And Thou wert left alone,
    Every existence would exist in Thee." [1]

When, however, we seek to ascertain the meaning of all this and relate it to our actual life, we are overtaken by a sense of disappointment, of longing destined to defeat, and of baffling contradiction. Whatever may be true of these values in themselves, since they neither rise out of experience nor have any bearing on experience, their meaning is remote; even the content of them, since it has no intelligible setting, could never be known; it would be the same to us as if it did not exist.

A second question is, whether the values with which we are concerned are simply those of human creation and are without meaning outside of the circle of human experience. That values have arisen in and have been created by the consciousness of men, is a fact. The natural history of values offers an interesting subject of study—the hour and circumstances of the genesis of particular values, their progressive modification, the disappearance of some, the transmutation of others, the persistence of many in practically unchanged form and content. The law of compensation holds good here as elsewhere in experience; one value is substituted for another with no loss, but instead a gain in appreciation and worth. The facts here yield themselves to historical inquiry with the same certainty that is true of other human facts. If, however, it were assumed that values have a purely human origination and exist nowhere but in the consciousness of man, it would

---

[1] Emily Bronte, *Last Lines.*

follow that before man appeared on the earth they were non-existent, and that after man has disappeared they will also cease to be.

Even if such a conclusion seems at first sight warranted, it may not be left unchallenged: it must be set in relation to several other questions: (1) Whether the human personality persists after death; (2) whether there are finite consciousnesses in other planets of our solar system or in other systems of worlds which may also be fitted for purposeful activity; (3) whether the universe is a congenial sphere for the creation, increase, and conservation of values. In respect to survival after death, while no demonstration is available to establish the fact, and arguments can only create an expectancy, yet if and in whatever form the consciousness continues to survive, by the same token its values will survive. As to the existence of conscious beings in other worlds than ours, when one considers the number of such worlds and the high probability that from everlasting to everlasting some worlds are becoming fit to support life, that some are inhabited with beings not unlike ourselves, and that others are passing into a condition unsuited to living beings, it is far from certain that the ultimate disappearance of terrestrial values would mean the total extinction of values in the universe. And this resolves itself into the third question, as to the place of values in the structure and functioning of the world. As we have already seen that the entire universe is of a piece, that it makes long preparations for the creation of values, that it lends itself to the increase and conservation of values, it should not be difficult to believe that values are not alien magnitudes in an inhospitable world, eking out a precarious existence, with annihilation staring them in the face as their final doom: they are as much at home as the infinite systems of worlds, as light, as evolution, as consciousness and purposeful will. If then, on the one hand, we have no place in the universe for absolute values, subsisting out of all relation to finite experience, on the other hand, we need have no fear lest all values will disappear if the human consciousness ceases to exist, whether here or in a future world. In the most pessimistic outlook only those values created by man would come to naught, and that, too, in a restricted, infinitesimal point of space and time in the universe. It may be objected to this that it will matter nothing to us whether values exist elsewhere in the event that we no longer survive to be conscious of them; but this objection has no bearing on the argument that values are an eternal fact in the universe, and that if these are, then God is.

III

Intimations are not wanting that in the earlier years of our era the idea of God was couched in terms of value, and indeed that there has been no moment since when the same fact was not in evidence. There is, for example, Jesus' reply to the rich young ruler in search of goodness wherein he referred the eager inquirer to God as the alone good. Near the close of the first century a writer declares, "God is love; and he that abideth in love abideth in God, and God abideth in him." He says also that "God is light." Augustine, following in the steps of his master, Plato, speaks with passionate accent of God as the Good, Truth eternal, and Love eternal.

"Yes, write it in the rock," Saint Bernard said,
"Grave it on brass with adamantine pen!
'Tis God himself becomes apparent when
God's wisdom and God's goodness are displayed.
For God of these his attributes is made."

To which Matthew Arnold, wholly agreeing, adds:

"*God's wisdom and God's goodness* —Ay, but fools
Misdefine these till God knows them no more.
Wisdom and goodness, they are God!—What schools
Have yet so much as heard this simpler lore?" [1]

A position having much in common with this is advocated by Fichte, who identified God with the Moral Order of the World—a view which to his contemporaries seemed so opposed to the common idea of God that he received and, indeed, gloried in the epithet "Atheist." Kant's notion of God was in large measure determined by the concept of value; having shown the untenability of the traditional theistic arguments, he yielded to the demands of faith by postulating God as the guarantor of immortality and a moral order indispensable to the realization of the "highest good." Schleiermacher and Ritschl are much in accord in the use of values in their conception of God; one finds the essence of God to be love, while the other holds that we know the essential nature of God only so far as this has value for our salvation.

IV

The recent study of religion from the point of view of psychology has shown how the idea of God has devel-

---

[1] *The Divinity.*

oped and is now defined by the consciousness of values. Beginning with Hoeffding, the principal later representatives of this position are J. H. Leuba, William James, Irving King, and Edward Scribner Ames. Hoeffding maintains that we must seek the idea of God not by the philosophical path which leads to an abstract goal, but by the way of experience, the distillation of which appears in the creation and conservation of values. God is therefore defined not by metaphysics, but by meaning; not by knowledge, but by value. Professor Leuba, describing the Protestant Anglo-Saxon in his relation to God, says, "Preposterous as it may seem, it is yet true that he cares very little who God is, or even whether he is at all. But *he uses him*, instinctively . . . for the satisfaction of his better desires. The truth of the matter may be put this way: *God is not known*, . . . *he is used*, . . . sometimes as meat purveyor, sometimes as moral support, sometimes as friend, sometimes as an object of love." [1] Professor James [2] defends a similar thesis. The God of the prophets "was worth something to them personally. They could use him. . . . They chose him for the sake of the fruits he seemed to them to yield. So soon as the fruits began to seem quite worthless; so soon as they conflicted with indispensable human ideals, or thwarted too extensively other values; . . . the deity grew discredited and was ere long discarded and forgotten. When we cease to admire or approve what the definition of a deity implies we end by deeming that deity incredible." Professor Ames; after exhibiting the dynamic character of ideas, says that "A person's idea of God may be taken as comprehending the highest ideal interests known or felt

---

[1] *Monist*, Vol. XI, p. 571.
[2] *Varieties of Religious Experience*, p. 329.

by him." The genesis of this idea is social and is followed
by the tendency toward suitable impulses; it, "like any
other general idea, signifies a system of habits, and in
this case as elsewhere, the presence of the idea has for its
normal effect the initiation of those habitual attitudes and
endeavors." [1]

V

If the truth of this position is allowed, and one does
not see how it can be gainsaid, then we have not to seek
outside of the human consciousness for a self-evidencing
"proof" of the existence of God.   Wherever one is conscious of values, there one is conscious of God; or, where
value is there is God.   If we discover truth, beauty, justice, goodness, sacrifice, service, we behold God.   And the
evidence is cumulative.   In its later stages it is more
cogent, but not necessarily more convincing.   To an
Isaiah or a St. Paul, God was as real as to any modern
theist.   To the theist of to-day, however, while the content of his idea is in part the same as that of the earlier
seer, it is in part new and richer, as more adequate interpretations of reality are developed through experience.
This principle is appealed to in the Fourth Gospel: Jesus
says that it is expedient for him to go away, so that the
Spirit given in his stead may guide the disciples into
all the truth.   They were to be handed over to the tuition
of experience in order that the values to which they had
already been awakened might unfold in higher degree.   In
these expanding values they were to be aware of the
Spirit.   St. Paul[2] declares that one is to search for the

---

[1] *The Psychology of Religious Experience,* p. **313.**
[2] Rom. x, 6-8.

supreme values neither in the heights above, nor in the depths below: "The word is nigh thee, in thy mouth and in thy heart."

This way of approach to the idea of God clears up a difficulty referred to on a previous page. It was there said that men have sought for proofs of the existence of God which they appeared to think were valid for any kind of being to which the name of God might be assigned —the God of Aristotle or Augustine, of Plotinus or Bruno, of Kant or Hegel. Here, however, God is primarily determined and defined only so far as values are actually in process of realization in human experience: as these are, so he is. No *a priori* proof is offered and none is relevant. As rapidly as old values are enlarged in meaning or new values emerge, they incorporate themselves into the idea of God; if, on the other hand, older values have undergone modification or ceased to function, the fact registers itself in a corresponding change in the idea. This does not imply that all thinkers will agree as to what is "value" in human life, but it does mean that whatever they recognize as value will, by virtue of that recognition, become an integral part of their idea of God. Conceptions of God will vary as the consciousness of values varies; and these will grow according to well known laws of development. But all "proofs" of the being, existence, or nature of God are superfluous, a misdirection of energy, and futile.

VI

A further question arises concerning the relation of these value-judgments to reality: Do they involve the existence of that which they affirm, or are they purely subjective? Several solutions of the problems have been proposed.   One with varying shades of emphasis was offered by Ritschl and his followers.   According to these thinkers, there are in general two kinds of judgments, each with a different intellectual function—theoretical judgments and value-judgments.   Theoretical judgments are concerned with causes which, existing independently of the individual, lie within the field of scientific observation, experiment, and verification; they involve that view of the world with which science and philosophy have to do, and that action of the mind in which cognition is disinterested, although not without the feeling of worth. Value-judgments are concerned with religious purposes and ends, which awaken feelings of pleasure and pain conditioned on their value for the self.   "Every cognition of a religious sort is a direct judgment of value." [1]   Accordingly, value-judgments are all those propositions which are held to be valid concerning the soul, the world, Jesus Christ, and God, if salvation is to be a realized hope.   An instance of this is in Luther's statement that "Whatever the heart clings and trusts to, that is really God."   Another instance of this is that in our contemplation of the grace and truth of Christ, his lordship over the world, and his success in founding his community, he has for us the value of God, and we therefore ascribe Godhead to him.

Ritschl [2] has been reproached, (1) with introducing a fatal dualism into knowledge, and (2) with insincerity in alleging that value-judgments create but do not guarantee the existence of that which they affirm.   Such a charge is from the Ritschlian point of view, entirely groundless;

---

[1] Ritschl, *Justification and Reconciliation*, p. 398.
[2] *Das Wesen der Christlichen Religion*, p. 102.

nor was anything further from Ritschl's intention. Kaftan says, "The truth of the propositions of faith mean and can mean nothing less than that they are objectively true." The upholders of this conception believe that reality may be more truly known in its dynamic than in its static aspect, that it is more adequately revealed in its purposive than in its causal activity. The findings of science are not questioned, indeed in their own field they are valid and trustworthy, but no scientist is capable of penetrating into and pronouncing judgment upon supersensuous spiritual realities—the world of meaning and ends. Fundamental to this attitude is Lotze's discrimination between mechanism and teleology. In religious experience and knowledge, therefore, one is always in the immediate presence of the object of his value-judgment. More real is the knowledge thus affirmed than that of the scientist by as much as knowledge that has reached the stage of interpretation is higher than that which is purely descriptive. This statement is, however, subject to a measured qualification, to the effect that no description, however bare, is wholly destitute of interpretation, nor can interpretation be entirely severed from description. The difference lies rather in the degree to which in the value-judgment the interpretation is carried.

A second way of solving the problem whether in value-judgments we are in touch with reality, is by an analysis of experience. This discloses the law that objects are real to us in proportion as they are active and purposeful. Knowledge does not lend itself to a sharp discrimination between factual judgments and value-judgments. Professor Ames offers two considerations in support of this position. (1) All thinking is essentially teleological, that is, it involves value. (2) We think of

God in terms of personality, that is, of purposive activity. Since we know a person only by what he does, it would be a contradiction in terms to define God as pure existence or as a static being. "The idea of God, when seriously employed, serves to generalize and to idealize all the values one knows. . . . It signifies the justice which government symbolizes, the truth which science unfolds, and the beauty which art strives to express." [1]

With reference to the question under consideration Professor Hocking [2] has made a unique suggestion. He first prepares the way for this by showing that ideas are not purely subjective but are themselves a disclosure of reality. There are many ideas which appear to involve objectivity, as space, causality, beauty, goodness, that which is sublime, holy, obligatory. Since these qualities are valid for others who contemplate them no less than for ourselves they may be attributed to the objects themselves. "It is not without precedent, then, that an idea should convey with itself some apparent title to reality; it is not impossible that some idea, as perchance the idea of God, should be able to make this title good." He then reverses the traditional method of the ontological argument. Instead of arguing from the idea of God to the existence of God, he declares, "I have an idea of God, therefore I have an experience of God."

If now we cannot escape the conviction that reality itself is present in our experience we may take the further step that it lies within our power to enlarge and correct our idea of reality, that is, the idea of God, by a more adequate experience. Analogies of this are found in other fields of interest. We may, for example, have a mistaken

---

[1] Op. cit., p. 318.
[2] The Meaning of God in Human Experience, p. 314.

or imperfect notion of an object; we may regard a rock or molecule as static. This is because the experience being crude and incomplete is taken at its face value and regarded as final. On the other hand, as experience becomes refined and avails itself of the tools which it has itself created, it beholds the static transmuted into the dynamic, rest giving place to motion, and the immutably fixed to ceaseless change; the solid earth melts, and the universe and every single thing in it appears in swift and eternal flux. Change alone is changeless and motion is rest. The experience of the idea of God has undergone a similar transformation and this reflects itself in the transformation of the idea of God. The idea thus follows and interprets experience. Soon after Jesus' death the apostle who had supposed that God cared primarily for the Jews and only in a subordinate way for the non-Jews were surprised by a remarkable display of divine grace and power among the Gentiles—an event which compelled a revaluation of the purpose and character of God.[1] In the fourth to the sixth century A. D. the church's experience of God seemed to repeat itself with a monotonous finality and the idea of God corresponding to that experience was fixed in the dogmatic formulas of the Nicene and Athanasian Creeds. In recent times, however, new experiences have overtaken and bombarded the Christian consciousness with disclosures from physical science, history, social studies, political ideals, and changes in national constitutions. In order to suffice for these vastly enlarged experiences, the idea of God has had to burst its fettered formulas and spread out over all the data which have forced themselves upon the human consciousness. The critical question for us is not whether we can argue from

---

[1] Acts x-xi, 18.

the idea to the existence of God, but whether we have the courage and the wisdom to interpret God in terms which shall be in harmony with the intelligence of to-day.

If we have rightly estimated the place of values in our experience and their meaning for our interpretation of the world, it is evident that we have no longer need of the ontological argument in its traditional form, and furthermore that we need not be disturbed by Kant's demolition of it. Ever since it was proposed by Anselm a suspicion as to its validity, at least in the way he presented it, has assailed every thinker who advocated it; many tried their hand at revamping it; and the time had arrived when some competent mind should either establish it on a secure foundation or else reveal its inherent and fatal defect. The present statement is in no way subject to the above criticism. Here is no inference from an idea to reality. One does not argue from an idea away to something which it is supposed to represent. One does not go behind or beyond the idea of God to the existence of God. In the very consciousness of value is the consciousness of God.

IX.   THE FINITE AND THE INFINITE

I

THEOLOGIANS are practically agreed that God is infinite. This has reference both to his being as self-caused and self-existent and as related to the world of which he is the Source and Ground. It is also applied to his attributes, as knowledge, power, presence, goodness, and truth. Infinity is thus conceived of not as an attribute in itself but as qualifying all other affirmations concerning the being and attributes of God. It might even be designated as an attribute of all other attributes. This position has, however, been subjected to criticism. One of the most serious efforts in this direction was in Mansel's famous Bampton Lectures. In his *Limits of Religious Thought*, following Sir William Hamilton's "Law of Relativity," he based his argument on the incapacity of the human mind to make affirmations concerning realities which lie beyond the rational understanding; definitions of the "Infinite," the "Absolute," and the "First Cause" logically nullify one another. If, therefore, only the judgment of reason were taken into account, the proper attitude toward these alleged realities would be a reverent agnosticism. That which is denied to reason is, however, possible to faith: God may reveal himself as infinite and this may become a subject of dogma. The philosophical part of this contention was threshed over again by Herbert

Spencer, who reached a conclusion concerning the Infinite similar to that of Mansel.

II

The conception of God as infinite has encountered two dilemmas. One concerns the relation of the Infinite to finite existences. Various solutions of the problem have been offered, two of which are here cited. (1) Since God is the alone real and all other existences are unreal, no reconciliation is necessary. Yet there is no existence without some measure of reality, and either this reality belongs to it or it is a form of the infinite Being. Moreover, since God's being is self-existent and all others are dependent upon him, the two magnitudes are of a different kind and hence again no conflict arises. (2) The other dilemma emerges with reference to the knowledge and power of God as related to the consciousness of Jesus and the free-will and redemption of man. The relation of the wisdom and power of God to the consciousness of Jesus has been presented in such a variety of forms that it would not be feasible to enter into the refinements of theological speculation on this subject. The general theory, that while in the incarnation the eternal Son of God, as the Second Person of the Trinity, retained in full the content and activity of his divine consciousness, yet at the same time, in greater or less degree, he limited the exercise of his divine in relation to his human nature. This doctrine maintains that not only does God manifest himself in three modes—Father, Son, and Holy Spirit— but as Triunity he eternally subsists in three essential modes. "Thus if the Son was 'upholding all things by

the word of his power' before the incarnation, he was no
less doing the same while he was making 'purification of
sins.' From any one of the three centers of life the whole
God is acting, . . . and from all at once, and from
each in many ways at once. All actions of each and all
move in the one sphere of the infinity of God." [1] This
presentation, which involves an intermittent and variable
irruption of the infinite divine consciousness into the finite
consciousness of Jesus, now in the way of knowledge, now
in the way of power, has, from the point of view either of
metaphysics or of psychology, never been able to effect
a satisfactory solution of the problem which it raises.
Either the divine is denied in the self-same terms in which
it is affirmed, or the human vanishes before the very definitions which would fix and preserve its meaning.

A theory proposed by D. W. Simon [2] deserves consideration by reason of its ingenious hypothesis. It is to the
effect that the incarnation is the last stage in the voluntary self-limitation of God. The first stage appears in
the creation of the world, by which event God limited the
infinitude of his being and attributes in order to produce
an "other" in which he could realize a purpose of grace.
In the creation of man with free-will he still further limited himself by voluntarily renouncing omnipotence and
foreknowledge, so that the future choices and action of
the human will might be free and to a degree opaque to
the divine intelligence. The two stages of God's self-limitation thus referred to are preliminary to a final stage—
the union of the divine with the human nature of Jesus
Christ in which the divine, as limited, gradually communicates itself to the human in the consciousness of Jesus.

---

[1] W. N. Clarke, *An Outline of Christian Theology*, p. 178.
[2] *Reconciliation by Incarnation.*

This conception, however, involves so many untenable presuppositions that it has to take its place with other inadequate solutions of the relation of the infinitude of God to
the world. It assumes that God is at the same time both
infinite and finite, that God is complete apart from the
world, that at a definite instant God changed from an uncreating to a creating activity, that by a volition God has
renounced omnipotence and omniscience in order that a
world and man may come into existence and be redeemed,
and that the "incarnation" involves the presence of two
natures in the person of Jesus Christ. If in order to
defend the thesis that God is infinite the only recourse is
to such arguments it is not strange that relief has been
sought in the conception of a finite God.

III

The theory that God is finite is by no means a purely
modern view, that is, if "infinite" signifies that God is all-
inclusive. Neither in the Old and New Testaments nor in
Greek philosophy was God other than finite. When under
Aryan influence in one circle of Hebrew thought God was
exalted to an unapproachable transcendence, requiring
mediatorial agencies between him and men, and evil spirits
were assigned a permanent place in human affairs, it is
evident that God was one, even if the Supreme One, among
many beings both good and evil. In the other circle of
Hebrew thought which was far less affected by speculative
interests, the God of the prophets still spoke to men
both afar off and also near. To Plato God was the
supreme Idea or the Good, but there were other ideas
equally self-existent, like the heavenly bodies in relation to

the sun; and, besides, he is not the author of all things: "God is not the author of evil but of good only." [1]   Aristotle conceived of God as a perfect self-consciousness, whose being was absolutely independent of the world which was equally with God self-existent and eternal.   For the Stoics, God was a pervasive dynamic force, a rational, purposive energy, immanent in all material things.   The gods of the Epicureans were utterly withdrawn from the world in a heaven by themselves.   Yet in spite of limitations which beset the highest object of thought, the term "infinite" in both Christian and Greek theology came into general use as "the constituent mark of the highest metaphysical reality; it belongs not only to the universe as extended in space but also to the inmost essence of things, and, above all, to the deity." [2]   It is unquestionably true also that it has become a matter of course "to conceive of the Supreme Being as the Infinite, in contrast with all finite things and relations."

A counter suggestion has in our time won for itself a hearing among serious religious thinkers. The main interest here is that of religion: religion suffers, if indeed it is not impossible, on the background of God as infinite. Religious experience and divine personality are two necessary poles of thought; if personality should cease, religion would also cease.   But personality and the Infinite appear to be irreconcilable.   A way has therefore been sought for conserving the interests of religion: many believe that this is found in the conception of the personal God as finite.   Accordingly if either is to be sacrificed and the Infinite is incompatible with religion, then the Infinite must be surrendered.

---

[1] *Republic*, Bk. II, p. 380.
[2] Windelband, *History of Philosophy*, p. 689.

IV

The modern inquiry concerning God as finite received a powerful impulse from David Hume in his *Dialogues Concerning Natural Religion*. This was continued and brought to a definite issue in John Stuart Mill's *Three Essays on Religion*. The motive of the inquiry was the existence of imperfection and moral evil. Hume intimated that it might exceed human capacity to form a judgment on these subjects and that our standards of truth and falsehood might not be applicable. However, he does not let the matter rest there. He first raises the question whether the word "infinite" might not, by reason of a certain unreality suggested by it, be replaced by a more exact and moderate term. On the ground of analogy "we must forever find it impossible to reconcile any mixture of evil in the universe with infinite attributes." On the other hand, the supposition that the Author of Nature is finitely perfect relieves every difficulty which springs from natural and moral evil. "A less evil may be chosen, in order to avoid a greater; . . . in a word, benevolence, regulated by wisdom, and limited by necessity, may produce just such a world as the present." Mill is still more specific in the way he meets the problem. He abandons the possibility of "reconciling infinite benevolence and justice with infinite power in the Creator of such a world as this." God is the Creator, not as originating matter and force and their properties which he has no power to alter, but only as author of their collocations by which purposes are realized. Assuming limitation of divine power, there is nothing to preclude the supposition of perfect knowledge, although the knowledge need not be infinite. In the sphere of moral evil the divine limitations are still more serious.

While the perfect justice and goodness of God are left unimpaired, there is proof of insuperable obstacles which baffle divine power in working out benevolent purpose.

These positions have been impugned by recent writers on Theism, as A. S. Pringle-Pattison [1] and W. R. Sorley [2] on the ground that both Hume and Mill judge the success or failure of a divine action wholly with reference to happiness; whereas a survey of the world makes several things clear: (1) that the world does not exist solely for the production of happiness; (2) that happiness and misery are not distributed according to individual desert; (3) that the world is to be conceived of as a sphere for the realization of ethical ends, as goodness through sacrifice and the triumph of the moral ideal. It is very questionable, however, whether the entire contention of these writers is valid, at least whether their emphasis does not require a revision. The world does indeed afford a theatre for the cultivation of virtue; there is a place in it for sacrifice in behalf of individual and social well-being. Moreover, in an estimate of the meaning of life we know of nothing higher or more desirable than moral goodness.

Yet (1) it is not clear that the argument which seeks to prove the infinite nature of God from a consideration of virtue or a moral order is any more successful than the argument of Mill and Hume with reference to happiness. If God is conceived of as solely interested in virtue as compared with happiness, it is a question whether he has been more successful in providing a sphere for it than for happiness. No one can ever prove that there is more virtue than happiness in the world. And we would have to make the same assertion even if the qualitative test were

---

[1] *The Idea of God,* pp. **331** ff.
[2] *Moral Values and the Idea of God,* pp. **331** ff.

applied. (2) Ever since Kant restored the Stoic emphasis on virtue as against happiness, the current has set strongly in that direction. The tradition has been continued even with those who acknowledge another master than Kant. They hold that if God is not perfectly successful in the production of happiness, this is because he cares not for it or at most cares for it in a subordinate degree. This, however, overlooks the incontestable fact of experience, that in the long run life presents a balance of virtue and happiness. On the broad scale, in the degree to which the divine order succeeds in creating virtue, it succeeds also in the creation of happiness. Virtue becomes unattractive, if not ugly and odious by setting it up as a thing apart, as the only aim dear to the divine will. Yet our hearts should teach us better. And the Master who trod the way of pain and renunciation which led straight to the cross, when its shadow was already darkening his steps, turned to his disciples with the wish that his joy might be shared by them and that their joy might be complete. Duty, the rigid and austere "daughter of the voice of God," not divorced from joy, is thus greeted by a great spirit:

"Stern lawgiver! yet thou dost wear
     The Godhead's most benignant grace;
Nor know we anything so fair
     As is the smile upon thy face;
Flowers laugh before thee on their beds;
And fragrance in thy footing treads." [1]

(3) If, therefore, any qualification of God as infinite is required on account of the limitation of happiness in

---

[1] W. Wordsworth, *Ode to Duty.*

the world, a like qualification is necessary by reason of the imperfection of virtue. Happiness has been treated as if it were a matter wholly within divine power, whereas virtue has been regarded as within man's power aided by divine grace. But happiness is no more determined or conditioned by the power of God than is virtue. Moreover, we have seen no reason for supposing that the Purposive Good Will has ever had a choice between the present world and any other, conceivably better or worse. There is no evidence that any degree of intelligence, however great, could more wisely control a universe than is the case in the one now existing. Virtue and happiness are only two, even if to us they are the highest, of the ends realized by the Purposive Will; including these there is an indefinite, perhaps infinite, number of ends forever in process of becoming. On the ground of the incompleteness or imperfection of happiness or virtue or both, we could not infer that the Creative Energy was finite.

V

One of the earliest attempts in America to show that God was finite was made by Horace Bushnell in his *God in Christ.* He conceived of God from two utterly disparate points of view: (1) as the Absolute, the Inconceivable, the Unrevealed, with respect to which no predicates could be affirmed; (2) as a dramatic impersonation, to be referred to a divine generative power to represent himself in the finite, coming forth in the interest of creation and redemption, presenting himself in three phases of activity, each of which is finite—Father, Son, and Holy Spirit. It is for him not so much a reasoned conclusion as the interpretation of an inner need: "my heart wants the Father, my heart wants the Son, my heart wants the Holy Ghost!" When this position is analyzed, it discloses affinities with second and third century gnosticism, with Neo-Platonism, and with certain speculations of the great mystics. Its genesis in Bushnell's mind is not, however, to be traced to these sources; instead it arose in response to needs similar to those which gave birth to the types of thought just referred to. Yet even if it appeared momentarily to answer to a deep craving of the religious spirit in relation to God, the price paid was too high; it was a device of the reason, but the reason will not be ultimately satisfied with this kind of pluralism of the divine. The reason will never be content with a permanent division in the nature of God, as if—a contradiction in terms—one part were infinite, another finite. Nor is the way paved for such a conclusion by designating one aspect of God as Absolute, the other as personal, one as unrevealed, the other as revealed. Either God is all infinite or all finite. The Infinite or Absolute so far as unrevealed is wholly negligible; it has simply the value of zero. According to Dr. Bushnell, therefore, the finite is the alone real; God is finite or he means nothing to us.

A conception having certain points of resemblance to the one just described but with a very different metaphysical background is advocated by Professor Bradley.[1] He distinguishes between the Absolute and God. The Absolute is the ultimate Reality in its undivided unity; God is the appearance of that Reality, to which we are related in our religious experience.

The view of Dr. Rashdall that God is finite does not differ in any essential point from the customary concep-

---

[1] *Appearance and Reality.*

tion of God. God's action is limited; he has, for example, no arbitrary power in respect to evil and pain, to change the past, or to be unjust. "There are necessities to which even God must submit." [1] These are not imposed upon him from without; they are parts of his essential nature. In addition to these necessary internal limitations are those which arise in the relation between God and human, and perhaps other, souls. Finite consciousness, if it is to have meaning, must be for itself; it may not therefore be invaded by another consciousness, even although that other consciousness is God. This does not mean that the soul is self-existent or is opaque to the divine intelligence. It is produced by God, is wholly dependent upon his sustaining will, capable of knowing God in part and of being wholly known by him. Besides these limitations which beset the life of God there are others which have their source in the world, whose peculiar constitution is to be referred to the divine will. God will not violate the nature of things which he has himself called into existence. Dr. Rashdall concludes his argument by remarking: "We may still say, if we please, that God is infinite because he is limited by nothing outside his own nature, except what he has himself caused. We can still call him Omnipotent in the sense that he possesses all the power there is." [2]

A theory presented by the late Professor G. H. Howison (*The Limits of Evolution and Other Essays*, 2d ed.) offers a unique setting for God as finite. He conceives of a harmonious society of minds united by a common rational intelligence, consisting of God and non-divine consciousnesses, who differ from him in the possession of a sensuous aspect of experience. God is the perfect person

---

[1] *Philosophy and Religion.*
[2] *Op. cit.,* p. 85.

eternally fulfilled; all the other selves are in a time-world, where they must forever strive toward a goal of fulfillment, yet they are also perfect in the sense of having power of self-recovery to wholeness after defect and even sin. Accordingly, God is the central member of the divine society, *primus inter pares.* He is not the Creator of other spirits, although if he did not exist they would not have come into existence; in their individual being they are self-active, with independent initiative. God is not the ruler of other spirits, since in this City of God both he and they have meaning only in relation to the same ideal, he perfectly, they in varying degree. Here are clear reminiscences of the Prime Mover and the self-moving souls of Aristotle and the independent yet harmonious monads of Leibnitz. The central spirit or God is perfect in love; finite spirits, as in Dante's Beatific Vision,[1] are forever drawn forward into higher reaches of experience, "By the Love that moves the sun and the other stars." If in spite of what has been said above God is called not finite but infinite, this is due to a peculiar use of the term "infinite." Professor Howison holds that both God and all minds are in a qualitative sense infinite, only God is pre-eminently so. For him infinity is interchangeable with eternity, self-existence, self-activity, freedom. He must, however, be classed with those who conceive of God as finite.

According to another presentation already described, God is working out his purpose not without hindrance from real obstacles to his will, as space and time, the inertia and intractableness of matter, the frailty and resistance of human and perhaps of infra-human wills. Thus God strives and suffers; it may be that even if he is

---

[1] *Paradiso,* Canto xxxiii.

ultimately successful he is for the time being and in part
defeated, sharing with us in our sorrow and struggle, our
repentance and victory. Thus in the alternative, "an
Immutable Absolute or a God who strives," we decide for
the latter. He is "progressive Purpose." Even if an
unfinished universe involved an unfinished God, this conception would be far preferable to a petrified and therefore changeless Absolute. The idea of God appears to
imply that he is to be regarded as in some sense capable
of existing apart from the world. The possibility is also
suggested that an unfinished world may not point to an
unfinished God: the perfect God may be hindered in working out his plan. On the supposition, however, that this
God is the Creator of the world, he must be accountable
for the intractability of the materials which he has brought
into existence and which prevents the realization of his
purpose except in the face of a more or less effective
resistance.

Two conceptions of God as finite which have so much
in common that it is difficult not to believe that one is
dependent on the other are those of Samuel Butler and
H. G. Wells. Both suppose an unrevealed Reality back
of the God whom we have experienced,—a veiled Being or
a God who called our God into existence. As to the Ultimate Reality, somewhat after the manner of Herbert
Spencer, we know only that it is, but not what it is. Each
describes with different and varying features the God with
whom we are concerned, but both alike subject him to
definite limitations in knowledge and power and perhaps
in goodness. In an earlier work,[1] Mr. Wells was much
more in accord with Butler than in his *God, the Invisible
King;* in this later book he detaches the finite God from

---

[1] *First and Last Things.*

all control of nature and restricts him wholly to human life with its aims and struggles; herein lies perhaps his chief distinction from Butler. The ultimate reference in both of these conceptions to an unknown Reality behind and separate from all appearance and activity has a long history. Neo-Platonism and Gnosticism are two earlier forms of this presentation: later, medieval mysticism furnishes many instances of the same way of thinking; to Kant, however, and those who were most immediately influenced by his theory of knowledge, we owe the more recent setting of this conception. Vivid and appealing as may be the picture of a finite God as active in the natural world and in human life, or in human life alone, it has never satisfied, and it will never satisfy the legitimate demand of religious faith or rational thought. Men will not be content with an irreconcilable dualism, either between God and the world or between one aspect of God and another, between appearance and reality, or between a finite God and the Absolute. Neither religion nor metaphysics will tolerate a permanent barrier between faith and knowledge. Religion postulates the unity which speculative thought seeks to explore and interpret. It does not alter the case that all the gods of primitive religions were finite, or that in spite of carefully phrased definitions to the contrary, Christian thinkers have in all other respects than that of definition treated God as finite. Nevertheless, in the last analysis, as Herrmann has shown, Christian faith involves a conception of God as omnipotent Love. The human spirit is, on the one hand, aware of an inevitable conflict between the forces of nature and the highest good and is, on the other hand, assured that since the God whom it trusts is superior to the natural world, its highest good is safe in the hand of Almighty

God as Father. Nothing less than a conviction like this will ultimately satisfy the Christian assurance of salvation.

Professor James's [1] idea of God as finite is a natural corrolary of the fundamental propositions of radical empiricism, that "our conception of the practical consequences is for us the whole of our conception of the object so far as that conception has positive significance at all." Accordingly, his definition of God grows out of certain irreducible beliefs: that the human will is creative; that evil is not merely apparent; that history is real; and that men have never regarded God as infinite. To these he adds other considerations: God has an environment; he is conditioned by time; he has a history of his own. The religious bearing of this conception appears in the statement that "the Divine personality and ours are consanguineous, at least in this, that both have purposes for which they care, and each can hear the other's call." Religious experience is sufficiently supported if only this power is "both other and larger than our conscious selves. Anything larger will do, if only it be large enough to trust for the next step." [2] It is precisely at this point that one hesitates and draws back; it is not only the next step, however, but what is involved in the next step that compels us to pause. Human life is not merely succession, nor does it move in individualistic straight lines which touch each other at points here and there, but it rises out of a larger unity to which one can assign no limit of time or space, and it endures as an integral part of the whole to which it gives unique meaning and expression. We are not to be deterred from calling God infinite by reason of

---

[1] *Varieties of Religious Experience*, p. 445.
[2] *Op. cit.*, p. 544.

the difficulty, even the impossibility, of reconciling the contradictions which arise between the infinite and the finite. The problem is as old as Parmenides and Heracleitus. The One and the Many can never be identified nor can they ever be separated. The One is not less One because there are the Many; and the Many in their infinite variety do not nullify the One. An idealistic mood finds the meaning of reality in a permanent and changeless identity which abides behind all its evanescent phenomena.

"The One remains, the many change and pass." [1]

When, on the other hand, experience interprets the world it falls back upon the atomic theory of Democritus or a mood equivalent to the same, or else upon the pluralism of Leibnitz, qualified by Kant's primacy of the will. As we have already seen, the scientific consciousness knows the world only as a unity. The philosophical interpretation of the universe, even that of Leibnitz, which seems to sanction pluralism, and that of Kant which appears to involve a dualism, rests upon a fundamental and indestructible unity. And theology postulates a Creative Good Will, a Purposive Love which reveals its presence in the ends in process of realization throughout all time and space. The question whether this Power is finite resolves itself into the previous question, whether the sphere within which it energizes is finite. If space is boundless and time without beginning or end, if the universe, both in extent and in duration, is infinite, the creative, ideal-forming Power within can be no less than it. We only follow the compelling suggestion of science and philosophy in affirming the infinitude of God.

[1] Shelley, *Adonais.*

VI

The term "Infinite" as applied to God requires more careful analysis. This may be undertaken from several points of view. (1) If, according to Neo-Platonism and Kant, as modified by Hamilton and Mansel and Spencer, the "Infinite" is to be defined negatively so as to mean all that the finite is not, then no positive affirmation as to its content is possible. One may declare it to be above the world and the human spirit, Cause of Causes, Transcendent, Primordial Being, Pure Form. In this case, since no intelligible property is to be attributed to it, its proper essence remains absolutely unknown, and its alleged existence is all the same as non-existence. If, with Spinoza, the infinite is quantitatively defined as embracing all reality, the infinite becomes the all, the finite a transient modification of the all. As to what God is in himself, Spinoza attempts no definition. When thought rises from mode to attribute and from attribute to the Most Real Being, all determinations fall away and the idea of God appears without content. God as we know him exists only as the essence of two infinite attributes and of the modes of these attributes. Thus God is Nature; on the one hand, in accord with Stoicism, God is the essential cause of all existence, *natura naturans*, or nature as active, and on the other hand, as the whole of that which so comes to existence, *natura naturata*. In a sense the God with whom we have to do is finite. An infinite number of attributes is indeed alleged, yet we know of only two, thought and extension, which are a partial expression of the being of God. Here, however, the term "Infinite" is used in so many significations that we have to be on our guard lest the infinite in one reference be only the finite in another.

(2) The term "Infinite" is used to designate the distinctive and essential characteristic of the divine Being. As a unity he is thus set over against the world of the finite as consisting of manifold contradictory elements. That which in the finite exists as fragmentary and inharmonious is in the Infinite reconciled and unified.   All possibilities which in the finite are as yet only possible or to be realized through God, find their perfect realization in him (cf. Aristotle). The Infinite is thus conceived positively; it gives to the finite all its meaning; and this is perhaps the most common form in which recent thinkers present God as the Infinite. The word "Infinite" which began as an adjective, has lost its adjectival reference and has become a substantive. As a substantive it has taken its place with other words, as the Absolute, the Unconditioned, and the Eternal, which have gone through a similar transformation.

(3) Another definition of the Infinite is more in accord with experience and its implications. This restores it to its earlier meaning. The Infinite is thus not something conceivably isolated from the world of reality as we know it, existing apart in a heaven by itself. Reduced to its adjectival form, it fulfills a more modest function—it assigns a further meaning to the realities of experience. We can form no image of Infinite Reality. However far we extend the limits of an object, as a line, from one stage to another, we reach only an arbitrary point beyond which advance is always possible. The imagination which necessarily deals only with outlines and limits cannot transcend its own nature. We are unable to grasp Infinite Reality as a concrete magnitude. There are no identification marks by which we can distinguish an infinite from an immeasurable entity. For a working theory of energy

or purpose, the immeasurable has the value of the infinite.
The universe extends beyond the reach, not only of all
existing, but of all possible instruments of human exploration; the question whether it is actually or only conceivably infinite is one which justly claims attention of physicists, astronomers, and mathematicians. If they decide
for an infinite universe, as a majority of them do, we shall
make such use of their position in its bearing on the idea
of God as seems warranted.

If we speak of infinite time and infinite space, of infinite
power and infinite purpose, we attribute to these all that
it is possible for thought to affirm of time and space, of
power and purpose as these exist anywhere in any shape
or degree. We must not, however, allow the negative
form of the word to deceive us, as if it were a denial or
a contradiction of what is given in the finite. In our
experience we are indeed aware not of infinite space and
time, but only of a concrete aspect of these, and the same
is true of power and purpose. We are content to believe
that all space and time which we have not yet experienced
would be the same to all possible as to actual experience,
and that the power and purpose which we are conscious
of in the narrow span of our earthly existence are an
integral part of a purposive activity everywhere present
and in process of expression. Just as the elements which
compose the individual atoms of an earthly body are
identical in structure with the atoms in any, however distant, star, and as life is a product of conditions which
exist not only on this planet but may exist in all the
realms of space, so every experience is what it is by
reason both of its immediate environment and of all that
has been and is in the universe as a whole. If, therefore,
we find order and intelligence in any form of existence, if

we discover purposive ends in particular events, we have a right to extend the range of their meaning to make them integral parts of universal order and purpose. We begin with the finite, but by an inner logic of interpretation we cannot stop short of the All. In this way we reach the sense of "Infinite" as we apply the term to God. If we define God as Nature, "the ideal tendency of things," [1] the "Creative Good Will," [2] then wherever we are aware of any becoming, of any movement toward higher ends or urge toward the production and conservation of values, we must follow the rational impulsion and pass beyond the single event to include the whole of reality in the sweep of our thought. Fitly to characterize this, the word "Infinite" springs to our lips.

---

[1] James, *A Pluralistic Universe,* p. 124.
[2] E. W. Lyman, *The Experience of God in Modern Life,* p. 36.

X. THE ABSOLUTE AND THE IDEA
OF GOD

I

AT THE present time the Absolute is approached from
three different angles—the metaphysical, the ethical, and
the pragmatic. The metaphysical approach is represented by Professor Royce, the brothers Edward and
John Caird, and Professor J. Watson. Professor Royce [1]
identifies the Absolute with Reality which is "the expression of a single system of thought, the fulfillment of a
single conscious purpose, or the realm of one internally
harmonious experience." In the most general sense the
Absolute is the totality of being viewed in its ideal aspect.
It may be defined in terms of thought, as perfectly fulfilled in the life of the world; of will, as eternally accomplished; of experience, as completely organized and self-
conscious; of truth, as transparent to itself; of life, as
in accordance with idea, "with no unanswered questions
and no unfulfilled desires." "This absolute experience is
related to our finite experience as an organic whole to its
fragments." [2] The very fragmentariness of our world
has meaning only with reference to a world beyond. All
that is finite—pain, ignorance, longing, strife, restless-
ness, the struggle to escape from our incompleteness—

---

[1] *The World and the Individual,* Vol. I, p. 40.
[2] *The Conception of God,* p. 44.

points beyond itself to its fulfillment and perfection in the Absolute; of each of these the "whole meaning is now and will always remain one with the entire life of God." [1] These are the authentic forms in which the Absolute longs and strives in us for the peace which we seek in vain on earth and find only in eternity.

Edward Caird holds that the idea of God is that of "an absolute Power or Principle." The religious consciousness "is the consciousness of a Being who embraces all our life and gives unity and direction to it, . . . the consciousness that our finite experience presupposes and rests upon a principle which comprehends all its various contents and transcends all its differences, . . . that, beyond all the objects we perceive without us, and beyond all the states and activities of the self within us, there is a unity which manifests itself in both, and from which neither can be separated." [2]

According to Professor Watson,[3] the marks of the Absolute, that is, of a rational universe, are: (1) It must be an absolute unity, (2) it must be self-differentiating, (3) its differentiations must form a coherent system. The unity is neither identity nor an aggregate of parts, but it comprehends all possible differences, even those which are finite. No differences can arise outside of the Absolute; and since the Absolute is perfect, no transition is possible within it to either better or worse. Moreover, since the Absolute is a coherent system, a change in any single aspect of it involves a corresponding change in all other aspects. (4) The unity is self-conscious and manifests its nature in all being, and particularly in man. (5)

---

[1] *The World and the Individual*, Vol. II, p. 276.
[2] *The Evolution of Religion*, Vol. I, pp. 67, 32.
[3] *The Interpretation of Religious Experience*, Vol. II, pp. 48 ff.

It may be designated as the Absolute or God; it is to reflective thought the Absolute, to the religious consciousness God.

The aim of these thinkers is to work out a unified theory of the world. In realizing this aim, two tendencies are in evidence: one springing from experience, the other from speculation. Unreflective experience breaks the world up into fragments, where everything is concrete, distinct if not separate, where the principle of individuation is the key which unlocks the meaning of reality. On the other hand, speculative thought never rests until it has discovered the identity in difference; the one of which the many are the expression; the law which explains particulars; the whole which embraces the parts; the Reason which is the essence of even the apparently irrational; the will which impels all partial and even conflicting purposes. Reflection is never content to remain purely empirical, but seeks to complete itself in the region of speculation. The different sciences push out, each on its own line, into the most comprehensive generalization; each also relates itself to the findings of other sciences to fill out its interpretation of the world. The result is a unified system of reality, predicated not only of that part of the world which has come under observation, but of that also which lies beyond the scope of present or even of possible human observation. In the region of consciousness, of intelligence, and of purposiveness, the same unity is sought as that which has been established by the physical sciences. On the other hand, the point of view and the method of speculation are radically different from those of experience—to ground the world in the principle of unity.

The great thinkers are unanimous in the conviction

that the world is susceptible of rational explanation—the world is intelligible.

"One God, one law, one element."

For Plato it was the idea of the Good, for Aristotle the perfect self-consciousness, for Augustine divine sovereignty, for Spinoza substance, for Leibnitz the Monad of monads, for Hegel the unity of thought and being, for Schopenhauer Will, for Schleiermacher the feeling of absolute dependence reflecting the Absolute Cause, and now for Royce and his fellow idealists reality is Absolute Experience and Unity. God is the Absolute Experience of which all finite experience is a fragmentary, although integral, part. God is the Absolute Unity which transcends and yet includes the oppositions of the finite. Accordingly, the Absolute, instead of being set free from all relations, as the term itself seems to imply, is necessarily inclusive of all relations.

To interpret the Absolute Reality as Professor Royce does in terms of Experience—a completely organized Experience—is beset with grave objections. The conception is purely arbitrary and incapable of verification. It is a new form of the ontological argument. It assumes that because we can combine words, each of which has in itself a definite meaning so as to make an intelligible statement, therefore a corresponding reality exists. When, however, the individual words of the statement are subjected to analysis and definition and then reunited as before, they seem to have changed their individual meaning and are no longer applicable to the reality which they were supposed to describe. In the new combination further terms, as thought and will, are indeed employed, but these present a static, not a dynamic entity; and even

such action as is suggested is self-identical and not that
of movement and action.   There is transcendent and
changeless fullness of being, but it has no history; it
never comes out on the field of human experience.   The
time-process, the irrevocableness of events, the development of personality may be true of the finite series, but
no more than in Aristotle can the Absolute be brought
within the category of experience, and hence be made
intelligible.

In attributing a completely organized experience to the
Absolute we simply do not know what we are talking
about.   Even if we were to allow the possibility of such a
condition, we have no knowledge of all that would be
necessary to fill up its measure.   The experience-contents
of the Absolute as alleged by Professor Royce consist of
the external world of science, that is, of atoms and their
mechanical whirl, of the field of consciousness in a small
corner of the universe, together with "the answers to our
present problems and the satisfaction of our present longings." [1]   Professor Menzes pronounced this representation of the Absolute to be inadequate, on the ground that
it seems to be lacking in spirituality and worth.   Contents
so impoverished fall far short of a commanding conception of God.   If one raises the several elements of human
experience to the highest degree, one is hardly justified in
regarding these as equal to the number of properties in
the Absolute or any of them as satisfactory in comparison
with the same quality affirmed of the Absolute.   The
writer just cited does not see how moral greatness is to
be reconciled with such an Absolute.   There is no morality without progress, and progress implies growth.   Morality is realized through struggle and achievement, and that

---

[1] Cf. *The Conception of God*, "Criticism" by Professor Menzes, p. 98.

too not at a point here and there, but in the whole range of action, and not merely with reference to the outer world, but in the entire inmost depths of the Absolute; thus the conditions for the realization of goodness are wanting. As between the two—an eternally complete experience and goodness—a choice will have to be made; their incompatibility precludes the retention of both.

A fruitful source of fallacy with reference to the Absolute lies in its supposed relation to time. There are two ways in which existence or reality may be presented—as static and its being or conscious life as eternally self-identical, or as dynamic and its action as eternally purposeful. If it is conceived as static it would in no sense be subject to the temporal order or in any essential relation to it. On the other hand, finite reality would be subject to the order of time. It is without bearing on the general question whether from one point of view time is relative to the various phenomenal existences according to the particular life-span or the rapidity of its response to environment. With Professor Bradley, one may even admit the existence of "any number of independent time-series." [1] Do what we will with time, however, there are two aspects of it which we shall never be in position to obliterate. One is the objective reality of time; the other is that whatever differences characterize the reaction of all existence-forms to their environment, there is for all alike an identical, instantaneous moment, a Now which divides future from past: behind it is the no-longer; before it the not-yet. This moment is not relative but absolute, that is, it is the same for all finite existences—the changing aspects of the infinite universe. It is indeed a "spe-

[1] *Appearance and Reality,* p. 211.

cious present," since it no sooner appears than it vanishes; nevertheless, its very instantaneity is real, unless we are ready to resolve this phenomenon into an appearance that is illusory. At this instant the physical atoms are in combinations which have never been before, and in an endless future will never be repeated. At this instant also the content of all finite consciousness, of the sub-conscious, and of the unconscious is unique in its long history, whether here or in other systems of worlds; this has never been the same as at the moment under consideration and will never be the same again. We place ourselves in an embarrassing position, however, if we persist in regarding the Absolute as complete and static and in referring the finite to the incomplete dynamic order. For if the finite is an integral part of the Absolute and the Absolute is static, the finite must be also static; but if the finite is dynamic we cannot refuse to the Absolute the same dynamic property.

If the question were otherwise stated, there might be a relative justification for the static as well as for the dynamic conception. If, for example, Being is regarded as a whole, whether as quality or quantity, it is an infinite fullness without diminution or enlargement, from age to age changelessly identical in its constitutive elements and potency. But if we regard the Absolute in terms of organized experience we behold its constitutive elements and potencies passing into an infinite variety and succession of forms; everywhere is activity, everywhere process, everywhere change, everywhere free creative action, tendency to equilibrium which dissolves again into instability, evolution fulfilling itself in ways which discontinue past achievements or merge them into other orders. In relation to this process with an endless variety of finite aspects there is a conceivable past and a conceivable future, but in reality there is no past and no future in separation from the present. Not that the past and the future are utterly without meaning. The present aspect of any and every part of the universe depends on all past moments and registers the issue of all the permutations and combinations which have marked the movements of the all-inclusive Reality; it contains also the promise and potency of all that is to be. If, on the one hand, we seek by a single word to characterize the complete scope of this process, either as a whole of which each momentary stage is a fragment, or as duration in its entirety as an undivided entity, we can designate it by no more adequate term than Eternity. But if, on the other hand, we regard the universe and every single thing in it from the point of view of either actual or possible change of movement and possible embodiments, we find it throughout subject to the time-process which is necessitated by the very structure of reality. The Absolute is therefore not complete without existence and this involves time; it involves also infinite possible changes which are accordingly never exhausted. An experience as completely organized is therefore out of the question. "The type of the highest reality is to be sought for not in any fixed Parmenidean circle of achieved being, but in an ideal of good which, while never fully expressed under the form of time, can never become actual, and so fulfill itself under any other." [1]

The theory that between our sorrow and longing and the Absolute is such a relation that each is necessary to the completeness of the other, is confronted with a two-fold difficulty. (1) From the side of the Absolute.

---

[1] J. H. Muirhead, *Encyclopedia Britannica,* Vol. XIV, "Idealism."

According to Professor Royce,[1] the Absolute is a completely organized experience with no unanswered questions and no unfulfilled desires, yet the divine experience is complete only through human pain and striving. "God who here, in me, aims at what I now temporarily miss, not only possesses, in the eternal world, the goal after which I strive, but comes to possess it even through and because of my sorrow." So many presentations leave the Absolute independent, self-sufficient, detached, and utterly beyond human knowledge, that it is a relief to find one who would overcome this isolated transcendence by holding fast the reciprocal dependence of God and man. We are, moreover, deeply impressed with the prophetic unction, the dithyrambic fervor, the measured and lofty diction corresponding to the elevation of the theme, a certain finality of utterance which belongs only to the seer. Yet in spite of all this we are not convinced. The position might win our qualified assent if we had only to reconcile the pain and sorrow of good men with the goodness of the Absolute; this would present a hard but not perhaps insoluble problem. The fact of moral evil, however, raises questions of a wholly different nature. On the one hand, Professor Royce says "that every finite purpose . . . is a partial expression and attainment of the divine will, and also that every finite fulfillment of purpose . . . is a partial fulfillment of the divine meaning." On the other hand, he affirms that, although we have all sinned and come short of the glory of God, "yet in just our life, viewed in its entirety, the glory of God is completely manifest"; our evil will is comprehended and reconciled within the perfect whole because it is "*supplemented, is overcome, is thwarted, is overruled*, by what

---

[1] *The World and the Individual,* Vol. II, p. 409.

expresses some other will; only in this way is the final perfection won." [1]

What is said here may be true of the Absolute from the point of the eternal world, but judged by experience it is only in part true. Unless we can reduce moral evil to ignorance and inattention, dissolving out of it as illusion those elements which experience as a mordant has fixed in the conscience of the race, we cannot assert that the glory of God is completely revealed in our life just as it is, or in our will in so far as it is evil. We should have also to ignore in the absolute consciousness all those moral qualities which the experience of men has found to be inexpugnable. It may be a correct psychological description of an evil deed to characterize it as attention to a partial good or by inattention to a larger good. It may be a just ethical estimate of sin that it is not wholly bad, since there is no absolute evil, and that there is a heart of good in things evil. It may furthermore be true that, whether they mean it or not, even despite themselves, the souls in hell, if such there be, serve God. Yet there is more in moral evil than a momentarily imperfect or mistaken idea. The descriptions of moral evil by the great moralists and tragic poets are by no means out of date. Aristotle, referring to the Socratic identification of knowledge and virtue, raised several objections to it which are equally valid when directed against Professor Royce's view. The simple fact is that every one does not always do as well as he knows even at the instant of evil action. And it is entirely possible that the evil-doer may persist in his course so that "a choice becomes an action, an action a habit, a habit a character, and a character a destiny." This position is not merely theoretical,

---

[1] *Op. cit.,* Vol. II, p. 365.

but is supported by experience; naturally, however, from experience no final judgment on this matter of destiny for every individual can be verified, yet one may follow strong indications. There may be moral evil as long as human life endures on the earth; and if human personality survives the shock of death, moral evil may go on renewing itself in the consciousness of the evil-doer. Whether or not moral evil is finally to be expunged from the human consciousness, it is here now, a fact not to be ignored nor explained away, as outstanding, as real as is goodness, and conceivably no less permanent. If, then, one admits that moral badness is a fact in present human experience—and one cannot deny this without denying experience itself—one gets no relief from one's fundamental problem by supposing that such badness may ultimately disappear. If in the eternal world the Absolute already possesses the fulness of knowledge and good and felicity which the finite strives for or perversely rejects, one does see how he can come to possess it through human experience.

When one considers both the altogether insignificant span of years in which the human consciousness has existed with its pain and struggle and sin, and the far longer and yet still insignificant span in which humanity is yet to survive on the earth, one cannot ignore the bearing of this consideration on the alleged consciousness of the Absolute. Again we ask, Is this eternally complete, or was it incomplete before man's appearance, and will it again be incomplete when man has disappeared from the face of the earth? It is hard to understand how completeness and incompleteness are compatible in the same consciousness, or how a goal eternally possessed can still be striven for by the divine will. To affirm that all finite sorrows and struggles, imperfections and sins are integral parts of the Absolute and are eternally present to the divine mind as distinct constituents of his unruffled and beatific consciousness, is to resolve finite experience into illusion and to construe the Absolute in terms of a static, eternal Now. In this conception of the Absolute the introduction of the will is an after-thought; as in all thorough-going idealism, it is superfluous. This entire point of view simply exchanges one set of difficulties which originate in the idea of time for another not less serious which have their source in the idea of the Eternal. It would be preferable to confess that the problem not only is not solved in this way, but is even insoluble, than to be content with an explanation which leaves all the essential questions unanswered.

(2) If, on the one hand, Professor Royce's theory fails to reconcile the Absolute with the facts of human experience, on the other hand, it is no less inadequate in its claim that the Absolute is necessary to explain the longing and struggle of the human spirit for the attainment of the ideal. He says that "we long for the Absolute," so far as this is "the longing of the Absolute in us for the peace which belongs not to Time, but only absolutely to Eternity." While we may not be able to prove or to disprove the part which the Absolute plays in our struggle for virtue and our desire for peace, we are at least in position to describe the psychological content and object of our longing. We most effectively desire only that which we can define. We use the term "perfection" or the Absolute, but the meaning we assign to it falls short of what is implied in it. To say that a denial of the Absolute involves a knowledge of it is hardly more than a play upon words. Attempts to win an idea of the Abso-

lute, as in the great mystics, have resulted in robbing it
of all intelligible content and resolving it into pure nega-
tivity. We do not long for perfection, for we do not
know what perfection would be, nor do we believe that
what we do long for will melt by imperceptible gradations
into final perfection. We can form no conception of a
perfect character or a perfect society. What is regarded
as final in personality or social structure for one period
becomes for a later time a transition stage to something
higher; and the further stage is judged to be higher with
reference not to an absolute standard, but to its more
adequate functioning and to undeveloped possibilities
which are felt to be immanent in the existing condition.
To say that we do not long for perfection, that we are
not and shall never be perfect, does not imply that we
know perfection, but it does mean that, however we are
related to the Absolute, we are finite still, and that all
our possible achievements, be they never so glorious, are
and must forever remain limited and imperfect. If the
Absolute be set up as our goal, then indeed are we doomed
to inevitable short-coming and defeat. Because not this,
but something more and better beckons us forward, we
live by hope which carries with it the energy of its own
fulfillment.

> "Thou are the Way.
> Hadst thou been nothing but the goal,
>   I cannot say
> If thou hadst ever met my soul.
>   I cannot see—
> I, child of process—if there lies
>   An end for me
> Full of repose, full of replies." [1]

---

[1] Alice Meynell, *Poems,* p. 28.

II

The ethical argument for the Absolute may be stated by Dr. Rashdall [1]: "An Absolute Moral Law or moral ideal cannot exist *in* material things. And it does not exist in the mind of this or that individual. Only if we believe in the existence of a Mind for which the true moral ideal is already in some sense real, a Mind embracing whatever is true in our moral judgments, can we rationally think of the moral ideal as no less real than the world itself. Only so can we believe in an absolute standard of right and wrong, which is as independent of this or that man's actual ideas and actual desires as the facts of material nature. The belief in God . . . is the logical presupposition of an 'objective' or absolute Morality. A moral ideal can exist nowhere and nohow, but in a mind; an absolute moral ideal can exist only in a Mind from which all Reality is derived."

We have here a restatement in terms of ethics of the well-known cosmological argument of Descartes, that since the mind of man could not originate the idea of the Perfect, another source must be sought for it, namely, a Perfect Being. If, however, the Perfect is interpreted as the ethical ideal, the immediate attention is transferred from the field of metaphysics to that of values, but the same logic is carried over to the new application. Since an absolute moral ideal cannot exist in an individual consciousness, on the ground that the individual thought is finite and hence limited and imperfect, its true source must be referred to an absolutely perfect Being; it is therefore self-evident, on the one hand, that a finite cause cannot produce an infinite effect, and, on the other hand,

---

[1] *The Theory of Good and Evil,* Vol. II, p. 212.

that if an infinite effect—an absolute moral ideal—appears in the finite mind, it must have been created by an Absolute Mind in which this ideal already exists. In support of this position, Professor Sorley [1] adduces two arguments. The first is drawn from analogy—the eternal validity of abstract truth which the mind discovers but does not create. The second is derived from the objective, eternal authority of ideals of goodness which are valid independently of human assent or even recognition, which accordingly demand a divine mind for their eternal realization.

Several considerations render this position exceedingly precarious if not wholly untenable. (1) With reference to an absolute ethical ideal. The assumption that a perfect ideal is a necessary implication of an imperfect ideal is a paralogism, yet one with a distinguished history. The term "imperfect" appears to have no meaning apart from the term "perfect." But when we refer to experience, we know and can know only the imperfect. All forms of existence are subject to ceaseless change; their nature is dynamic; they function with a greater or less degree of regularity, harmony, and efficiency which may conceivably be enhanced indefinitely. The Patent Office demonstrates that improvement in all kinds of machinery is under way; breeders of animals are continually bettering the quality of their stock; horticulturalists are constantly aiding nature to produce more beautiful flowers and more excellent fruit. We rightly think of all of these physical adjustments and living organisms as perfectible; not that they either will or can attain a stage beyond which nothing higher is possible, but that they are susceptible of yet further degrees of development. This does not mean that

---

[1] *Op. cit.*, pp. 352-353.

at some moment in the future there will be a perfect ship, a perfect horse, a perfect apple, or a perfect rose. Still less does it imply that any one of these exists anywhere perfectly as an idea. Outside of the field of the ethical ideal no one would think of saying that there exists a perfect idea in the mind of the Absolute, toward which creative evolution strives but never attains, and at last only approximates. One does not therefore see why an exception is made in the case of the ethical ideal.

(2) A further difficulty arises concerning the content of the Absolute Moral Ideal. We are acquainted with some of the values which belong to finite moral endeavor, both individual and social, but we are far from being able to define them with any degree of adequacy. Even the great principles can be stated only in the most general, and hence very indefinite, terms. We can speak of "an absolute standard of right and wrong," but the words refuse to convey an intelligible meaning. The only standard that we know is relative and therefore progressive— a flying goal. If, then, we are ignorant of what is included in a perfect ethical ideal, how can we affirm the existence of such an ideal in any mind, however great?

(3) We have already seen that the conditions under which such a consciousness is postulated forbid the existence of the very thing in question. To conceive of the divine Mind as static and self-identical, or even with Aristotle, as eternally active with an eternally unchanged content, is to contradict both the meaning of consciousness and the fulfillment of purpose. If we are to discover the nature of God in the nature of the world—and we have no encouragement to look in any other direction— we shall never come upon the track of an Absolute Being. Even if we regard the Absolute as all-inclusive, we have

no monotonous, self-repeating activity, but the revelation
of a Power renewing its energy in an endless variety of
changing forms, symbol of an exhaustless capacity of
creative differentiation.

III

The impression one receives from pragmatic pluralism
is that between it and any doctrine of the Absolute a
great gulf is fixed; if the pluralistic theory is true, then
idealistic monism under whatever form is excluded. We
are therefore at once interested when the most unrelent-
ing advocate of radical empiricism says, "The Absolute
is not the impossible thing I once thought it. Mental facts
do function both singly and together, at once, and we
finite minds may simultaneously be co-conscious with one
another in a superhuman intelligence. It is only the extravagant claims of coercive necessity on the Absolute's
part that has to be denied by *a priori* logic. As an
hypothesis trying to make itself probable on analogical
grounds, the Absolute is entitled to a patient hearing." [1]
As we read such words, we begin to ask ourselves whether,
after all, even if a complete understanding between the
contending camps is not feasible, a truce may not be
arranged so that peaceful communications may pass from
one to the other and perhaps a revaluation of each by the
other lead to further friendly approaches. This anticipation is weakened when we read further in reference to
religious experience: "The believer finds that the tenderer
parts of his personal life are continuous with *a more* of
the same quality which is operative in the universe outside
of himself and which he can keep in touch with; . . . a

[1] William James, *A Pluralistic Universe*, pp. 292-293.

wider self from which saving experiences come." [1] And
he adds, "The drift of all the evidence we have seems to
me to sweep us very strongly toward the belief in some
form of superhuman life with which we may, unknown to
ourselves, be co-conscious." He is referring to the analogies with psychology, with the facts of pathology, psychical research, and religious experience. These when taken
together establish a decidedly formidable probability in
favor of a general view of the world nearly identical with
that of Fechner.[2] Thus proceeding from lower to higher,
we have a unified psychical life which embraces all partial
beings, rising to include the heavenly bodies, and these
in turn becoming members of a cosmic, universal life. The
outlines of this superhuman consciousness thus probable
remain very vague and the functionally distinct selves
involved in it are left problematical.[3] Professor James
shows further that the improved idealism of the present,
instead of dissolving the many in the One, preserves the
many as the eternal objects of the One. It begins, therefore, to look as if pluralism in its scheme of the universe
might provide a place for the Absolute. But the promise
is deceptive. As, on the one hand, the absolutist represents the Absolute with a pluralistic object, so, on the
other hand, Fechner, in spite of his finely wrought web
of panpsychism, advocates an idea of God who in conflict with evil is not essentially different from the God of
ordinary theism.[4] After having apparently yielded so
much, Professor James [5] withdraws all that he seemed to

---

[1] *Op. cit.*, p. 307.
[2] Cf. *Zend Avesta,* passim.
[3] Cf. *A Pluralistic Universe,* pp. 309-310.
[4] Cf *Zend Avesta,* 2d ed., Vol. I, pp. 165 ff., 181, 244 ff., cited by
James, *op. cit.,* pp. 294, 344.
[5] *Op. cit.,* pp. 310-311.

concede: "The only way to escape from the paradoxes and perplexities that a consistently thought-out monistic universe suffers from . . . is to be frankly pluralistic and assume that the superhuman consciousness, however vast it may be, has itself an external environment, and consequently is finite." Thus disappears the last hope that pluralism can come to terms with any sort of an Absolute.

IV

The question whether the Absolute is without further ado to be identified with God has received opposite answers. With some thinkers as Bradley, God and the Absolute are two different entities. All that we know presents itself in experience under two aspects—Appearance and Reality. Every aspect of the world is characterized as appearance which, when we try to think it through by itself, gives rise to contradiction. This is true of space and time, of motion and change, of activity and passivity, of self and the not-self. We are compelled to conceive of each of these, on the one hand, as individual, independent substance, and, on the other hand, as in relation to other things; neither of these interpreted by itself is, however, the entire truth, but must be supplemented by the other—the relative by the self-subsistent. According to the law of contradiction, we are held within the world of appearance, unable to reach Reality. For in Reality itself all contradictions are annulled, all oppositions reconciled, all imperfections done away. There is but one Real; plurality of Reals is impossible; in this Real all differences are embraced, all discords dissolved, all phenomena unified and perfect. The Real is therefore independent, unrelated, self-consistent, a complete individual experience, that is, it is the Absolute. In relation to the Absolute the world, the self, and even God as personal are resolved into appearance. Accordingly, there is a discrepancy between the God of religion who is a "person," an object to man, and therefore a finite being, and God identified with the Absolute. Hence one must choose; one may retain the God of religion, but if so, one will have a being who is incomplete, inwardly contradictory, ever striving to pass beyond himself and to be absorbed in the Absolute. If, on the contrary, one identifies God with the Absolute, one satisfies his metaphysical demand, but parts with his religion. "We may say that God is not God, till he has become all in all, and that a God which is all in all is not the God of religion. God is but an aspect, and that must mean but an appearance of the Absolute." [1]

With this position of Bradley, although with varying shades of difference, many thinkers are in accord. It will serve our purpose to cite two. Professor A. E. Taylor defines the Absolute, or as an alternative name, the Universe, as "a conscious life which embraces the whole of existence, all at once, and in a perfect systematic unity." This is not necessarily, however, the same as "God." We can prove neither that the Absolute is the God of religion, nor that God is a finite individual within the Absolute. [2] Dr. Inge, [3] who follows Eckhart in distinguishing between the Godhead and God, says that "the God of religion is not the Absolute, but the highest form under which the Absolute can manifest himself to finite creatures." Ac-

---

[1] *Appearance and Reality,* pp. 446, 447, 448.
[2] Cf. *Elements of Metaphysics,* pp. 60, 404.
[3] *Personal Idealism and Mysticism,* pp. 13-14.

cording to Dr. Rashdall,[1] "The Absolute cannot be identified with God," but "must include God and all other consciousness . . . as forming with him a system of unity.
. . . The Ultimate Being is a single Power, . . .
manifested in a plurality of consciousness, one consciousness which is omniscient and eternal, and many consciousnesses which are of limited knowledge, which have a beginning, and some of which, it is possible or probable, have an
end." This doctrine of God belongs to the group which
we have already considered—the conception of God as
finite. Here, however, the background is the Absolute,
which embraces the totality of being or existence, from
which indeed evil is not wholly excluded.

This differentiation of God from the Absolute has not
commanded the assent of all competent thinkers. Indeed,
until a comparatively recent time the God of traditional
theology has been identified with the Absolute, but without subjecting the position to critical inquiry. For
Anselm, God was the Absolute Reality. Calvin, in his
postulate of the divine sovereignty and the several doctrines derived from this, leaves no room for and indeed is in
no need of any Absolute beyond God. For Spinoza in
his definition of substance, for Leibnitz with his central
Monad originating pre-established harmony, for Hegel
with his philosophy of Idea or Spirit, and for his followers of the right wing with their identity of thought and
being, God is the Absolute, and no property of the Absolute lies beyond his being. In Spinoza and Hegel the
formal definition of God is far removed from the common
doctrine of the church. The idea would have been more
fully represented with Spinoza by the All-Real, or Nature,

---

[1] *Theory of Good and Evil,* Vol. II, pp. 239-241. Cf. also *Personal
Idealism,* "*Personality Human and Divine,*" pp. 392-393.

or the Absolute, and with Hegel by the Absolute Spirit or Idea. Yet they continued to employ the term "God" partly, perhaps, out of deference to its traditional value and partly on account of their own religious interest. More recently the question has become acute, and the identifying of God with the Absolute is accompanied by considerations and arguments not less carefully drawn than are presented by those who distinguish between God and the Absolute. Pringle-Pattison [1] maintains that the Absolute, instead of an all-embracing, self-centered life, is an eternally purposive Being who communicates his life to individual spirits capable of spiritual response; in such beings the Absolute becomes known in the qualities which we attribute to God. According to Mr. Webb,[2] when one has attained to that degree of intellectual development at which the problem of the relation of God to the Absolute emerges, "no conception of God which takes him for less than Ultimate Reality will satisfy the demands of the religious consciousness." He corroborates this position by the assertion that the religious consciousness will never be satisfied with anything less than identifying God with the Supreme Reality or the Absolute. On the one hand, on the ground of the distinction between philosophy and religion, there need be no question that the Absolute is a valid object of speculative philosophy, as is witnessed to by a long line of great thinkers; on the other hand, it is only for the religious consciousness that the Absolute can be known as God. Here is laid bare both the connection and the distinction between these two permanent fields of human interest. Moreover, there is no more serious obstacle in regarding the Absolute as an object of relig-

---

[1] *The Idea of God*, Lectures XIV, XV.
[2] *God and Personality*, pp. 137-138.

ious devotion than as an object of metaphysical speculation. God has been distinguished from the Absolute in
part to relieve him from responsibility for moral evil;
either the Absolute is not incompatible with moral evil,
since in it is found the reconciliation of all discords and
the perfection of all mistaken and imperfect endeavors,
or else God is of boundless goodness, but of limited power.

Particular questions involved in this position will come
up for discussion later when the personality of God is
considered. In the meantime, it is to be said that the
Absolute, if it is to be all-embracing, so that the totality
of all forms of existence is to be included within it, com-
ports with evil as well as with good. "The Absolute
seems to be tolerant of any kind of world-contents and
experience-contents whatever." [1] No evil of any sort can
be separate from the Absolute except by denying its existence or declaring it "unreal." If, however, we are to
appeal to experience for our test of reality, evil appears
to be not less "real" than good.

The idea of God as the Absolute has arisen in response
to two deep and permanent longings: first, for stability
in a world of change; secondly, for completeness in a
world of fragmentary experiences. "Being" is thus contrasted with "Becoming," and perfection with what is
partial and incomplete. Reality is thought of as the
unchangeable and eternal, as the Absolute beyond the
limitations of the finite. The pious heart has voiced this
feeling in the prayer:

"Change and decay in all around I see;
O Thou who changest not, abide with me!"

---

[1] W. E. Hocking, *The Meaning of God in Human Experience*, p.
184.

If men are to live, they must find a refuge which abides through all the fluctuations of experience, the same yesterday, to-day, and forever. Plato discovered this in the metaphysical idea of the Good, transcendent and changeless. The Hebrews found it in the all-powerful will of a redeeming God, the same through all generations. For them the idea was dynamic and functional; later, owing to the feeling that it needed a basis and justification from metaphysics, the static was welded to the Hebrew and early Christian dynamic conception. Now, after so long a time, the static conception has become a part of the very structure of our thinking about God. The present need is therefore twofold. (1) To set the idea of God free from the static conception which has for centuries dominated the definition of the Absolute. The point at which the static and the dynamic have been fused must be discovered and a solvent applied which will once more separate them and leave the moral values free to function. (2) To transfer the values associated with the static into the dynamic conception of the Absolute or God. This will take place when we look for the Absolute not beyond the world, but in it: in its flux and change and becoming; in the order and intelligence within it; in its permanence, changelessness, and "duration." Here, if anywhere, we find God. And here, too, is all that we require of the stability, and so far as possible, the completing of the progressive individual and social ideals.

The question of the relation of the metaphysical Absolute to God is partly a matter of definition. If, for example, we regard such an Absolute as self-relating, that is, as creating his own relations, then naturally his relations will be those only which are willed by himself or which spring from his necessitated action. If in any respect the world conditions the exercise of his wisdom or power, this must be traced to his will, since the existence of the world and the action of every single thing in it have their source in him. If, moreover, free, responsible persons further his will or even hinder it, both their being and their activity must be referred ultimately to him. When, therefore, God is defined as the Absolute Creator and the Absolute Sovereign, he is the source of all power, the ultimate source of evil and sin. This is essentially the Augustinian-Calvinistic doctrine of God. Thus the relations which subsist between the Absolute Will and all forms of the finite originate in that will and may at any instant be terminated by it. This view is, however, invalidated by several untenable assumptions. (1) That before the creation of the world God as the Absolute was a solitary, self-sufficient Being, wholly absorbed in the intercommunion of the divine nature, embracing, according to the Trinitarian formula, Father, Son, and Holy Spirit. (2) That the Absolute Power passed from an uncreating to a creating activity. (3) That the world therefore had an absolute origination. (4) That it exists outside of the Absolute Being. (5) That, accordingly, the creating action gave rise to no reciprocally necessary relations between the Absolute Will and the world; for whereas on the side of the world these relations are necessary, on the side of the Absolute Will they are arbitrary: that Will is as perfectly free to annihilate as to create the world of time and space and human spirits. We have seen that these definitions of God as the Absolute are unwarranted whether by scientific, philosophical, or religious considerations.

Those who like Professor Royce do not shrink from attributing to the Absolute a causal relation to sin and evil awaken a revolt in the moral sense at the implications of such a view. This theory is no more acceptable when urged from a metaphysical than from a purely theological point of view. The moral consciousness will not tolerate the notion that sin originates in the will of God. Forever repugnant is the suggestion that the declarative will of God requires sin as a necessary condition of revealing the divine justice; equally repugnant is the supposition that sin both originates in and is overcome by the Absolute Will.

A religious relation to a metaphysical Absolute, if indeed this is possible, must be extremely attenuated. Neither prayer nor gratitude, neither the sense of sin nor a healthy longing for virue could arise in connection with it. No churches are built to perpetuate and extend its power over men. No altars have been reared for sacrificial offerings to it. No social service has been undertaken in its name. No missionary has ever gone forth to win converts to its saving influence. And it is inconceivable that any one should lay down his life for it. If religion is to survive on the earth, the quickening spirit in human hearts must be not the Absolute but God.

XI. TRANSCENDENCE AND IMMANENCE

I

THE doctrines of the divine transcendence and the divine immanence have had a long and checkered history. They have been associated with many philosophies, many experiences, many theories of the world. Sometimes they have been consistently worked out, each on its own line to the exclusion of the other, and again, under the conviction that transcendence and immanence are complementary aspects of reality, efforts have been made to reconcile them. Just now this is the popular point of view; but the endeavor to harmonize them is often beset by confusion of thought and the result, being unsatisfactory, invites to renewed attempts in the same direction.

Until the Hebrews came under the influence of Aryan thought, whether from Persia or from Greece their idea of God was free from those elements which later became integral and essential parts of it. Their God was in a semi-detached relation to the world, neither rising out of it nor bound absolutely to it; whenever he would he manifested himself in natural phenomena on the land, in the sea and sky, in storm and flood, in famine and plenty, in pestilence and war, now letting his people go their way and now aiding or punishing them, giving victory or defeat to their enemies. He was free to work his will

both in the hosts of heaven and among the inhabitants of
earth.   He was a God who was near and yet afar off.
Their pragmatic idea of God left no room for, as it had
no need of, those subtle, speculative conceptions which
arose among a people to whom the reason meant more
than the will and speculative thought was more prized
than moral action.   In this matter Jesus differed in no
respect from the prophets.   God was for him One who had
all power, who as Father answered to every need of his
children, who fed the birds of the air, clothed the grass of
the field, and established his kingdom in the earth.   Such a
question as "What and where is God?" would have seemed
strange to Jesus, and if answered by him at all must have
derived its content from his experience and the ideal hopes
of his people.   But transcendence and immanence, as these
were conceived by Greek thinkers, by Jewish theologians,
and by Christian apologists, never emerged above the
threshold of his consciousness.

II

In Greek thought transcendence in an extreme form is
the doctrine of Aristotle, immanence the doctrine of the
Stoics; traces of both appear in the Old, and especially
in the New Testament.   Plato in different moods may be
cited as representative of both immanence and transcendence, and the Platonic-Stoic philosophy has affinities with
each.   In the early Christian centuries the thought of God
was powerfully influenced by the Alexandrian school as
may be seen by a study of Plotinus and his followers, of
Clement, Origen, and, not least, of Augustine.   To the
same source may be attributed the point of view of Justin [1]

_____

[1] *Apology*, I, 61 ff.

with which one may compare Philo[1] and the Hermetic writings.[2]   The development of the idea of the divine transcendence may be traced along three main lines— theological, mystical, and philosophical.   These are not always clearly separated from one another but often flow together; yet even so the central interest will lie in one rather than the others of these three directions.

From the theological point of view there is a metaphysical aspect of God which is remote, unrevealed, inconceivable, the Absolute, to which only negative terms may be applied.   For the majority of those who represent this position, transcendence is not the whole of God.   Many of these theologians, as Augustine, conceive of God as personal, revealing himself in the most intimate and loving way in redemption.   All of God that can become active for the salvation of man comes into play; and, so far as man is concerned, if this were all of God, there would be no feeling of the inadequacy of the divine.   For in relation to the world God is all-wise and all-powerful; all causes are the expression of his will; in relation to men all events are the fulfillment of his purpose.   But theology is not merely practical; it is in part the product of speculative thought.   And this is satisfied only with alleging a transcendent element in God.   The interests supposed to be served by this conception are various.   There is first the feeling that God must be far more than any expression of him.   For Augustine "God is more truly thought than he is uttered, and exists more truly than he is thought."   It is regarded as the height of irreverent presumption to suppose that the plumb-line of our reason or imagination can fathom the utmost depths of the divine.

---

[1] *Leg. Alleg.*, 47a.
[2] *Poemander*, 4.

To the words of the prophet a metaphysical meaning is assigned: "As the heavens are higher than the earth, so are my ways higher than your ways, and my thoughts than your thoughts." [1] Those who would scale the heavens in order to comprehend God are sobered by the warning: "Canst thou by searching find out God? canst thou find out the Almighty unto perfection?" There is an element of mystery in the nature as in the ways of God that man cannot comprehend; since he cannot know what this is, he can give it no name. It is more and other than what he has experienced; yet if it could be apprehended it would in no respect contradict but only complete what the soul has already found to be true. The value of this assertion of the transcendence of God lies less in its contribution to theology than in its influence upon the theologian himself, in creating a modest reserve, an attitude of reverence, even of awe toward this Reality of realities.

One conception of the divine transcendence arises from a distinction between the secret and the revealed will of God. The biblical warrant for this is sought in part in a word in the Old Testament: "The secret things belong unto the Lord our God; but the things that are revealed belong unto us and our children forever." [2] There are also many other references to which appeal is made in support of the position, that within the divine nature is a wealth of wisdom and purpose which is known only to God, which is of such a nature or degree that it either has not been or cannot be communicated to men.[3] To this hidden source is to be referred the decree not only of election to holiness but of reprobation to damnation. Only

---

[1] Isa. iv, 9.
[2] Deut. xxix, 29.
[3] Cf. Rom. xi, 33-36.

the impious and incorrigible could reject the latter decree, since it originated in the secret and adorable counsel of God. This transcendent aspect of God is opaque to human intelligence and will remain forever impervious to human inquiry. Although it is irreconcilable with what we otherwse know of God, yet it is maintained that since it is given by revelation there is no recourse but to accept it and bow before its awful mystery. Such a tension in the divine nature cannot, however, be tolerated by us, some way must be found to solve the contradiction and render God either all transcendent, or else so known that the contradiction disappears. "God is light, and in him is no darkness at all." [1]

Another way of conceiving of the divine transcendence appears in the common doctrine of the Trinity. This takes two forms. In the first, God is presented under two aspects: (1) for the sake of redemption, God appears to men as Father, Son, and Holy Spirit,—all revealed and active in delivering men from sin, each with a definite function which may be intelligibly defined. (2) He is represented as existing in an eternal super-mundane form, with an inner-Trinitarian life, essentially and unchangeably Father, Son, and Holy Spirit. Of that life the revealed Trinity is a faint and far reflection. This life was real and complete before the creation of the world; nothing was added to its fullness or felicity by the creation of life; and if the universe were to sink into nothingness, this would in no way affect the consciousness of God as Triune. We have no language to describe this life of God. We cannot penetrate to its inmost secret.

"God only knows the love of God."

---

[1] I John i, 5.

Naturally such a conception has but slight bearing on our idea of God. Its only claim to recognition lies in the theory that the Trinity of redemption is grounded in the eternal transcendent Triunity.

In the second form of conceiving of God as transcendent in relation to the Trinity, the Trinity is defined as follows: the Father is the source and ground, and is manifested in his Son Jesus Christ and in the Spirit which is the quickening principle of the consciousness both of the individual and of the community. So far as we interpret Fatherhood through Jesus Christ, we know what qualities to ascribe to it. This could, however, be only a partial description of God, for the term God signifies immeasurably more than is embodied in Jesus, and that "more" is either the ideal-forming Energy by which the world is carried forward in the development of meaning, or it is the unrevealed, unexplored element in the divine nature which lies beyond our present and even possible intelligence. In either case we are brought to acknowledge a transcendent aspect of God.

III

If we seek a religious valuation of the transcendence of God we have recourse to the mystics. There are two types of mysticism, one of which brings to full expression the doctrine of the divine immanence. This makes much of the "inner light." It has affinity with a pantheistic view of the world. It elevates the feelings to a commanding place in religious experience. An indescribable sense of oneness with God is the seal of its consummation. There are moments here below when the feeling of this union is intense and seems on the way to complete and permanent realization; ideally this is not an exceptional experience but an enduring state of the personal life. None of the powers of the self are quiescent, but while all are brought into full play, the sense of effort is wanting. God who is to be real for the inner life is not far off.

"Closer is he than breathing, and nearer than hands and feet." And yet, as another has said, "near is too far." Instead of losing, one finds, himself in God. This type of mysticism flourishes under the shelter of the divine immanence.

The other type draws its very life-blood from a theory of the transcendence of God. For the great mystics, as Dionysius the Areopagite, John Scotus Erigena, St. Bernard of Clairvaux, and Eckhart, the essence of God was beyond human apprehension, indefinable, ineffable, inconceivable. Its content cannot be bodied forth by the imagination, fathomed by the reason, or disclosed by revelation. In the earthly life there are moments when the soul as in a swoon sinks into union or identification with God, but the moment quickly passes, the waking memory recalls nothing of its secret; only in heaven can it reach its consummation, from which no lapse is thereafter possible.

This conception of the divine transcendence, which is connected with a postponing of the Beatific Vision to the celestial world or an absorption into God does not, as might be supposed, vacate the earthly life of positive content. For in the interim there are many things to do and much to enjoy. Life here is intensely active. By prayer, by discipline, by contemplation, the spirit moves toward its divine destination. The stages of the journey are both religious and ethical. As religious the spirit directs its aspiration and longing, its prayer and praise, its peni-

tence and thanksgiving to God; as ethical it seeks to
purge itself of sloth and self-indulgence, to cultivate
every excellence and all virtue.   As religious there is
Christian fellowship, communion of saints, desire for "the
better country."   Hymns like those of St. Bernard of
Clugny, "The Celestial Country" and Faber's "O Para-
dise!" voice this longing for release from the body and
presence with the Lord.   Professor James in his *Varieties
of Religious Experience* has introduced us to a score of
mystics with their vivid and intense scorn of earth and
their unfulfilled, impatient longing for the consummation
of bliss.   Yet in spite of the insatiate other-worldliness
of their aspiration, their activity in respect to the present world was of astonishing volume.   In corroboration
of this one has only to mention St. Francis of Assissi, St.
Catherine of Siena, St. Theresa, and Madame Guyon.
St. Bernard of Clairvaux would have been content only if
he might found one new monastery every day.   Their
mortification of the flesh, their fidelity to every task, their
rigorous discipline of thought and desire, their practise
of "recollection," their vigils of fasting and prayer, were
the steps by which "they climbed the steep ascent of
heaven."   Inextricably associated with this is the Platonic
ideal that life's goal is reached only by the "practise of
death."   The aim is to divest one's self of all that constitutes one human in order to rise into union with the
transcendent God.

IV

The chief representatives of the philosophical view of
the transcendent God are Kant, Hamilton, and Spencer.
As this has been already described, we do not need to

expatiate upon it at length.[1] For these men the transcendence of God is only another way of saying that he is unknowable by the human reason, first, on the ground of a theory of knowledge by which we are limited to a knowledge of phenomena, and, secondly, on the ground of the unresolved antinomies which beset the terms Absolute or Unconditioned, Infinite, and First Cause. According to Kant, we regulate our conduct and our view of the world "as if" God existed; according to Mansel, the spokesman of Hamilton's logic, the veil which hides the knowledge of God from us may be lifted by revelation; according to Spencer the Infinite and Eternal Reality is of the same nature as that which wells up in consciousness.

Several other definitions of transcendence, partly metaphysical, partly personal, have been proposed: (1) the many depend on the One; the One is neither the sum of the many, nor the material of which they are composed;[2] (2) God's essence is infinite, whereas the essence of nature is finite both in quantity and in quality;[3] (3) the divine life is not exhaustively revealed by any temporal or spatial or personal expression of the divine Mind or Will; (4) the perfect spirituality and personality of God constitute his transcendence; (5) the absolute freedom of the divine action proves transcendence.

V

Immanence rightly understood is metaphysical or cosmic; it is therefore to be distinguished from personalism,

[1] Cf. pp. 57-59.

[2] Bowne, *Theism*, p. 245.

[3] Paulsen, *Introduction to Philosophy*, p. 257.

and also from a naïve doctrine of omnipotence. It has been interpreted in terms of substance, thought, causality or force, consciousness, the contingency of free will, and the Logos doctrine.

1. The principal modern advocates of cosmic immanence, based on the idea of substance, are Bruno, Jacob Boehme, and Spinoza. According to Bruno every individual thing is an existence-form of God. Since God is the universal animating principle, each thing follows in part the law of its particular nature and in part the law which holds good of the world as a whole. Boehme thought of the world as an organism, with God as its life, a conception reflected in Fechner's *Ueber die Seelenfrage*. For Spinoza God is the only life. All the forces of existence are either extension- or thought-modes of the one Substance. All of nature is God, although all of God is not included in nature. Thus a basis is laid for a theory of transcendence as well as of immanence.

2. According to Hegel, to whom the essential nature of reality is thought, all phenomena are referred to an inner, necessary logic of development. In this metaphysical pantheism the many are only forms of the One and the One is identical with the many. No influences can come from without, since there is nothing from which such influences would originate. Aside from the universe there is no self-existent Being who before the creation dwelt in solitary grandeur or who from an unseen region sends forth "light and truth." The nature of the universe is rational, and this is also the nature of God.

3. When God is regarded as Force or Causality we have a different approach to the idea of immanence. Schleiermacher, for example, bases his conception of Immanence on certain definitions: (1) religion is the feeling

of absolute dependence which is man's response to God as the absolute Causality; (2) the omnipresence of God, itself unspatial, conditions what is spatial and even space itself; (3) the individual and limited things in the universe are the immediate expression of the causality of God. For Professor Royce [1] the immanence of God is secured by a reconciliation of individuation with the reality of the Absolute. Each finite self-consciousness is a portion of the divine self-consciousness. "The one will of the Absolute is essentially and organically composed of many." The harmony of all is due to the freedom of each acting in unison with others. Bowne holds that a system of interacting members requires a unitary Being by which they are posited and maintained in harmonious relation; that is, the One, conceived of as causality instead of as substance, is the power by which the many exist.

4. In the theory of evolution as advocated by Herbert Spencer, John Fiske, and Joseph Le Conte the idea of immanence is essential and is defined by reference to consciousness. Spencer [2] has been cited as an advocate of transcendence; he is also and equally on the side of immanence. In his ultimate theory of the world he declares that "all things proceed from an Infinite and Eternal Energy which is of the same nature as that which in ourselves wells up in consciousness." According to Fiske the world is not a machine but an organism with an indwelling principle of life. Each organic life is a specialized form of the Universal Life. The evolutionary movement toward psychical life, the dramatic tendency in

---

[1] Cf. *The Conception of God*, p. 293. *The World and Individual*, Vol. I, Chapter X, Vol. II, Chap. VII.

[2] Cf. *Sociology*, Vol. III, p. 172: "Religious Retrospect and Prospect."

history, and the development of the moral ideal are the manifestations of the indwelling, living God. For Professor Le Conte God is resident in nature. All phenomena are modes of his consciousness; all natural forces are forms of his consciousness; all laws of nature are regular methods of the operation of his will. God is the only independent reality and his action throughout the universe is direct and constant. An analogy of the immanence of God in the world is seen in the inner psychical aspect of the activity of the brain. Thus the veil of nature hides a person, infinite and self-conscious, whose perfection is revealed in the universe.[1]

5. A more or less confused doctrine of immanence is based upon the divine will yet is regarded as essentially real. The totality of God pervades and fills the universe: God is present not potentially but essentially and as a whole in every part of the world. His immanence is, however, conditioned by his purpose; it depends on his free creating and conserving will. Such a relation is necessary to the world but not to God.[2]

6. According to the Logos-doctrine as interpreted by Hegelian dialectic, in the Son God is objectively immanent, revealing himself in nature and history, and especially in the incarnation; in the Spirit God is subjectively present and immanent in his redeeming action in the human soul and in the community of believers. There is, however, nothing arbitrary about this. It is not a matter of choice whether God will sustain this relation to the human consciousness; it is essential to his very being; on man's part therefore it is radical and indefeasible and can

---

[1] *Evolution in its Relation to Religious Thought*, pp. 338 ff. Cf. also Lyman Abbott, *The Theology of an Evolutionist*, p. 13.
[2] A. H. Strong, *Systematic Theology*, Vol. I, pp. 79 ff.

never be wholly perverted or destroyed. Humanity is rooted in God. God's highest self-expression, indeed his very self-realization, is through the universe and especially through man redeemed.[1]

7. A conception of immanence appears in literary form in many modern writers, as Wordsworth, Coleridge, Carlyle, Emerson, Tennyson, and Walt Whitman. No one has defined this attitude more fitly than in Wordsworth's oft-quoted words [2] which became classic the moment they were penned. Those who see in Nature a physical fact only are blind to its greater meaning; he is aware of

> "a sense sublime
> Of something far more deeply interfused,
> Whose dwelling is the light of setting suns
> And the round ocean and the living air
> And the blue sky, and in the mind of man;
> A motion and a spirit that impels
> All thinking things, all objects of all thought
> And rolls through all things."

This feeling has been associated with the Romantic movement in poetry, with the evolutionary view in science, with the metaphysics of one type of idealistic philosophy, and with certain interpretations of religion from the point of view of experience and the consciousness of values. Its permanent appeal to the human spirit is witnessed to by its long history and its prevalence among many races of men; and that too not alone in the earlier animistic stages but in the highest circles of human development—

---

[1] Cf. A. E. Garvie, *A Handbook of Apologetics*, pp. 157-158. Cf. A. H. Strong, *Christ in Creation and Ethical Monism.*

[2] *Lines Above Tintern Abbey.*

Hindu, Greek, Mohammedan, and English.   In some quarters it seems to have reached the saturation point, as in Emerson, Whitman, John Burroughs, and in many Russian and French novelists.   That the ethical ideals associated with this general attitude are at times naturalistic or at least not marked by the vigor and rigor of Kant's categorical imperative is easily understood.   These writers think of the universe as animated throughout by a single Principle or Power, so that morality is everywhere and always, even when tinged with Stoic fortitude, relative to time and place and degree of evolution.

VI

The entire question of transcendence and immanence requires restatement and revaluation.   The classic form in which each of these ideas appeared arose from different sources and as ideas are incapable of reconciliation. They cannot be harmonized in any being so as to become constituent parts of a personality.   Attempts have been made in this direction, but the result is a clumsy piecing together of incongruous elements.   Devotional hymns render this incongruity less conspicuous, partly because they express what the pious heart feels and partly because they envisage reality in concrete representative forms.   This has never been more finely put than by Dr. Holmes, who has given to transcendence and immanence and all that lies between them their full value.

> "Lord of all being, throned afar,
>   Whose glory flames from sun and star;
>   Center and soul of every sphere,
>   Yet to each loving heart how near."

The theories of transcendence and immanence originated on Greek soil. The conceptions of them which have been most in vogue among later theologians seem to have forgotten their source and have wandered off into confused and incoherent formulas. To be in earnest with either one of these has always resulted in a reduction of the other to a meaningless framework, or if the intention was to retain both, they were subjected to an interpretation far removed from their historic and intelligible setting. Transcendence has been evaporated into a spiritual freedom of activity, immanence into a willed omnipresent energy. At a time when second causes were set over against the First Cause, immanence was defined as the divine providential activity which "energizes in the second causes." [1] A recent writer says that through the divine immanence the "whole organism of humanity is environed and saturated with the Spirit of God." [2] In such presentations a distinction between transcendence and immanence melts away and the same definition serves for both. In case, however, one seeks to maintain the common distinction between transcendence and immanence, the divine nature is separated into two unrelated and incongruous parts.

If we are to assign any meaning to transcendence we must avoid the assumption that God is independent of the universe, that his life would be complete without it, and that he is any degree separated from it. Apart from the universe God is inconceivable; no content can be attributed to his being. All that we know or can know of him is conditioned on our knowledge of the world. Moreover, we believe that there is no "beyond," no Epi-

---

[1] L. F. Stearns *Present-Day Theology*, p. 268.
[2] J. H. Snowden, *The Personality of God*, p. 109.

curean heaven removed from the world, as a dwelling-
place for the divine. Prayer is often conceived of as in
the formula of the dedication of Solomon's temple,
addressed to a Being far above the earth: "hear thou in
heaven thy dwelling-place." A New Testament writer
refers to God as "dwelling in light unapproachable."
For such a Being intermediaries would be necessary, even
as for the Olympian Zeus, flying from heaven to earth,
from earth to heaven. It is not, however, so much the
precise conceptions of an earlier time as the attitude of
feeling enshrined in these conceptions which lives on in
the popular mind. The intermediaries have disappeared,
unless indeed Jesus and the Holy Spirit are regarded as
such, but prayers still go "up" to God, between whom
and the worshiper is some mysterious means of communication. To those who are thus disposed, wireless teleg-
raphy has been seized upon as an analogy, suggesting
that distance is annihilated between the aspiring soul and
God. On the other hand, there is a vague sense of relief
at the thought that God is far off rather than near;
otherwise the soul's most private sanctuary is invaded and
thoughts and feelings, which one likes to believe are known
only to one's self, are open to the gaze of another of
whose presence one is unaware. Every one has secrets
which he not only does not but even cannot lay bare to
his most intimate and sympathetic friend; how much more
would he shrink from freely exposing them to the sight
of the Most Holy and the Most Loving. Many comforting assurances have grown out of that word in the Revelation: [1] "Behold, I stand at the door and knock; if any
man hear my voice and open the door, I will come in to

---

[1] iii, 20.

him, and will sup with him, and he with me." Although this may be the feeling and language of religion or of the naïve consciousness, it is not true to reality. It is the survival of a conception of God which lingers in the popular mind after the view of the world in which it arose and was once at home has ceased to function in the scientific and philosophical consciousness.

On the other hand, quite as far removed from the truth is that theory of the divine immanence which conceives of God either as identical with the universe, himself Nature in all its contents and operations, or as so imprisoned within the physical order as to be determined forever by physical necessity. We have already seen that while there is an element of invariable mechanism, there is also a purposive element in the universe, everywhere present and everywhere active, to which all the meaning of the universe is to be referred. Accordingly, mechanical necessity does not swallow up the freedom of this all-pervasive Power, for the sphere of freedom is the realm of ends.

If the terms immanence and transcendence are still to be valid, they must grow out of our view of the world and be interpreted so as not to be mutually contradictory or to nullify each other when referred to the same Reality. It would perhaps be preferable to dispense with both of these terms in favor of some word which has no embarrassing implications. Since, however, the terms in their present-day use have no fixed and uniform connotation, we need not hesitate to seek a meaning which shall justify our use of them. Accordingly, we shall find immanence in a universal purposive principle or activity, and transcendence in the ideal meaning which has been and is to be developed in distinction from the immediately actual. The two are therefore not essentially different from each other: they are different aspects of the same Reality. If we may seek an analogy to the divine in the human experience, we shall say, on the one hand, that at every instant consciousness continues its purposive activity and is characterized by a definite content; on the other hand, that there are ideals and potencies within it not yet realized, which await future actualization. There would be no present content if there were no ideal aspect, and there would be no ideal aspect without the actual content, of experience. While these two points of view may be distinguished from each other, they cannot be separated. It is as if the ideal hovered over the actual and beckoned it forward to new stages of achievement, or as if there were in the actual an indefeasible urge toward further and higher forms of the actual (cf. Heb. xi, 16). God is immanent so far as he is the pervasive principle or energy by which the creative process is carried forward; he is transcendent so far as there are infinite possibilities in the creative process which may be realized under temporal, spatial, and conscious forms. The immanent God is

"The God of things as they are";

the transcendent God is the God of things as they are to become. Since, however, being is ever passing into becoming, God as immanent is not static but dynamic; and because becoming rises out of and fulfills being, God as transcendent is not detached from the actual. If he is the changing, he is also the permanently, real One.

In different systems of worlds in the universe the transcendence of God has different meanings; whether in a given world there is life and personal consciousness; in some worlds this may have existed and have disappeared;

in one system and another this or a different expression
of the creative energy may be in process of realization.
Here is life and consciousness, in perhaps a single planet
of our solar system; in Orion or Capella a divine impulse
may be working out an even more wonderful result. The
resources of God are various and inexhaustible; we know
those only with which experience has made us aware.
Some of these are disclosed in flashing insights of scientific research; others are conjectured on the ground of
analogy. The question as to how far there is a divine
memory and a divine anticipation, distinct and separate
from the world-process, is one of deep interest but one
which we may not be in position to solve. Whether the
divine memory is registered in the present dynamic tendencies of the universe, as these have arisen out of the
past, enriched by continuous accretions from creative
evolution, and the divine anticipation is to be identified
with all that is involved in the existing movements of the
present hour, must be left an open question. In any
case, no other memory or foreknowledge than this is susceptible of proof. To speak of an infinite fullness of
knowledge in the Absolute, out of all necessary relation
to or dependence on the universe is to use terms which are
purely a matter of definition. No defensible doctrine of
revelation could guarantee the validity of belief of an
absolute foreknowledge of all events which lie in the bosom
of the future. Nor can it be shown that any tenable
theory of salvation requires such prescience on the part
of God. It is enough if the individual self and the social
organism are both quickened to higher ethical and spiritual activity by the divine purposive will and find an adequate response in it to their ever-renewed endeavor. This
resource from which life draws its meaning is none other

than the immanent yet exhaustless and therefore transcendent Creative Good Will.

One of the most significant aspects of transcendence is seen in the evolution of life on our globe. It would have been a reasonable supposition that when vegetable and animal existence appeared the Purposive Will operating in nature had reached its goal. But as one traces the long process in which higher forms have emerged, he becomes aware that reserves of power and adaptation have been drawn upon until man comes forth to begin his struggle for existence, the development of his moral ideas, and the creation of a social organism which is to embody his instinctive and conscious aims. If this evolution had been arrested at any of its lower stages, who could have imagined the potencies for good which have later come to manifestation—justice, sacrifice, social service? We are told not alone by social dreamers but by sober students of history that humanity is only just now entering upon an era of well-being, vaster and more splendid than all that has gone before. What forms this higher good will assume it is vain to conjecture. Even more impotent is one's imagination to picture the high moral and spiritual achievements of the race many hundreds of thousands of years hence. Nor may we form any notion of the nature and attainment of those beings who are yet to dwell in other worlds of space. All this belongs to the region of the divine transcendence, the so far unrevealed and measureless potencies of the Source of all good. On the other hand, as we observe the movements of the world-order and the progress of historical events, we see something of the divine transcendence passing into immanence, and the immanent aspect continually changing, as the world, especially man, becomes susceptible to finer adjustments and the realizing of more spiritual ends. The supreme instance of this is Christianity in its relation both to other religions and to its own background. The potencies of the divine operating in it carry to a further stage the essential ideals of other religions, including the Hebrew religion, while it is at every moment scarcely more than the promise of what it is to become. It is what it is because the immanent God has wrought in and with the human spirit; it will press on toward its consummation because of the infinite riches of grace which await fulfillment from a transcendent aspect of God.

XII. THE PERSONALITY OF GOD

I

EARLY Christian writers made no more attempt than did non-Christian writers to analyze and define personality. They regarded man as personal. Since man was made in the image of God, God was also personal, that is, of the same nature as man. Not that they did not believe that there were qualities in God which man did not possess, but they were chiefly interested to attribute to God what they conceived to be the highest in man. The highest names they gave to him represented the supreme character and functions of man—King, Lord, Ruler, and best of all, Father. Their discussion centered not in the personality *of* God but personality *in* God.[1] As their doctrine of sin was that of "Original sin," so their doctrine of God was that of the Trinity—three persons in one God. They were sensitive as to the use of the term "person," but their sensitivity was limited to the definition and defense of the "persons" of the Godhead. It is only recently that the focus of discussion has shifted from personality in God to that of the personality of God.

II

From its first appearance the word person has been a disturbing presence in theological usage. It is purely

---

[1] Cf. C. C. J. Webb, *God and Personality.*

technical, "convenient," so it was labeled by St. Thomas
Aquinas.[1] It has, and indeed it has always had, a different meaning when applied to the persons of the Trinity
from that applied to men, and hence often leads to confusion of thought. Fairbairn says that it belongs to "the
category of the schools," which is true. Much trouble
would have been avoided if it could have kept its academic
seclusion. It comes forth, however, into the light of day,
forgetful of the limitations imposed upon it. In a work
intended for thoughtful readers, one comes upon these
words: "there is a true sense in which God in his unity is a
person. . . . Accordingly, we must understand tri-per-
sonality as existing consistently with the unipersonality of
God." Referring to personal distinctions implied in the
terms Father, Son, and Holy Spirit, the author continues:
"We cannot suppose that these personalities, these Egos
or selves, are bounded off and separated from each other,
as is the case with men. Rather are we led to suppose
that in the one self-consciousness of the infinite God there
are three distinct centers of self-consciousness, three distinct Egos which spring from and are merged in the one
divine Ego. . . . The closeness of the relation between
the three persons is indicated in the teaching of Orthodox
theologians, that in each act of every one of the persons
the other two participate.[2] This is only one instance
among many which might be cited from contemporary
works on the same subject.[3] However circumspectly,
even meticulously, a writer guards the preliminary definition of the term "person," and hedges about his statement
as to the use he will make of it, he invariably neglects to

---

[1] *Summa* I, Quaest. 29, sec. 3.
[2] L. F. Stearns, *Present-Day Theology*, pp. 196-197.
[3] Cf. J. H. Snowden, *The Personality of God*, pp. 86-87.

observe his own restrictions. In general this type of
thought is found only in works on dogmatic theology; it
rarely ever appears in treatises on theism.

Although to the word person or personality wholly
different meanings are assigned when referred to God from
those applied to man, yet as in the above quotation we can
see precisely where the confusion arises. Personality is
subjected to two different meanings, yet there is no indication that the same word is not valid for both uses.
Father, Son, and Holy Spirit are called persons, and God
as a unitary Being is also called a person. This two-fold
usage has arisen in response to two situations, one ancient, the other modern. We shall first indicate the origin
and meaning of the term "person" in early Christian
thinking, and then show how more recently the same term
has acquired a different significance.

In order to defend the doctrine of the Trinity the early
church had to discover in the nature of God a dual aspect,
one of which represented the essential reality, the other a
multiplicity of forms or entities which laid a basis for a
two-fold distinction in the one undivided Being. This
was expressed in the Greek creeds by the use of three
terms, one of which represented being or reality in its
widest reference ($οὐσία$), the others, concrete differences in the divine nature which yet involved the possession of a common essence ($ὑπόστασις$ and $πρόσωπον$).
When the discussion of the Trinity was carried over to
the Latin church, by a singular fortune the term "Substance" which would naturally have been equivalent to the
second of the Greek terms referred to ($ὑπόστασις$)
came to stand for being or essence, and another word
was introduced to signify the three distinctions in the
Godhead, namely, "Person." Thus, Father, Son, and

Holy Spirit are persons, although possessing a common substance:

"God in three persons, blessed Trinity."

Until recently the definition of "person" which has been generally accepted, owes its formulation to Boethius in the early part of the sixth century: *"Persona est naturæ rationalis individua substantia"*—person is the individual subsistence of a rational nature.[1] Two aspects of the definition are to be noted: (1) a person is an individual, yet not necessarily of a fixed and changeless character; (2) a rational nature is a universal property common to many individual persons. Accordingly, while all persons are individuals, all individuals are not persons. Moreover, in the traditional doctrine of the Trinity, while the persons of the Godhead are individual, there is one rational nature common to all alike. This, then, is the standard or official doctrine of the Greek and Roman, the Lutheran and Reformed churches.

The history of this doctrine in the Christian church shows that it is beset with inner difficulties which have never been and perhaps can never be resolved—logical, metaphysical, psychological, ethical, and religious. The confusion and the contradiction inherent in the definition of persons in its traditional setting is apparently so serious that at present interest in it is hardly more than academic. It is for the most part confined to theologians who are more intent on conserving the past than finding truth for the present, to theological students in the early stages of their training, and to controversial preachers who make it a point to defend all the dogmas of the

---

[1] Cf. Webb, *op cit.,* pp. 47-48.

church, regardless of conditions which have rendered these dogmas if not obsolete yet inactive. The average layman, whether he is college-bred or not, is ignorant concerning the doctrine of the three persons in one; or, if he chances to know, he passes it by as something which his pastor may preach about but which has for him no pragmatic value.

It is conceivable that if the doctrine of the three persons in the Godhead were to survive and once more resume its ancient supremacy, belief in the personality of God might be seriously endangered; indeed all interest in the personality of God might cease, having been concentrated on personality in God or the three persons of the Trinity. At present, however, this danger is far from imminent, the tendency is all the other way, and unity rather than triunity is the trend of the time.

These remarks are subject to slight qualification in view of a particular theory of the Trinity. Its aim is to provide a basis in the Godhead for the social relations of men—the family, the church, the state, and indeed all the forms of association in which humanity realizes its destiny in a social organism. According to this conception God is not a unitary Being, solitary in an insulated felicity; he is a social Being, Father, Son, and Holy Spirit—an eternal society. Before the creation of the world the inner fellowship of the Trinity was complete and perfect. And since man was created in the divine image, his ideal is to become through social union and activity what God is. And as Father and Son are not complete each in himself without the other or apart from the Spirit, so every man is incomplete except as he shares a common good in a social family patterned after the divine Family, between which and humanity is the reciprocity of love.　Even if one hesitates to yield assent to this conception, one cannot fail to be attracted to the aim for which it is put forth.　For the social is among the very first of all present-day interests.　He who surrenders himself to social as distinguished from purely individualistic aims,—and the hope of the world lies in the social gospel,—must find in the nature of man, in the structure of the universe, and most of all in the constitution of God the ground of his confidence.　Whether such a theory of the nature of God as this conception of the Trinity offers provides the basis desired is questionable.　Whether the theory itself is a true interpretation of the inner life of God is more than questionable.　That the theory is imaginatively conceivable does not guarantee its truth.　It is not necessary that the good, the conserving power in the realization of human well-being, be already in existence in perfect actuality; it is only necessary that it be in process of development, endowed with the promise and potency of renewal and advance.　The evidence for the social life of God as described above is unconvincing because in the nature of the case it is inaccessible to the human mind.　On the other hand, all those to whom God is real believe that he is the source and inspirer of all the social ideals in which lie the future of humanity.　For the divine purposive will is exhaustlessly rich in impulsions toward all those ends in which the highest good is realized.

III

The solution of the problem under consideration is not advanced by setting up a distinction between person and personality; as if there were a difference between the per-

sons of the Godhead and the personality of God.   Nor
does it meet the case to say that the Father, Son, and
Holy Spirit are persons, but that God is a super-personality which somehow embraces the three in a mysterious
unity.[1]   The confusion into which this whole matter has
been plunged is seen in treatises on the Person of Jesus
Christ, and the Personality of the Holy Spirit, where the
aim is to formulate a doctrine of the nature of Christ and
the nature and function of the Spirit as individual and
also as members of the Trinitarian life of God.   In treat-
ing of Christ the method is first to describe Jesus as a
historical person, and then to investigate the meaning of
his person in a metaphysical realm.   This results in three
very different descriptions: (1) his human nature; (2) his
divine nature in union with his human nature in the incarnate state; (3) his eternal nature in the being of God,
in no way dependent upon the incarnation.   The Holy
Spirit is presented as an eternal subsistence in the life of
God, as a cosmic spirit immanent in the life of the world,
and as an agent in the work of redemption.[2]   Our attention is, however, detained by several suggestive facts:
first, complete treatises are devoted to one or another
member of the Trinity, Father, Son or Jesus, and Holy
Spirit, as if each of these was practically independent of
the others; secondly, there is the person but not the personality of Jesus Christ; thirdly, instead of the person it
is the personality of the Holy Spirit; fourthly, Fatherhood is substituted for personality in God.   Between 1860
and 1900 this was the well-nigh universal practise of
writers on these subjects.   It still continues in many quarters.   Recently, however, another path has been struck

[1] Cf. Snowden, *op. cit.*, p. 36-37.
[2] Cf. F. B. Denio, *The Supreme Leader.*

out. This variation in the use of terms as applied to the different aspects of Christian experience is, to say the least, confusing. One result is that the reader of average intelligence, perplexed at a use of words and a method of argument which he meets with nowhere else, withdraws attention and becomes indifferent to the whole matter. He is not unwilling that his pastor preach an occasional sermon on the subject, but he feels that while it may be a part of the church's faith, it lies entirely beyond the circle of his understanding. An opposite result is that many readers whose uncritical opinions have been received upon authority, supposing themselves to be in possession of the truth, become vehement advocates of the teaching they have imbibed. Unless we are prepared to regard "person" as a function of the Deity,—in which case another word should be substituted for it,—it would be better to dispense with it altogether. Until this is done, we must expect confusion to continue, and the confusion will become more serious by as much as the present tendency develops to fix attention exclusively on the personality of God.

IV

In more recent times this question has been approached from a different, one might almost say, a revolutionary angle. This path has indeed been already trodden by philosophers, although not without the companionship of theologians. The philosophers have compelled a revision of the whole inquiry concerning the personality of man and God. Except in the case of Hegel and his followers of the right wing, little or no attempt has been made to find in the personality of God a place for the "persons" of the Trinity.   The question has been generally although not wholly detached from its relation to the Trinity; and God is thought of as one.   It is not so much what God might be in himself,—this had occupied the attention of the theologians of the early church,—as what might be his relation to the world and to the religious consciousness of men.   The scientific spirit is abroad, the world is conceived of as a unity; an adequate cause must be sought for its production.   The Creator of this vast mechanical order must be one.   Since the universe bears traces of power and wisdom and goodness, the Source of it must not only not be less but more than it; he must himself possess in the highest degree the properties found in the universe.   But power, wisdom, and goodness are the marks of personality.   Passing from the natural world to the moral order Schleiermacher [1] found in religious experience a warrant for ascribing personality to God.   He makes no attempt to analyze the content of personality, save only as it is related to the religious consciousness. Later his outline of personality became more vague and shadowy and the reality as objective yielded its place to the postulate of religious experience.

The common, one might call it the naïve, way of reaching a definition of the divine personality is by attributing to it the properties which are characteristic of the human consciousness.   When, for example, by Snowden [2] these properties are described as intellect, sensibility, and will, the method of procedure is to set these free from their finite limitations and thus raise them to the highest degree of excellence and activity.   The personality of God is defined in terms of consciousness.   This consciousness is

[1] Cf. On Religion, pp. 93 ff., transl. by Oman.
[2] *Op. cit.,* pp. 40 ff.

fundamentally intelligence, feeling, and will, but it has no
need of the processes which are necessary to the human
mind. God knows by an infinite and immediate aware-
ness. His relation to time and space is beyond our comprehension. His emotional life, although real, is both
higher and deeper than that of man, and perhaps different
in kind. His will acts without the use of means.
Thought, feeling, and will are in perfect unison. His intelligence is omniscience, his will omnipotent; no similar
term is, however, found for the divine feeling. Such is the
common doctrine of the divine personality.

V

When this subject is approached from the idealistic
point of view, as for example, that of Professor Royce,
we have a conception of God as the Absolute in terms of
thought, will, experience, and life. It is fully in accord
with this idea of the Absolute to regard God as personal.
It is true that conditions which appear to us to be essential to constitute personality are wanting. Thought, will,
experience, and life are affirmed, yet each is so defined
as to leave it radically different from anything which we
are familiar with as personal. Moreover, an effort is
made to reconcile the various meanings assigned to these
terms, but the idealistic point of view from which the
argument proceeds maintains the primacy of thought,—
thought which is absolute and perfectly fulfilled in the
life of the world. Will, although not absent, is subordi-
nated to thought: the will, instead of achieving, is eternally accomplished. Co-ordinated with thought and will
are experience which is completely organized, self-consciousness and life in perfect accord with idea, "with no

unanswered questions and no unfulfilled desires." This is essentially the doctrine held by the Calvinistic Dr. Hodge and Edwardean-Augustinian Dr. Shedd, although it has its source in a very different metaphysics and is expounded from the theological rather than from a philosophical interest. The ultimate question is perhaps not so much whether a Being so defined is personal as whether such a Being exists. If the fact of its existence could be established, then no doubt the term "personal" in some transcendent sense might be employed to designate the character of this Being. A further question may be raised, whether, if this is the meaning of personality, some other word than personal should not be applied to man.

It would be more difficult to associate personality with the idea of God as the Absolute as advocated by Professors Caird and Watson. The characteristic terms, Principle, Unity, a coherent system, and others like them, lend themselves less readily to the notion of personality than is the case with Royce's will, experience, and life. And although according to Professor Watson this reality is self-conscious, yet both self and consciousness find little or no analogy in human experience; the meaning assigned to these hardly raises them above a non-personal pantheism. If, however, the Absolute is all-embracing, it must be characterized by consciousness, so far at least as there is consciousness in man. It is also claimed that the human consciousness would have no intelligible content but for the fact that it rises out of and expresses in part the Absolute Consciousness; for all finite thought presupposes Infinite Thought which alone gives it rationality. When we have allowed to these terms all the values they will bear, we are still far from personality. The terms themselves are abstract. Thought implies a thinker, but the thought is neither discursive nor intuitive, and it does not, any more than the Idea of Plato, involve a personal background. There is a Principle which pervades the universe, to which its unity and development are to be referred, but nothing is added to it by calling it personal. The doctrine here in question is more a philosophy, even a theosophy, than a basis for religion. And there are many points of contact between it and Christian Science. It is a late instance of Greek idealism with intelligence as the key-note, salvation by knowledge, and the elimination of all that appears in consciousness save thought alone.

VI

Personality is much more truly attributed to God by those theories of reality which assign primacy to the will rather than to the idea. In this group the Hebrew religion is the forerunner. On the whole the New Testament conception, omitting a few references, flows in the same channel. St. Augustine, on the side of his theology represented by the *Confessions*, gives to the personality of God its full value, although he does not discuss the question of personality as such. This is, however, out of harmony with his presentation of the Trinity in his great treatise on that subject; in that work he reserves the term Person for Father, Son, and Holy Spirit, yet in a qualified sense; he used the term not because it was equivalent to the reality, but in order not to keep silence when something, however beyond human speech, must be affirmed.

Among later thinkers new initiatives have given a powerful impulse to the conception of the divine personality.

One is to be traced to Leibnitz, the other to Kant. Leibnitz has his doctrine of finite monads—creative reproductions of the Supreme Monad, each with its possibility of consciousness, depending upon an inner principle of development into full personality, according to the type of the Great Monad, God. From this conception has grown the pluralistic theory of the universe, with many centers of independent initiative yet with interchanges of activity. Although the human is patterned after the divine, yet the human monads are developing personalities; the divine is an eternally complete and perfect personality. To the other impulse, derived from Kant, are to be referred all those notions of the divine which represent it as a purposive activity, whether the activity be finite or infinite. Both pragmatism and pluralism are at home here. A contrast is drawn between "an Immutable Absolute or a God who strives." Under this head we must group the recent doctrines of God as finite, developing, struggling, suffering, sharing with man his defeats and victories, identified with the ideal tendencies of the world, having a history, and aims not less real than those of man. The two most fascinating advocates of this conception are Professor James and H. G. Wells; but they are only the leaders of an increasing number to whom the static God of traditional theology offers an unsatisfying notion.

In order more adequately to account for the opposing tendencies of good and evil in the world one writer has suggested "a Cosmic Soul, a struggling God . . . who has striven up out of the blind but not merely mechanical action of physico-chemical atoms, into the instinctive, spontaneous, half-conscious life of the planet. From there he has struggled up to the consciousness of the animal; and from there with ever growing power, purpose, and will, with the faint stirring of a definitely moral life within him, into the consciousness of the cave-dweller and the primitive savage. From there, with ever widening vision, with an acquisition of mental power and moral will, with an increasing determination to conquer those physical propensities which have clung to him since the time of his brute existence, but are now hindering his progress up the heights of righteousness and purity, he has struggled up and up until he has expressed himself in a Buddha, a Socrates, a Jesus, a Tolstoi, . . . in every human being." [1] Here is presented a conception of God which includes all the elements of personality. To substantiate the position appeal is made to Christian experience, which involves communion with a sympathetic because a struggling God, fellowship with him in his great task, a sense both of sin against him and of his forgiveness, a confidence that, despite evil and defeat, all the essential values will not only survive but ultimately triumph.

While the above view conserves the elements of personality and lends itself to an explanation of many baffling facts of evil as well as of good in the life of the world, it is a high price to pay for what is gained. It finds in God, however, what the human mind has never been and, it is safe to add, will never be satisfied to find there, namely, evil. In Zoroastrian thought Ahriman was invented to relieve Ahura Mazda of evil. In Hebrew thought evil spirits and in Christian thought Satan clear the skirts of God of all complicity with sin. Because God is holy, a gulf yawns between him and all evil. It is his shepherding love which goes in search of and brings back the wander-

---

[1] J. W. Macdonald, *The Christian Register*, Vol. 100, No. 30, pp. 206 ff.: "The Problem, Is God Omnipotent?"

ing one. If it is essential to the personality of God that
evil as well as good be included in the finite, struggling
God, we shall have to choose between personality and goodness, and it would not be hard to say which shall be
retained. Is there not some way by which evil and the
downward tendency here alleged may be eliminated from
the idea of God, and all that is essential to personality
remain?

With reference to this need two paths have been
opened; in one, personality is not denied to God but
rather affirmed in a higher degree. Replying to a charge
that his idealistic pantheism deprived God of properties necessary to support religious faith, Paulsen [1] vindi-
cated his position by saying: "It will not permit us to
define God by the concept of personality, simply because
the concept is too narrow for the infinite fullness and
depth of his being. Still, in order to remove the apprehension, we might call God a supra-personal being, not
intending thereby to define his essence, but to indicate
that God's nature is above the human mind, not below it.
And pantheism might add that it finds no fault with any
one for calling God a personal being in this sense. In so
much as the human mind is the highest and most important thing we know, we can form an idea of God only by
intensifying human attributes." Herbert Spencer says
that the Infinite and Eternal Energy from which all
things proceed is probably psychical and hyperpersonal.
Bradley,[2] replying to his own question, whether the Absolute has personality, says: "We can answer it at once in
the affirmative or negative according to its meaning.
Since the Absolute has everything, it of course must pos-

---

[1] *An Introduction to Philosophy*, p. 254.
[2] *Appearance and Reality*, pp. 531, 533.

sess personality. And if by personality we are to understand the highest form of finite spiritual development,
then certainly in an eminent degree the Absolute is personal." On the other hand, he adds: "If the term 'personal' is to bear anything like its ordinary sense, assur-
edly the Absolute is not merely personal. It is not personal, because it is personal and more. It is, in a word,
superpersonal. . . . It is better to affirm personality
than to call the Absolute impersonal. But neither mistake
should be necessary. . . . But it is better in this connection to call it superpersonal."

The motive of these writers is perfectly sound. Tested
by the highest degree of personality attained by man, we
have not reached the measure of God. We are told that
God is like Jesus Christ, and he is reported as saying, "He
that hath seen me hath seen the Father." And this is
true. But God, while he is like, is yet both other and
more than Jesus. Personality, so far as it is affirmed of
God, is far richer and more inclusive than the personality
of Jesus. If, as St. Paul declares, Christ is the head of
man and if he represents the highest achievement of
human personality, then we must call God super-personal,
a being who embraces all the essential properties of Jesus
and of all men, and possesses others which are beyond
their capacity.

The disparity between man and God has given rise to
an ingenious and widely accepted theory of the relation
between the two. Lotze took the position that human
personality is far from perfectly developed. He supported this by showing that our feelings and passions
which rise out of an obscure background never attain complete self-consciousness, and that the finite consciousness
does not contain within itself the conditions of its exist-

ence; it has to depend upon the stimulus of the cosmic whole or the non-ego for the initiation and growth of its activity. These are, so Professor Bowne who is Lotze's enthusiastic pupil and expounder affirms, limitations rather than sources of our self-consciousness. In our inner life are similar limitations before which we are partly passive and which in any case we cannot wholly control. Personality in us will always be incomplete, an ideal which is ours only conditionally and imperfectly. Since the ground of our existence is not in ourselves, we have never absolute control of our states. This is not, however, true of the Infinite Being; for since this Being has the ground of its existence in itself, it is independent of all outward conditions; it is therefore eternally self-sufficient. Accordingly, Lotze [1] turns the tables on previous conceptions of the relation of the human to the divine personality by saying: "Perfect personality is in God only; to all finite minds there is allotted but a pale copy thereof; the finiteness of the finite is not the producing condition of this Personality but a limit and hindrance to its development."

VII

May we hold that God is personal but is also less or more than personal? A position not wholly unlike this is taken by those who as Bradley have a doctrine of the Absolute of which God is part but not the whole. There are in the universe vast stretches of both space and time which but for the presence of man contain no intimation that a personal Being is at the heart of things. In sys-

---

[1] *Microcosmus*, Vol. II, p. 688. Cf. B. P. Bowne, *Theism*, pp. 167-168.

tems of worlds in process of formation or dissolution, in which perhaps no rational being has ever existed, none that could form social relations, or lift a face reflecting the glory of God, there would be no occasion for such a question to arise as that of the personality of God. If it were conceivable that a human consciousness had standing-place at a point of time far back in the evolution of the solar system where were only atoms with their exact and unvarying mathematical and mechanical relations, the formation of gases, of water, of mineral compounds, and the beginning of life in the sea, on the land, and in the air, looking forward, there would be nothing in the view to suggest the idea of personality in the Power to which these phenomena owed their appearance. Not that there was no material in these which later might contribute elements to this idea and be essential to its completeness. When, however, at another and later moment in the process of evolution, in that part of the universe with which we are most familiar and at the present hour, one looks back upon the unfolding of plan, the idea of personality rises and shines with clear and steady light. We see now that the latest crown the earlier stages, and contain a promise the full scope of which staggers the imagination. As we have already become aware, when life was less developed the full disclosure of God in its farthest ranges of spirit was not possible; yet this was immanent and only awaited the "fullness of time." When we consider, what is certainly possible, that always in some worlds in the universe there are beings to whom ethical and spiritual values are real, we do not have to think of God as himself developing step by step with the planetary life with which we are familiar and so becoming moral, whereas he was before ruled by necessity or driven on by a struggle for existence. On the contrary, moral values were from eternity essential elements of his nature and were revealed to such beings as were susceptible of response. Even if we find no warrant for the doctrine of angels, which has played a large rôle in Jewish and Christian theology, as giving to God a conscious environment where his glory might be felt, yet the aim which inspired this conception was worthy. The modern view of the world fully justifies the conjecture that if there are not angels, there have always been and will always be spiritual agencies wherever in any world conditions for such beings are ripe. If in those other worlds there have been sin and sorrow and death; if such souls are seeking to realize the aim of individual and social well-being, then we may believe that in the will of God they find forgiveness and comfort, the impulse and strength for living which mortals experience here. This may be stamped as an attenuated speculative notion, and it does not claim to be much more. It cannot be proved to be true, but it also cannot be disproved. If it is true, it greatly encourages the conviction that the good will of God has not sprung up first with the advent of man on the earth but is eternal and the source of good wherever goodness is found.

The question whether God is super-personal needs perhaps a more adequate putting. If it means that God is wholly above the personal plane, the answer must be a negative one; for we have just seen that there are elements in the divine nature which are also highest in man. Man may be regarded as the standard of personality. The personality of man has been defined as "selfhood, self-consciousness, self-control, and the power to know." [1] This definition shares the defects which shadow all definitions

---

[1] Bowne, *Personalism*, p. 226.

which are concerned with the highest values. The concrete personal life would hardly recognize itself under this scheme. The human selfhood is in the making and never comes to more than the bud or at most to the blossom stage. Self-consciousness, widened out to embrace the un- and the sub-consciousness, is in its farthest development fragmentary and incomplete; if not discontinuous, is intermittent; now and then like lightning flashes illumining its world yet disclosing the darkness out of which it rises. Self-control is never more than an imperfect mastery of the unfolding personal powers—an ever renewed struggle to unify the aims and especially the spirit of life. As for the power to know: with all his achievements man stands, an eager child, on the threshold of inquiry, with key in hand which experience alone can shape—the greatest secrets of the universe as truly hidden from him as from his most distant ancestors gazing with dumb awe at the show of things. In the nature of the case, human personality as we know it, however splendid its attainments, can never be anything else in the individual than transient and incomplete, in the race pressing on toward a receding goal.

If this is to be the standard of personality, then God is both sub- and super-, perhaps extra-personal. The sub-personal aspect of God appears in purposive activity in all such phenomena as the play of atoms, the formation of carbonic-acid gas, and the metereological cycle; the super-personal aspect is related to those purposive aims which lie beyond the comprehension of human intelligence. However far science pushes the boundaries of knowledge, the mystery, the wonder, the appeal to faith is not less than in the time of Job—the unconquerable faith that will not let go. God is not less than man, since man is one of the forms in which God reveals his creative will; but he who is the all-creating, the all-embracing One is to man as the infinite compared to a mathematical number low down in the scale. Something of God is beheld in the movement of atoms, something in the majestic sweep of worlds in space, and something in the spirit of man, but in none of these nor in all together at any single instant of time may one discover the entire meaning of God.

VIII

To assert that God is perfect personality of which man is but a faint copy is open to many objections. The path by which this definition is arrived at has been frequently traversed. The characteristic properties of the human personality are first ascertained; these are found to be imperfectly developed; their very existence as imperfect implies a perfect archetype. We are reminded of Aristotle's contingent motion which implies an Absolute Prime Mover, and of Leibnitz's finite monads and the Infinite Monad of which they are copies. But apart from the matter of terms the imperfect does not imply an actual perfect. The conception to which Lotze lent the influence of his great name has won assent more by its bold and startling paradox, which strikes one with the force of a discovery in a field where much confusion prevails, than by its correspondence with reality. It could be true only by the denial of features which are as essential to personality as those which are affirmed. It has to be assumed that to be a person one must have a self-centered existence, independent of an environment, having all of its resources within, every element of its being transparent to itself, all subsisting in changeless harmony and perfection. But we know nothing of such persons; persons that we know or indeed would wish to know belong to a very different order of experience. Sensations and perceptions; imaginations and memories; discursive reasoning and flashes of interpretative insight; dependence upon a physical organism which conditions birth, growth, animal spirits, and decay; love and hate; struggle, defeat, and success; friends and social ties; hopes and dreams of a life after death,—these and many other inner and outer conditions are inseparable from persons. We can form no conception of what a person would be from whom these were absent. And now one of two things; either we must redefine the idea of personality so as to eliminate all that gives zest to life, leaving only a bundle of attributes, such as selfhood and the power to know, or else, if we retain that which makes life personal and vivid, we must carry this over to God and find in him one who shares our struggle and suffering, our momentary defeats and glorious victories, himself the great Protagonist on the battlefield of the good.

The latter alternative is chosen by all those who advocate a finite God. They have brought God down from the heights where he has dwelt in secure isolation, inaccessible to all but speculative thinkers, and domiciled him among men; they have welcomed him who works and suffers and overcomes with them in the adventure of life. Thus endowed with human attributes and thereby raised to a vastly higher degree of excellence, he is the Person of whom all other personal beings are but faint copies; and he is this, not because he exists apart from men, but because he is one with, and yet in his very oneness superior to, all other persons. On the other hand, those who have

stripped God of the amazing variety of interests which
lend to human life its charm, and find in Intelligence or
the Trinity the secret of the life of God, and then assure
us that, in virtue of such qualities, God is the Supreme
Person, and that at best we are but imperfect reflections
of his personality, have removed God so far from us that
it matters little whether or not he exists as a Person.

The human heart in its hunger for God is not so easily
satisfied. It will never long accept stones for bread. Baffled in one direction, it strikes out new paths. At present
two of these are hard trodden by eager spirits. One is
the attention given to Jesus Christ. Despairing of a
direct and rewarding approach to God, men have turned
to Jesus. The word God is still often on men's lips, but
their intimate and most happy thought is about Jesus;
whatever else God is he will at least be as good as Jesus
was; indeed, Jesus is gradually taking the place of God
in the reverent affection of Christians. One has but to
read our hymns and books of devotion, to listen to popular sermons, scan Sunday-school lesson helps, examine
courses of lectures offered to theological students, and
converse with educated laymen to discover that interest
in God is secondary to interest in Jesus Christ.

The other path is that of social service. An increasing
number of serious people do not question that God is real,
a fit subject for metaphysics and for theological study,
but they believe that life is short and human need urgent;
by higher ideals of justice, by education, by sympathy
and co-operation society may be reorganized so that all
that was contemplated by the coming of the kingdom of
God may be realized apart from a definite reference to
God. It is not so much what God may be in himself,
that is, whether he is the Absolute Person of which human-

ity is a faint copy, as whether the value, which found expression in the life of Jesus, which have been all along associated with the idea of personality, and are in process of development in the social organism, are to be the creative forces in the new moral order of the world. Not infrequently the two paths are merged into one, and Jesus, as representative of personal values, is made the leader in the recreation of society. But however highly we estimate the power of Jesus and the social ideal, we cannot fail to recognize that in this program the dynamic of belief in a personal God as an impetus to individual and social regeneration is hindered and repressed.

There are still others who would wholly dispense with the idea of God, whether personal or not. They believe, on the one hand, that increasing knowledge will do away with the need of any reference to him as accounting for the world, and, on the other hand, that as the sense of social solidarity grows, the idea of God as personal helper will become unnecessary: men will find in their fellow-men what they formerly supposed they found in a superhuman Power. Unless, therefore, by a fresh definition of personality God is felt to stand in some most intimate and inseparable relation to men, he will take a diminishing place in the experience of men.

IX

We wish now to approach the idea of the personality of God from a different angle, not by way of analysis of the content of personality, but by relating it to purposive ends. If one confines himself to an analysis of the idea of personality, he reports his findings as selfhood, self-consciousness, self-control, and the power to know.

Without these the idea would be lacking in completeness. Unless, however, we can establish the personality of God on other grounds than the logical completeness of the idea, we are met with the same difficulty which confronted us in Anselm's famous argument. In order to avoid this, we shall interpret personality with reference to ends. Our proposition is that the notion and degree of personality are determined by the number and quality of ends which are connected with it. Ends exist in infinite and ever-changing profusion, and they are of all grades from lowest to highest, dissolving only to be renewed. Some are concerned with physical relations only, others are bound up with the process of life. A larger number and a higher grade of ends are involved in animal than in vegetable existences, and among animals there are also varieties and degrees. Yet among animals there are none which have purposive ends either high enough or numerous enough to make life personal; there are in them, as comparative psychology discloses, the beginnings of personality. It is only when we rise to man that we discover ends of such a character that we designate the one in whom these appear as personal. Even here they exist in manifold variety, at their beginnings hardly personal; in some individuals developing only in feeble degree, leaving them at the end of life only slightly personal; in others unfolding in splendid profusion, constituting them richly endowed persons. Purposive ends are, however, only partially present in any man, or indeed in all men together, but to the extent to which they are present, men are persons.

In the argument for the existence of God from ends in the universe, we saw that the universe gave abundant evidence of purposive activity, and that this purposive activity defined the nature of God. The character of the ends reveals the personal character of the Power operating in the world. If we could transport ourselves backward in the history of our planet to a time when we beheld only waters and barren rocks and encircling clouds, we should have no reason for raising a question concerning the personality of God, for no values had yet appeared to suggest or support such a thought. And even after vegetation sprang up both in the sea and on the land, and life emerged with its brood of swarming fish and huge beasts and fowls of the air, there was little or nothing to indicate the personal nature of the Power by which all these were brought into existence. It is only with the advent of man that moral values begin to play a part. There are indeed ends in the material realm connected with atoms and physical forces. The omnipresent Power cares for rhythmic motion and for beauty, but if this were all, it is doubtful if the personal character of this Power would ever have been suggested. Beyond the non-moral and the esthetic there has been created in our world in the development of human life a scale of moral and religious values. And we have a right to believe that what is true on our planet is not unique, but is duplicated in countless other worlds. While these values have come to birth in the human consciousness, they are not limited to the human consciousness alone. They have arisen in a universe which is not hostile to them, but is on their side. The Power inseparable from the world energizes mightily in their behalf. To man belongs much credit for great achievements in virtue, for his gains in purity of heart, for his love of truth, for his sense of social justice, and not least for the refinement and elevation of his religious sentiments. But these are not achievements of man alone. They have been partly created and partly forced upon him by an ideal-forming activity resident in the world. And because they are never complete, but are susceptible of indefinite expansion, they witness to an inexhaustible push in the Will that called them into being. So irresistible was this impetus felt to be that the Greeks called it Fate, so infallibly retributory that the Buddhist called it Karma, so superior to all earthly custom and authority that the Hebrew called it King of Kings and Lord of lords, so like the spirit and aims of the Saviour that Christians have called it the Father of our Lord Jesus Christ. In each instance the name was taken from the ends which are supremely active in the lives of men. This Power is not detached from these ends; it does not exist independently of them. It is personal to the extent that they are personal. It is not necessarily exhausted in the ethical and spiritual ends which appear in our experience. It would be idle to look primarily elsewhere for the personality of God than in the ends which are being realized in our world. But having found personality here we cannot limit it to our globe. Wherever moral beings are, there these ends are and there personality is. If our personality is constituted by the number, variety, and character of the values which emerge in our experence, this must be likewise true of the Reality in whom we live and move and have our being, only in a higher, even in an immeasurable degree.

Wherever there is truth there is God; wherever there is justice, loyalty, sacrifice, parental affection, co-operation, wise charity, religious devotion, there too is God; and he is both the source and the guarantor of these. In the deeper moments of our experience, when we are caught in the drift and whirl of dangerous seas, mast and rudder swept away, and we are threatened with swift and remediless overthrow, an inner voice is heard speaking in words as unmistakable as those of human speech, "Lo! I am with thee; be not dismayed; I will hold thee; in me thou art safe." The words are indeed of human origin and have come down from those who before us have passed through the deep waters, but they are the continued human response to an authentic inner yet objective Presence. The sense of guilt, the feeling of release from sin, the urge to conserve and increase moral values—these are the echoes in the human soul of a creative purpose in the soul of the universe. The social movement, with its conflicting tides of emotion and interest and aim, expresses not merely the diverse ends of many individuals, but the one end of a mighty Power whose impetus tends to originate, correct, enlarge, and complete all human endeavor. Such ends as these, saturated with ideal meaning, are the very essence of personality.

Looking backward upon the process of evolution, we can now see that the personal values which have arisen in man's life are only higher forms of that purposive Energy which appeared earlier in animal existences, for there, too, ages before man came into being, were the struggle for a fuller life, sympathy, sacrificial self-giving, the group consciousness, and co-operation.[1] In their mute acceptance of man's superiority and dominion they unconsciously confess that what they have realized in part is yet more richly fulfilled in man. Their development, occupying millions of years, is a silent prophecy of the continuation if not completion of their upward push in the fuller life of man. One vital impulse runs through it all—to express and fulfill itself in ends which are constitutive of personality.

-----

[1] Cf. Henry Drummond, *The Ascent of Man*, pp. 215 ff.

Not less significant is the further fact that the physical world is so organized and controlled as to be not only a congenial home for the ideal ends of animal and human life, but also to create that life of which the ends referred to are its characteristic notes. And since our planet is not independent and self-sufficient, but is an integral part both of the solar system and of the infinite systems in space, we must extend our conception to embrace these also, and see in the ends we discover here an instance of ends which are universal. And since these ends are purposive and culminate in ethical and spiritual values, we must pronounce them personal and the Reality of which they are the expression as personal.

In this presentation we have left at one side the common conception of personality, as selfhood, self-consciousness, self-control, and the power to know. Whether these are true of the Reality which is the indwelling and directive power in the universe, we may not be in position to say. It is not true in any sense which these words bear in our human experience and speech. This view of the personality of God may leave much to be desired by those who would psychologize the consciousness of God. But as this appears to be a task beyond us, we feel that we do not lose anything in renouncing the attempt. Since our conception of the personality of God rests not on a theory of the divine consciousness, but on the character of the ends which are disclosed in the universe, we are content to seek for no other definition or ground of belief in conceiving of it.

XIII. THE LIVING GOD

I

WE ARE now near the end of our task. It remains to
gather up the meaning of our discussion into a definition,
with a further interpretation of the implications involved
in it. The aim has been to expound ethical monotheism.
By ethical monotheism is meant a doctrine of God defined
in terms of purpose. In the discovery of purpose we have
discovered God. For us the question is not what God
may be as a metaphysical Absolute, but what he is as
active in relation to the world and to our highest good.
The ultimate ground of our belief in God is therefore not
metaphysical but moral—the necessity of God for the
completion of the meaning of our life: first, to provide a
principle of unity for our intelligence in relation to the
world; secondly, to guarantee the validity and fulfillment
of our ethical and spiritual ideals; finally, to ratify our
religious yearnings for redemption and union with God.

The principle of unity is a universal purposive Will
which is active in all worlds, its fundamental constituents
like the atomic constitution of the universe the same everywhere, entering into an infinite variety of combinations,
but under all circumstances a Creative Good Will. We
do not first formulate this conception of God and then
project it into the changing world, but we find it there
in the facts of the world and interpret these into a rational

302

ideal. So far as we believe that our ideals of individual and social development are in harmony with the "Power, not ourselves, that makes for righteousness," we are confident that they will not go down in defeat, but, corrected and enlarged, will find their fulfillment in the continued life of men. Our deepest need is to be set free from the narrow and debasing aims of self, from the passion that burns but does not purify, from the cleft will, from the unsocial spirit, the irreverent, Godless temper. We need to know that at the heart of things is a steadfast, righteous, almighty Will which tolerates no deviation from its rigid way, but sometimes violently arrests the transgressor, and tenderly draws him back into paths of peace. We need also to be assured that, while social regeneration may be delayed, it cannot be killed; it will surely make its way, and that too by a thousand agencies, some conflicting, some co-operating—the church, the state, the school, the family, industrial reforms, commercial treaties, political agitation, the printing-press; through all "worketh the same Spirit," urging toward the goal of a redeemed humanity. To believe in a glorious future for the race, we must believe in a God whose purpose of good can never know defeat. To believe in such a God carries the fulfillment of our dearest hope.

II

Our idea of God is partly a postulate of faith. This is the Reality which must be, if our hopes are to attain their fruition. Here we follow in the path of the Old and the New Testament. The supreme characteristic of the prophets, Jesus, and the apostles was the clearness, certainty, and enthusiasm of their faith in God. Yet this was not the product of theoretical reason, but an attitude, an affirmation, an expectancy, in which they gathered up the meaning of their own future and that of the world in terms of a Purpose, at first in part other than their own, but with which they identified their will. They knew that their faith must be true, not because they had experienced its full truth, but because without it life would be robbed of content,

"And dust and ashes all that is."

They were unconsciously practicing Anselm's dictum, "*Credo ut intelligam*"—I believe in order that I may know. Had they waited for their idea of God until they had fully explicated it by experience, they would have been forever destitute of it. It was the necessary presupposition of this experience; without it, the experience would have been entirely different. It was indeed a postulate, but it was something more, and in that "more" lay its secret. One may believe something to be true, but at the same time be cold or neutral toward it. To these men, on the contrary, their belief was like a fire in the bones; it renewed its energy in every new experience, however resistent and contradictory; for the most part developing itself in the common social tasks, yet in the hour of extremity and anguish disclosing its richest content. This is and must remain a permanent feature in our idea of God. Not that we shall follow Kant in a will that there be a God, without the hope that we shall ever be in contact with the Reality which we thus assume to exist. Naturally, if God is defined by ends, and these ends are progressively realized, one who stands at the beginning of the ways can know only what has been actualized. When a man and a woman plight their troth at the altar, they understand little of what it means—"for better for worse, for richer for poorer, in sickness and in health, till death do us part,"—but the energy of their love contains within itself the fulfillment of their pledge. To-day, however long the idea of God has been cherished in human hearts, we are still only on the threshold of our knowledge of this infinite and eternal Good Will. Yet even so, our devotion to it is measured not by our knowledge, but by our inward surrender to what is implicit in our faith.

Ethical monotheism, instead of remaining merely a postulate, presents itself to experience for verification. It is an assumption on which the great adventure of life waits. It holds in its hand the good of all the days to come. If it begins in faith, it is transmuted by experience into knowledge.[1] It has to be held fast in the face of seeming contradictions. For in the first place, circumstances which are not of our choosing, over which, too, we have no control, appear at times utterly to confute its truth; and in the second place, fidelity to this Will forces us into conditions in the midst of which the very survival of faith in it seems impossible. But, on the other hand, one condition of its being permanently true for us is that we are true to it. Naturally, if the postulate of the Good Will were ultimately to be discredited, it would have to go the way of other exploded assumptions; such a contingency, in view of the meaning which this idea has already acquired, is so remote as to be entirely negligible. Since it involves the entire scope and all the values of human experience, not only now but also hereafter, its verification is necessarily progressive and always incomplete. It is therefore continually susceptible of enlargement and also of correction. Accordingly, we need never

---

[1] Cf. Ps. xxxiv, 8; John viii, 31-32.

be disturbed that the concrete definition of God changes with each new generation, becoming richer in proportion to its experienced content; we should be profoundly thankful that it can never be embedded in a fixed and final dogma. When through experience that which was a postulate of faith becomes an object of knowledge, the knowledge becomes a basis for further ventures of faith and wider expectancies and fulfillment: "*Intelligo ut credam*"—I know in order that I may believe.

Of these two poles of the idea of God neither can be dispensed with; one is not less essential than the other. The idea of God as a Purposive Will may be true, and if so, is worthy to command the supreme devotion of the human will. It can be known to be true only if in response to that devotion it proves itself valid by filling life with a divine content and eternal meaning.

This must not be understood as if at any conceivable stage of advance in our knowledge of the divine Good Will we shall be able to include all reality within its scope. There will always be something to say for naturalism, for dualism, for an immanent and conscious tendency in things. Strive as we may to bring all refractory elements into harmony, some still prove recalcitrant. In every religion is such a remainder which has been handed over to an alien and hostile power—demonic spirits, Satan, Ahriman, Fate, intractable matter, a place of everlasting torment for the obdurately bad. It would be of no use for us to blink this age-long, unresolved conflict; it is with us still, in forms no less benumbing to faith than at any earlier day. Yet in spite of all untoward and unreconciled facts, we ally ourselves with those of all ages—prophets, poets, philosophers, founders of commonwealths,

saints—who believe that goodness is the heart of things,
and that it has creative power to penetrate and transform the life of man; and this not without recognition of
the evil which confronts and withstands it, and not ignoring the struggle in which evil gives place to good. A
light-headed girl, upon whose steps the shadows have not
yet fallen, may come tripping down the primrose path
with lilting song:

> "God's in his heaven,
> All's right with the world!" [1]

But those to whom

> "Years have brought the philosophic mind"

know that unless God comes down out of his heaven, and
awakens and confirms in men the will to good, the world
will not be right. Jesus beheld Satan falling as lightning
from heaven, and in the instantaneous vision was concentrated the victories of a million years; yet to his followers
was committed the task of fragmentary and age-long realization of his dream.

No doubt it is this motive which has originated the
more recent conceptions of God. Instead of a Being who
dwells in undisturbed felicity in a transcendental world,
God is here, among men, in the very midst of their experience of good and evil; one who strives, who struggles, and
fights with men on the side of the good; who suffers pain
and sometimes defeat in the conflict, yet undaunted by
momentary failure ever renews the attack and progressively wins. However inadequate such a picture may be,
it has probably done more than any and all other concep-

---

[1] Browning, *Pipa Passes.*

tions of God to bring him back and down into the struggles of our human world. Centuries ago Jesus, whose name was to be Immanuel (God with us), ate and drank with men, and they felt that God was in very truth with them. But after his death, they believed that he was taken up into heaven, "a cloud received him out of their sight," and he was gone. Although he bequeathed his spirit to his followers, yet it has always been far more difficult for them to realize his spiritual than his bodily presence. The Father was remote and unseen; the Son had withdrawn into the heaven whence he came; the Spirit, if among men, was an impalpable presence which came and went. It was natural for the heart of man to turn to the Virgin Mary, the apotheosized woman with the mother-heart to be to troubled souls what Jesus had been. But now the tide has turned; the barriers have been thrown down; once more all that Mary, the "Mother of God," the Spirit as the comforting Presence, and Jesus as the incarnate Savior, stood for as ministers to human need, is provided in this newer conception of God. He has come down from his inaccessible heights and has joined himself to men, making common cause with them in their endeavors after the greater good. He is the Great Adventurer; he is the unconquerable Fighter; he is the Intimate Companion; in sickness he is the tender Nurse; in death with soothing touch he draws the soul forth into an ampler realm. Some of these suggestions may seem crude and irreverent, and perhaps they are so; they may err on the side of familiarity as much as the older doctrine erred on the side of exaltedness; and they may diminish the spirit of worship which was begotten by the thought of God as "high and lifted up." But at any rate, there is now no partition-wall between God and man: God is the immanent Spirit in the spirit of man, Life of his life, Love of his love.

At the same time, there is no ground for disquietude lest the other aspect of God be lost sight of. We shall never be so arrogant as to claim to know all. There will always be an unexplored remainder—the Unknown beyond experience, inviting but impenetrable; and in the presence of the Great Mystery the spirit will give expression to its hushed feeling in reverence and awe. In the New Jerusalem the seer beheld no temple; but so long as human hearts are on this side of the veil, there will be churches and altars and worship. In all our world there is no sight so impressive as that of a multitude, or even of two or three, bending low in adoration before the unseen, unfathomable God. There will always be the great hymns of the church, breathing out aspiration, confession, thanksgiving, in which man brings his frail and yearning self to the Eternal. And the greatest thinkers, as Plato and St. Paul, will not cease to attribute to God more than our human measuring-rod can compass. After completing the most elaborate theodicy which issued in the cry, "O the depth of the riches, both of the knowledge and the wisdom of God!" a deeper hush falls upon the spirit of the brooding apostle, and the cry completes itself: "How unsearchable are his judgments, and his ways past finding out!" The drama of the world-history, written in rocks and stars and the vanishing tablets of human experience—who can decipher it? Who is worthy to break the seals and to open the book which holds the secrets of the future, even of man's life on the globe?

Those who, as Horace Bushnell, Samuel Butler, and H. G. Wells, advocate a finite God, are not satisfied to leave the matter there. They, and indeed all who think of God as finite, feel the need of an infinite background of reality out of which rises the divine personage whom we call God. Here we have again a witness to the inexpugnable conviction voiced by Job: "Lo, these are but the outskirts of his ways; and how small a whisper do we hear of him! But the thunder of his power, who can understand?" (Job xxvi, 14). Such words carry an unanswerable rebuke to the smug complacency of those to whom, as to Job's friends, the entire will of God lies bare—and as barren—as the sands of the desert. More reverent is Mr. Wells, with all his seeming irreverence, than are those who profess to have sounded the abysmal depths of the divine Will. Ethical monotheism is partly a postulate of faith, presenting itself for verification, and partly an attitude in which "deep answers to deep," with no articulate words to voice its meaning—

" . . . with no language but a cry."

III

The conception of God as an ideal-forming Principle, a Creative Good Will, retires into the background, if it does not wholly dispose of several points of view from which theories of God have been framed. 1. God is defined as Substance, a notion advocated by nearly all theologians, with the exception of Duns Scotus, Leibnitz, and Schleiermacher. It was felt that there must be some permanent basis in which the various properties cohered and which therefore gave them their indissoluble unity. It did not matter that there was no conceivable relation between the rational nature and the individual substance. The doctrine gave rise to many positions which have been provocative of controversy, which but for this doctrine of substance would never have arisen. The doctrine of the Trinity in its traditional form is a case in point. A recent statement [1] of it runs as follows: "The three Persons in the Trinity are truly persons in the sense that each one has a degree of independent thought and feeling and will, and yet these three cohere in the higher synthesis of one unitary spirit and life." If we substitute the word "Substance" for "spirit and life," we shall find the meaning clear, and we shall see perfectly the background from which the conception rises. A very different meaning would, however, be assigned to the Trinitarian doctrine, providing it was retained, if we think of God not as Substance, but as Creative Will. If, on the other hand, the unity of God is in question, it is not the unity of substance, but of purposive action which embraces all ranks of being and endures forever.

2. The conception of God as Purposive Will relieves us of the attempt to reconcile and unite the metaphysical and the religious interests of the traditional idea of God. Both of these notions—the metaphysical and the religious —have been held by great thinkers at the same time, and because they were supposed to be homogeneous have on equal terms been incorporated into the dogmas of the church and in theological teaching. But these notions have really nothing in common. They belong to different universes of discourse. They have lived together in peace only when and because their incompatibility was not perceived: one is rational, the other ethical; one static, the other dynamic; one is abstract, the other living and personal. To the static aspect of the idea of God have been referred the divine properties conceived of as at rest back

---

[1] J. H. Snowden, *op. cit.*, p. 36.

of the active properties; to the ethical or religious aspect
has been referred the activity by which the kingdom of
God is established among men. For us, however, this distinction does not exist. In God is no potentiality beyond
the actual energy of willing. There is perfect rest, but
this is as Schopenhauer pointed out the tireless action of
will. There are indeed potentialities in God, not, however,
as latent power, but precisely those ideal-forming activities which have been eternally operative and will yet bring
forth other forms of beauty and goodness in the world of
his delight.

> " . . . God fulfills himself in many ways,
> Lest one good custom should corrupt the world."

3. In addition to the idea of Substance as characteriz-
ing the nature of God, various other conceptions have
been suggested, as, for example, the Godhead distinguished
from God; an ineffable Reality back of all manifestation;
a perfect self-consciousness complete apart from the universe. These conceptions come to us with a variety of
backing—by a theory of revelation, of being, of experience, of knowledge, and of language. (1) We are told
by Mansel in his *Limits of Religious Thought* that the
entire content of dogma, relating to God as the Trinity
and the Person of Christ, lies beyond the reach of our
rational power and can be known, if at all, only by revelation. We are in a field of mystery where unless God
draws aside the veil we are shrouded in darkness. The
use of the reason is purely regulative, that is, it is limited
to reducing to logical order what has been received by
revelation. This appears to be the common position occupied by theologians in expounding the doctrine of the

Trinity. (2) There is also a theory of being which is essentially that of the mystics. From Plotinus on to the latest advocate of mysticism, man in his most awakened moments hears, not authentic sound, but only its echo, beholds not light, but only the shadow of light, stretches forward to a goal which withdraws itself as he approaches; his deepest longing is to sink himself in the ineffable One where all differences are annulled and all movement forever stilled. (3) From a very different point of view we are told that we are so limited by the nature of experience that here below we can have no knowledge of aught but the phenomenal world, yet are so constituted that we must postulate a transcendental world in which God is eternally real, although we are incapable of entering into personal relations with him. This position is supported by a theory of knowledge which offers a rational justification of it. (4) We have finally a theory of language according to which all ideas are compelled to clothe themselves in words, and words have only a representative value. Even the Trinity is no more than an instrumental manifestation of the divine for the sake of redemption; what God is in reality back of this dramatic representation lies beyond the power of man to know.

From our point of view, the dualism involved in these and other theories of God does not exist. Not that we know or can comprehend the entire meaning of God. Our actual knowledge is, however, summed up in Purposive Will realizing itself in ends. So far as these ends are known, God is known. And there are not two sources of knowledge of God, one referred to natural revelation which is shared by all men, another referred to supernatural revelation as communicating truth about God which the human mind cannot otherwise become aware of. The

being of God is not other than his will, and his will does
not exist outside of a world of space and time and conscious beings.   Nowhere is God more real and never will
he be more active than in the immediate circle of our
conscious life.   If our experience is not in contact with
his energizing activity here and now, we shall not elsewhere and at another time be in touch with it.   And if our
language concerning God cannot extricate itself from
its earlier function as representing physical objects, and
it is still compelled to body forth its meaning in imagery
which betrays its sensuous origin, this does not signify
that the Reality, if we could know it, would be something
essentially different from what our words enshrine.   The
attempt to separate the Godhead from God is futile—the
Godhead incomprehensible and ineffable, God revealed in
creation and redemption.   There is no God back of God.
To hold with Augustine, on the one hand, that God is the
unmoved and inconceivable Absolute, and, on the other
hand, that he is the sole predestinating cause of salvation,
or with Calvin that the will of God is utterly inscrutable
and yet is the source of both election and reprobation, or
with Herbert Spencer that the Ultimate Reality is Unknown and Unknowable, and yet is an Infinite and Eternal
Energy, the First Cause, and of the same nature as that
which wells up in the human consciousness—this is to
divide a unity which admits of no cleft.   All of these conceptions originate in a common fallacy, that the world of
our experience is different from a theoretical world which
transcends our experience.   With a world which transcends experience and a conception of God which alleges
something in him which is other than what is manifest in
our world we can have no concern.   Speculation regarding
such supposititious matters is unproductive.   Exceedingly

happy are the words of one who was of all men perhaps the greatest sinner in this regard: "Cold and frivolous are the speculations of those who employ themselves in disquisitions on the essence of God, when it would be more interesting to us to become acquainted with his character, and to know what is agreeable to his nature. For what end is answered by professing with Epicurus that there is a God who, discarding all concern about the world, indulges himself in perpetual inactivity? What benefit arises from the knowledge of a God with whom we have no concern?" [1]

There is no intention here of warding off a speculative in favor of a positive doctrine of God. Speculation is of high antiquity and numbers among its adherents the most famous thinkers; it is an inalienable prerogative of the human reason. But whatever lustre attaches to it by reason of age or splendid achievements, it must not usurp the seat of authority when truth near at hand and adequate to support life is available. However prolonged our existence and in whatever world passed, we could never know that God is Absolute Thought or that there is an abysmal Godhead back of God, but every day in any sphere we can be aware that God comprises the sum of our ideal interests, and that he is not only *a*, but *the*, Creative Good Will. When we try to thwart that Will, our deed reacts upon us with abortive and fatal futility. When we work with it, individual aims and social endeavors are furthered and confirmed. To have discovered this is the immemorial glory of the Hebrew prophets. Jesus gave expression to it through all his ministry, but most in the shadows of Gethsemane and the cross. And history is one long confirmation of it.

---

[1] Calvin, *Institutes of the Christian Religion*, Vol. I, p. 50.

IV

Our idea of God disposes of another misconception, namely, that there is in the divine nature a tension between justice and mercy. This misconception has been thus stated: "God may be merciful; he must be just." This assertion raises the whole question of justice and love and the forgiveness of sins, and the relation of these to the divine will. The question is made more difficult by reason of two considerations: one, the statements of the Scriptures, the other, the experience of life. The sacred writers are at one with the greatest of the Greek tragedians, that retribution for both good and evil is a universal law, and they are agreed in referring it to such a source as guarantees its inviolable execution. A prophet of the Old Testament avers that "the soul that sinneth, it shall die," and an apostle of the New Testament announces that "Whatsoever a man soweth, that shall he also reap." The entire Bible may be regarded as an illustration of the truth of the words here transcribed—stern, pitiless, and without exception, involving the innocent no less than the guilty in the sweep of its resistless law. It presents the will of God as indeed "a consuming fire." [1] His jealousy for obedience to his law—the progressive social ideal of the time, his bringing to naught the deeds of evil-doers, sometimes with fierce and terrible destruction, always infallibly just, often rough in execution, reveals a will whose very structure is justice. The impression created by the Scriptures is carried to a complete confirmation in the wider continued experience of men. It may happen that men do not know what justice is, they may even be striving to realize it, but, choosing the wrong

---

[1] Heb. xii, 29.

path, go more or less blindly to their aim; yet this neither delays nor bends the justice of the divine will. This is invariable, inexorable, inescapable. And we are ever held within the circle of such a God: "His justice which knows no flaw and brooks no evasion and cannot be swerved; . . . his hatred of sin, terrible and flaming, a hatred which will send men through a thousand hells, if they will have them." [1] Such is the justice of God, sometimes secret, at other times open, always sure as the conservation of energy and the swing of atoms.

Experience reveals another law not less pervasive than that of justice, namely, that of love. Side by side with the stern demands of justice and its penalty for transgression, the Bible comes to us freighted with its love, its sympathy, its compassion, its persuasive gentleness—a revelation of the heart of God. And from the day when our first parents began to suffer the long doom of sin and "God made them coats of skin and clothed them," to the last vision of the redeemed when he shall clothe them with "fine linen, bright and pure," there is never a moment in between when the divine loving will is not pouring out its wealth of good. In spite of devastating physical forces and ferocity of animal life, we may still say that the structure of our world is beneficent and in the animals below man are the beginnings of beautiful love. Appalling is the contrast between the unweaponed gentleness of the dove and the tearing beak of the eagle, the trusting simplicity of the lamb and the cruel strength of the tiger; and one does not wonder at the poet's startled question as he contemplates the two—

"Did he who made the lamb make thee?"

---

[1] Albert Parker Fitch, *Preaching and Paganism,* p. 161.

It is not less hard to feel that to the same source are to be traced justice and mercy. Almost by instinct we believe in a rigorous and unbending righteousness; but only by an effort do we convince ourselves that love is equally fundamental in our world; particularly is this the case when we think of the forgiveness of sins. For here we meet a double difficulty: first, we seem to require an exception to the inexorable law of justice, and secondly, we do not see how love can supplant justice. There is, however, incontrovertible evidence of the arrest of wicked purposes in the hearts of men, the beginning of new impulses, desires, and aims. There is release from the bondage of the past. There is emancipation to a better spirit. There is a sense of oneness with God. Most persons connect this experience with a particular theory of God's relation to it, alleging an atoning deed on the part of God as a condition of the forgiveness of sins, in which justice is satisfied, in which too a different attitude is created in God toward the sinner, even that of clemency. Yet the fatal tension between justice and love continues— they never meet.

The antinomy thus set up in the divine Good Will between these needs somehow to be resolved. This cannot, however, be brought about by any expedient in which the divine justice is relaxed, deflected, arrested, transmuted, or in any way becoming other than it is, but only by holding fast its principle in undeviating operation. We no longer define miracle as suspension, interruption, or violation of a law of nature. "Justice is man's dearest possession." Once let an exception be acknowledged in the working of the divine will and we may as well throw overboard reliance on any principle or law of the divine order.

Love has been defined as the opposite of justice. Justice holds the even scales of desert and reward; love would ignore desert and turn reward into a gift. Justice would punish; love would arrest penalty and confer blessing. Justice would kill; love would make alive. Justice would reduce all to law; love would annul law and draw men into the realm of grace. But love is not to be so contrasted with justice. If love is anything, it is a higher justice. The father of the prodigal, having made the utmost expression of his love to his younger son, replied to the elder son's charge of injustice: "It was meet to make merry and be glad; for this thy brother was dead and is alive again, and was lost and is found."

Thus love does not violate justice; it is an interpretation and expression of justice which reveals more fully its essential nature; it is not love until it is justice in the highest degree. Perfect justice would leave nothing to be desired in the relation of man to man and of man to God; and perfect love could offer neither more nor less than this. To join the word "holy" to love adds nothing to its meaning when applied to God.

In order to realize the force of the contention that justice and love are two names for the same divine quality, we may consider the relation of the justice of God to sin and the forgiveness of sin. Sin is not what the antinomy of justice and love assumes, nor is it what that theory of the atonement based upon this opposition requires. Sin is not the completely individual thing, involving the degree of knowledge, capacity, and responsibility which this doctrine demands. No one has ever been willing to find the entire source of sin in the individual, not even in the first man. It has been explained as originating in our first parents, in Satan, in ignorance, in untrained will, in weak and diseased physical bodies, in untoward environment. It has been described as an anachronism, wherein men continue actions of animals under conditions which are unsuited to their performance, and the legitimate habits of an earlier social condition live on when they have been outgrown or outlawed. Whatever explanation we have to offer for the fact of sin, we cannot load exclusive responsibility on any man or on all men. Man with his frailty, his failure, and his sin is the product of the universe, that is, of the indwelling Power which has shaped our world and all that is in it. In the long process of the evolution of life and well-being, in one corner of the globe

> "out of darkness came the hands
> That reach through nature, moulding man."

Man did not ask to be born; he has chosen but little of the conditions in which success and defeat arise; he aims at a good and mistakes the path to its accomplishment. He is rarely as guilty as his envious or pharisaic fellowman adjudges him to be. In his sorrow for his sin and despair of release from the bands of habit and debasing social ties, he looks upward and still more deeply within, and there he comes upon the Power to which he owes his being, his circumstances, and even his temptations, the Power which has beset him behind and before, in which lies all his hope, and he cries:

> "Thou wilt not leave us in the dust;
> Thou madest man, he knows not why;
> He thinks he was not made to die;
> And thou hast made him: thou art just." [1]

---

[1] *In Memoriam.*

Between these two poles of human frailty and the justice of God our lives are passed. For the truth of this we do not have to resort to a weak sentimentality; the sober insight of prophets, poets, social workers among the submerged tenth, those who seek to reform men and women with criminal record, the leaders in religious education of the young,—all find in this a key to their outlook upon human life. To our own poet Whittier [1] we owe a beauful wording of this truth:

> "He who knows our frame is just,
> Merciful and compassionate,
> And full of sweet assurances
> And hope for all the language is
> That he remembers we are dust."

In the forgiveness of sins we are in the presence of the same sense of justice. For forgiveness is not less an act of justice than of love; indeed, it is justice under another name. Forgiveness does not annul the past; it does not abolish the consequences of sin; it does not transmute acquired dispositions; it only initiates but does not complete the substituting and transforming of the stored-up content of the sub-conscious self into a heaven of holy tendencies. He who feels that his sins are forgiven begins to fulfill those ends both individual and social which are to constitute him a person; these ends are the only justification for bringing him into existence, for forgiving his sin, and for making him part of that moral and spiritual order in which the greater glory of God is revealed and realized. He has now begun to conserve and advance the values which give to the world and human

---

[1] *Snow Bound.*

life their highest meaning. Jonathan Edwards has a flaming discourse on "The Justice of God in the Damnation of Sinners." We would substitute for this "The justice of God in the Salvation of Sinners," initiated as this is by the forgiveness of sins. Two writers of the New Testament have stated this in words which have formed the theme of a hundred thousand sermons and have led millions of souls to the new life. One said that God had taken in hand the doing away with the sins of men, "that he might be just, and the justifier of him that hath faith in Jesus;" [1] the other, who was not blind to the deadly nature of sin, wrote, "If we confess our sins, he is faithful and just to forgive us our sins, and to cleanse us from all unrighteousness." [2]

V

We turn now to the more personal relations involved in our conception of God—prayer, co-operation with God in the tasks of life, divine sympathy and comfort in sorrow.

Our idea of God will bring about a profound change in the conception of prayer. It would be difficult to formulate the various notions and especially feelings which are commonly associated with this experience; these differ with the individual groups as influenced by tradition, experience, education, and the world-view. We shall not attempt a description of them or an explanation of the reason for their divergences. Ours is a more modest task, —to show the attitude of prayer which is involved in our

---

[1] Rom. iii, 26.
[2] I John i, 9.

idea of God.   This will be limited to three particulars:
adoration, confession, petition.

1. When we think of adoration there rises before us
a prostrate form symbolizing a spirit overladen with a
sense of the majesty of God.   The feeling is inarticulate,
or if it utters itself in words, it is aware how inadequate
these are to convey its meaning.   We give expression to
this attitude in song, as in the great processional which
echoes the adoring praise of a scene in the Revelation:

"Holy, holy, holy! all the saints adore thee;
   Casting down their golden crowns around the glassy
     sea;
  Cherubim and seraphim falling down before thee,
   Which wast, and art, and evermore shalt be"

In a previous paragraph we have seen how such a feeling
will never be outgrown.   Now we wish to point out other
avenues along which this spirit will move in our time.   As
the earlier adoration was begotten in the great crises of
experience where the Deliverer immeasurably surpassed the
world and all its forces of evil, so now our attitude toward
God will take its rise in experience not less rich in meaning to-day.   There are three of these.

The first is the new appreciation of the natural world
which is a late product of the human spirit.   Not that the
Psalmists, Homer, and Vergil have no eyes for the beauty
and the terror of the universe.   But the conscious seeking
for the strange and wonderful, the going in search for
beauty as one searches for hid treasure, exploring foreign lands to come in sight of new visions of loveliness
and grandeur is something which had its birth with the
Romantic spirit.   A new worship has arisen.   It is not

now God in his transcendent isolation and in the puritanical sternness of his ethical demands, robbing life of half its charm, but beauty that draws men on into the shrine of worship.

> " 'Beauty is truth, truth beauty,'—that is all
> Ye know on earth, and all ye need to know." [1]

A new temple is therefore reared, a new altar consecrated, and the worshipers bend low before the strangeness, the mystery, and the splendor of the spirit that makes "everything beautiful in its time."

Another attitude is created by the discoveries of physical science. The infinitely great and the infinitely little; the play of hidden forces which have begun to yield up their meaning to the painstaking inquirer; the perfect obedience which Nature demands of him whom she will serve; the complete emptying of conceit and presupposition; the humility and teachableness which she will reward with knowledge; the assurance that we are only on the borderland of a yet more wonderful world than imagination has dreamed; and withal, that however far we penetrate into the heart of things, we are still and shall always be in the presence of an Infinite and Eternal Mystery. Here again is another temple and another altar, and hither come worshipers, some in academic robes, others in the rough garb of those who are busied with metals and gases, with earth and rocks, with bodies both living and dead. Here are no blatant voices, but spirits alert with expectancy, silent with surprise, hushed with reverence and awe.

Another group rises before us, who confess to the elevation of the ethical ideal and the sanctity of the moral

---

[1] Keats, *Ode on a Grecian Urn.*

order,—a moral order not finished and complete, like the New Jerusalem, hidden in heaven, some day to be let down bodily to earth, but an order progressively realized among men, whose realization may be delayed but not destroyed —"which eye hath not seen, nor ear heard, nor hath it entered into the heart of man to conceive." Here again is a temple, with altar and worshipers bending low in recognition of an Almighty Power, who out of the struggle and confusion in our social world, is creating a new Humanity in which his Spirit shall completely dwell.

These are the newer forms of the adoring mind as real to men and as dear to God as was the worship of Ezekiel or of the Revelation. To this ideal-creating Power, Beauty and Truth are not less precious than are Moral Values; those who adore in one or other of these temples are equally dear to the God of all.

2. According to our idea of God confession of sin will complete itself in two aspects—word and deed. There is oral confession to one who has been wronged. If one repents of an evil action or course of life, this may be all that is required to set his feet in the path of virtue. But a word of confession carries the resolve a step further; it is a fuller expression of the purpose of good; it commits one to the fulfilling of his intent; it brings the social influences into play; it carries with it the force of a spoken contract and the creation of a new social expectancy. Much of what is said here is valid for the "confessional" where the confession of sins is voluntary and sincere and the priestly confessor represents the moral and spiritual values which are involved in the transaction. Still more significant is the deed of him who repents of his sin. He is now active on the side of the moral order; he assumes relations with good men, which will reinforce

his own good intentions and make it harder for him to fall back into his evil past; he begins to be at one with the Good Will in its creation of good in the world. In some quarters there is a tendency to disparage good works, but there is no danger that there will be too many of these. It is only by good works that good will can be expressed and established among men. As there is no sin against God which is not at the same time a sin against one's fellow-men, so there is no good which embraces one's fellow-men but at the same time involves God in its sweep.

3. Our hardest problem confronts us in the matter of prayer as petition. Volumes have been written on such questions as, How to pray, What to pray for, Remarkable answers to prayer, Prayer and the laws of nature, and the Reflex influence of prayer. These and other questions like them we leave at one side. We shall ask only what is the meaning of prayer and what its relation to the Purposive Good Will.

We pass by the prayers of the church, venerable, stately, fitted for every occasion, distilling the experience, the wisdom, the aspiration of the greatest souls. We shall best reach the heart of the subject by analysis of two prayers, one, the Lord's prayer, the other, the prayer of Jesus in Gethsemane. The Lord's prayer is divided into two sections, in the first of which is a recognition and surrender to the divine will. In order that the nature of that will may be more clearly perceived it is addressed to a paternal Being; it is social in its scope; ideally fulfilled in heaven; to be reverently accepted and obeyed. Such is the attitude toward the divine Good Will with which one begins his day, takes up his tasks, and relates himself to the world of men and things around him. Then comes the second section which concerns personal needs: first, physical, those which belong to the providential order of the world; secondly, spiritual, those which are related to the fulfillment of the moral and spiritual ideal. Central to this prayer is the divine will which prescribes our ideal, provides for our need, and judges our spirit. Its use by every variety of believers in God and its connection with all the Liturgies of the church, show that men have found it to be, what in reality it is, a universal prayer. Although Jesus said, "Thus pray ye," yet in the Garden of Gethsemane we have a very different type of prayer. The order of petition is reversed; instead of the will of God as first, we have at the outset the most urgent thrusting forward of an individual wish, so pressing and violent that it expresses itself "in strong crying and tears." This, however, at length gives place to another mood, the will of God swings back into the forefront of the field of desire and aim, and the cry is heard, "Not my will, but thine be done!" And now the strangest of all paradoxes appears: Jesus' will finds its fulfillment in the divine Good Will!

Different as these prayers seem, they are at heart one. They equally lay bare the nature of all petition,—to seek and to find the meaning of the Purposive Good Will in every particular condition, and then to make that will our own. This may give rise to a struggle, a fierce and bitter conflict between the lower and the higher self, the individual and the social well-being; the human and the divine may at the outset seem in sharp, irreconcilable opposition; but the prayer is not ended until the lower is merged in the higher, the individual finds his larger life in the social realm, and the longing completes itself in the infinite and eternal Good Will. A self-willed child takes no account of the wise purpose of a good father but

insisting upon his own claim defeats the fulfillment of any
part of his wish. But this is not prayer. The first condition of fruitful prayer is to accept the world we live in, in
every way to strive to ascertain the meaning of it and how
to realize its ends,—and this is the function of prayer,—
and then with heart and soul give oneself to the furthering
of the Divine Will in which alone our wish comes to its
consummation.

VI

Our conception of God as Purposive Will throws light
on our part in the realizing of ends in the world. 1. We
shall not think of ourselves as pawns on a chess-board,
moved to and fro at the will of a master hand. However
we minimize the initiative of the human will, we cannot
reduce it to zero, save at the price of exchanging a person for a thing. In the analogy suggested by Jesus, "I
am the vine, ye are the branches," while the branch cannot
wholly originate its fruit, yet it has a unique and indispensable part in the production of it.

2. In the task which we engage in we do not work in
companionship with the divine will only. We can establish no exclusive claim nor acquire any patent right to
material or method of work in association with God alone.
We are indeed fellow-workers with God, but he does not
lend himself to any private enterprise with which he and
we are exclusively concerned. This was the fallacy of the
mystics. St. Simeon Stylites and the Blessed Henry
Suso, one on his pillar, the other in his cell, renouncing every common interest with their comrades in the task
of life, dreamed that they were having God all to themselves, acquiring sainthood by abnegation of all social

relations and every physical good. It has been said that
the secret of the profound religious experience of Augustine lay in the reciprocal relations "God and the soul, the
soul and God." If one judged by the *Confessions* alone,
this might seem to be true. It is, however, only half of the
truth, as one may discover by a study of Augustine's
exhaustless labor both by pen and by the oversight of
his great See. Peter would have three tabernacles reared
on the Mount of Transfiguration, that so the glory might
be continued and confined to the happy disciples; but
Jesus, in the strength born of the new experience, would
go back once more to the valley, there to resume his social
ministry. There can be no permanent solitary enjoy-
ment of God. Many of Faber's poems which are attuned
to this note are not only fallacious but even malign.
Dante's final view of Beatrice, as she turns from her lover
to face again the vision of God, is beautiful as a picture,
but it is neither human nor Christian. The human will
does not lend itself to such self-centered, insulated enjoy-
ment. The "Legend Beautiful" floating down to us from
Medieval days shows how such an expectation frustrates
itself. The convent bell has rung the signal for distribut-
ing alms, and the monk, about to obey its summons, is
startled by a vision of his glorified Lord standing in the
middle of the room as if to bless him with a word and
touch from the heavenly world. Hesitating for an instant
between his desire to stay and his duty to go, reluctantly
and without a word he leaves his Lord and goes on his
errand; having fed the hungry, with perturbed spirit, he
returns to his now thrice-deserted room, and to his immeasurable surprise beholds his Master still standing
there: "Hadst thou stayed, I must have fled!"

3. So far as personal relations are concerned we serve

God in proportion as we serve our fellow-men. We speak of our hymns and prayers and the sermon at church as "divine service"; we announce that "divine service" will be held at morning and evening hours; and we speak of the prayer meeting as the "service" of prayer. This is a reminiscent relic of the time when men supposed that worship could be perpendicular, ascending straight to heaven. We, however, in our day, know that all our "services" are social. We know also that the Spirit of God is a social spirit, and that all service of our fellow-men is service of the social will of God. In the parable of "The Great Assize" those who had been kind to the needy were all unaware that in their service they had ministered to Christ; while those who had turned a cold heart to the destitute implied that they would not have withheld mercy from Christ if they had known that in distress he had appealed to them for aid. We cannot say that one should serve God and afterward his fellow-men; no one can serve men without at the same time and in the same deed serving God. "If we love one another, God abideth in us."

4. The Creative Good Will is unable to bring to expression the infinite multiplicity and richness of its ends without us. Jesus said, "Apart from me ye can do nothing;" it is no less true that apart from us he can do nothing. A thousand volts of electricity may be developed, but unless there are tiny filaments in every room, it cannot light the house; it remains a potential energy or flows off in other channels. The significant thing at Pentecost was not the rushing of a mighty wind and the fire —a potential, undistributed good; but the fresh gift of enthusiastic interpretation of the gospel, symbolized by the wind and by the flame parting itself into individual tongues resting upon each of those who stood on the

threshold of their mission. The principle of individuation finds its meaning here. There is no such reality as an undifferentiated universal; the One exists only in and through the Many. So far as the ends are concerned which make for personality, God is as impotent without man as man is impotent without God. The only way he can "raise up children unto Abraham" is not by changing stones into persons but by the free surrender to his will of those who incarnate the spirit of Abraham. Tender and gracious and willing as was the power of Jesus, "he did not many mighty works there because of their unbelief."

5. In this task of realizing ends which are in line with the Creative Good Will, we can create nothing new but only aid in carrying further those ends which are already partly fulfilled; we use natural means and social agencies which await our hand. The landscape gardener has only to look around him if he would discover his material: the earth and grass, flowering plants, shrubs and trees, rocks and sloping land,—out of these he makes beauty where ugliness reigned before. The sailor who would gain a distant port has but to assure himself that his ship is seaworthy and to trim his sails, letting his compass rule his rudder, and sea and wind will bear him on to his desired haven. The divine will which energizes in the human will controls all natural forces and guides other human wills, and this provides both the opportunity and the reinforcing aids for completing or at least furthering our highest personal aims. On the cross Jesus cried, "It is finished!" and yet the work which he had scarcely more than begun he left for others to carry on. Our lives are so intertwined with others that we really begin no tasks; we only continue what others have undertaken, perhaps able only to conserve the talents intrusted to us and at

our death leaving them for alien hands. "Other men have labored and we have entered into their labors."

VII

Perhaps the problems raised by our conception of God as Purposive Good Will culminate in our experience of sorrow and loss. It is not so much that a speculative solution of sorrow seems to be beyond our reach, as that we find it hard to adjust our feelings to those conceptions of the divine will which appear to be well-grounded. We have, however, certain fundamental convictions which we know to be unassailable. 1. This is on the whole a good world. This conclusion remains after making allowance for all the untoward and evil things in it. The untoward and evil things are real; they are not less real than is the good. They may give place to more favorable conditions; they may be modified so as to be endurable. But if old evils disappear, new ones rise up: a new disease takes the place of one which has been vanquished. Still, in spite of physical evils and the morally bad, this world with its sickness and deformity, its cruelty and deceit, its disappointment and sorrow, its death which brings every life however brilliant and happy to an inexorable end,— in spite of these and all other unfortunate things, all, save those who were born with an incurably sour taste in the mouth, unite in saying, This is a good world.

2. In this good world sorrow and loss are integral to its existence. It is written that in the New Jerusalem God shall wipe away all tears from their eyes, and sorrow and sighing shall flee away. But this is spoken of a dream-world which when we waken to reality vanishes like

the phantasms of our sleep when the day dawns. In the only world that we know, sorrow is inescapable—an experience created by the same life that creates joy. We cannot conceive of a human existence from which all sorrow is completely barred. There are indeed those athwart whose path its shadow is not yet cast; there is no one to whom sorrow and loss are not imminent, who, if he lives long enough, will not feel its aching and benumbing touch. "God has one Son without sin, but none without stripes."

3. This, then, is the way that the Creative Good Will constitutes and controls the world, or at least that part of it where we pass our days; and we have no power completely to change it. We may alleviate pain, we may prolong life, but when all is done we have only broidered the garment of sorrow and lightened by a little the spirit of heaviness. Sorrow abides still, a constituent part of our life that we did not make and cannot change.

4. And yet sorrow is somehow reconcilable with the Purposive Good Will. Speculatively we may not see how, but in experience the two co-exist in a harmony created by faith. Sometimes one holds fast the Good Will in spite of the sorrow: "Though he slay me, yet will I trust him!" At other times the sorrow is a form of the Good Will, as in Gethsemane and on the cross. Again, the sorrow is transmuted into joy by the lapse of time and the alchemy of a loyal spirit; the letters of St. Paul abound with this promise and its fulfillment. This elemental faith has been thus expressed: [1]

"I doubt not that the passionately-wept deaths of young
    men are provided for—and that the deaths of young

---

[1] Walt Whitman, *Leaves of Grass*, "Assurances."

women, and the deaths of little children are provided for;
(Did you think Life was so well provided for—and
Death the purport of all Life, is not provided for?)
I do not doubt that wrecks at sea, no matter what the
horrors of them—no matter whose wife, husband,
child, father, lover, has gone down, are provided for,
to the minutest points;
I do not doubt that whatever can possibly happen, anywhere, at any time, is provided for, in the inher-
ences of things;
I do not think Life provides for all and for Time and
Space—but I believe Heavenly Death provides for
all."

What then is the attitude toward life which goes along
with this conception of the divine Good Will? 1. It is
partly expressed in the title of the latest book by John
Burroughs, "Accepting the Universe." Our task is to
know the universe we live in; what it offers and what it
demands; what it gives and what it takes away; how to
adjust ourselves to its conditions and how to shape these
to our use. Here is birth, here too is death. Joy is here
and also sorrow; love, memory, hope, disappointment,
struggle, defeat, victory; and, crowning all, desire for
continued life after death; but whether we shall realize
this in prolonged individual consciousness or only "join
the choir invisible," experience here below offers us no
lighted torch. We may read fairy tales, we may listen to
marvelous prophecies of the future unfolded by men who
talk in their sleep; such things signify nothing. Our task
is single and perfectly simple—to ascertain what kind of
a world the Creative Good Will is actualizing here and

now in the short space of our earthly life, to calculate
the "risks" which are probable and the events which are
sure, and then adjust ourselves, not with the hard temper of the Stoic, but faithfully and bravely, even if at
times sadly, to our task.

2. When the shadow falls and sorrow and loss have
darkened all our world and we sit alone and disconsolate
by the ashes of our hope, we may still recall the light and
joy of other days; we may comfort our hearts with the
assurance that the world as it is is created by a Good
Will, wiser than our wisdom, more just than our measuring-rod of right, more tender than our gentlest compassion, and more worthy of our trust than all our imperfect conceptions of his goodness.   A Psalmist [1] has
coupled two words which at first seem removed from each
other "as far as the east is from the west."

> "He healeth the broken in heart,
>   He bindeth up their wounds.
>   He counteth the number of the stars,
>   He calleth them all by their names."

Here is, however, no chance connection.   Only that Good
Will could heal the broken hearted with whom lay the
control of the infinite worlds of space and time; and he
alone would be worthy to guide the universe in its track-
less path through eternity without the loss of a single
shepherded star to whom a broken heart is among the
most precious of all values.   In this confidence we go forward to meet what life has to offer, even its sorrow and
loss, safe in the will of the Living God.

---

[1] Ps. cxlvii, 3-4.

"Oh living will that shalt endure
    When all that seems shall suffer shock,
    Rise in the spiritual rock,
Flow through our deeds and make them pure.

"That we may lift from out of dust
    A voice as unto him that hears,
    A cry above the conquered years
To one that with us works, and trust,

"With faith that comes of self-control,
    The truths that never can be proved
    Until we close with all we loved,
And all we flow from, soul in soul."
        —Tennyson, *In Memoriam*, Canto cxxx.

INDEX

INDEX

Absolute, The, 69, 75; and the Trinity 60; and the finite, 69; and God, 88; 244; as Power, 105, 215, 219; as immutable, 218 f.; and experience, 226, 229 f., 234; and time, 231 ff.; as dynamic, 232, 242 ff.; as static, 232; and moral evil, 234 ff., 250; and perfection, 237; and Pluralism, 242; and dynamic values, 249; and transcendence, 254; and personality, 282 f.

Adler, Felix, 83.

Ahriman, 165.

Ahura Mazda, 165.

Ames, Edward Scribner, 61, 198 f., 202 f.

Anselm, 110, 205, 246, 297, 304; on the cosmological argument, 97; on the ontological argument, 97 f.

Aristotle, on God, 40 f.; as the Prime Mover, 40, 96, 217; as realized ideal, 96; on final cause, 129; on perfect self-consciousness, 210; on self-moving souls, 217; on knowledge and virtue, 235; transcendence, 253.

Arnold, Matthew, 59, 197.

Aryan idea of God, 18, 40, 209.

Ascent of Man, The, 300.

Augustine, *Confessions,* 48; and Manichaeism, 48; and Neo-Platonism, 48; and the Absolute, 49; and Dionysius, 49; and experience, 50; on evil, 166; on divine sovereignty, 229; on predestination, 328.

Augustinianism, 26.

Authority, 10.

Bacon, 129.

Banks, J. S., 104.

Bergson, 160.

Bernard of Clairvaux, 197, 258.

Bernard of Clugny, 123, 259.

Blatchford, Robert, 86.

Boehme, Jacob, 261.

Boethius, 276.

Bosanquet, B., on mechanism and teleology, 132.

Bowne, B. P., 262; on the ontological argument, 108; on personality, 289, 291.

Bradley, F. H., on the Absolute and God, 215, 245; on the Absolute and personality, 287 f.

Bronte, Emily, 194.

Bridges, Horace J., 83.

Bridgewater Treatises, The, 103, 111, 128.

Browning, Robert, 171, 173, 307.

Bruno, 55, 261.

Bunyan, 123.

Burroughs, John, 86, 265, 334.

Bushnell, Horace 60, 214 f., 309.

Butler, Samuel, 71, 218 f., 309.

Calvin, 26, 54, 141, 246, 250, 314 f.; on predestination, 92, 99.

Carlyle, 264.

Cause, Meaning of, 100, 119, 132; efficient, 129; final, 129, 132.

Christ, Deity of, 31; Person of, 66 f.

Christian Science, 87.

Clarke, W. N., 104.

Clifford, 85.

Coit, Stanton, 83.

Coleridge, S. T., 264.

Comte, A., on religion of humanity, 75.

Confessions of Augustine, 48, 328.

Consciousness, 120, 142 f., 159; in God, 141.